Vita Sackville-West's

SISSINGHURST

THE CREATION OF A GARDEN

Vita Sackville-West
and
Sarah Raven

virago

VIRAGO

First published in Great Britain in 2014 by Virago Press

7 9 10 8 6

Original gardening columns by Vita Sackville-West, as first published in the
Observer newspaper, Copyright © The Beneficiaries of Vita Sackville-West 2014
Selection and new material Copyright © Sarah Raven 2014

A CIP catalogue record for this book
is available from the British Library.

ISBN 978-1-84408-896-6

Typeset in Bell by M Rules
Printed and bound in Great Britain by
Clays Ltd, Elcograf S.p.A.

Papers used by Virago are from well-managed forests
and other responsible sources.

Virago Press
An imprint of
Little, Brown Book Group
Carmelite House
50 Victoria Embankment
London EC4Y 0DZ

An Hachette UK Company
www.hachette.co.uk

www.virago.co.uk

CONTENTS

Harold and Vita standing in front of the fireplace in the newly restored South Cottage in the early 1930s.

INTRODUCTION

Gardens do not normally survive their creators, but Sissinghurst remains one of the most heart-rendingly beautiful spectacles in England. It's a garden in a romantic place, a ruined Elizabethan hunting palace flanked on two sides by a moat, in the pretty wooded part of the Kentish Weald. Enveloped in its own orchards and cornfields, it's full of intimacies and, in summer, what its creator called 'the dark blue and gold' of long views to distant hills. The combination of the buildings, the walls, and the planting around and within them has an extraordinary effect. There is very little else like it in the world for abundance and fullness: its fountains of roses, voluptuous, delicious-smelling, out-of-control geysers of flowers; the Purple Border, the White Garden, the Cottage Garden, all set within the terracotta brick frame. It is one of the twentieth century's greatest creations, made eighty years ago in the course of about a decade by the writer Vita Sackville-West and her husband, the diplomat-cum-politician and writer, Harold Nicolson.

I remember my first sight of Sissinghurst when, just under thirty years ago, I was invited to a party on a Bank Holiday Monday, when the garden used to be closed. I was living in west London and, unusually for someone in their mid-twenties, I was already keen on gardening. I was training to be a doctor in the white-coat sterility of the Charing Cross Hospital wards, but I came from a plant-loving family and to keep me sane, I'd started to grow things in my own back garden.

The party was held on a lovely sunny day in May, and I was excited to see this famous garden. I had not expected the beauty of the buildings. People had talked about the garden, but not the place, which as you approach from the narrow lane feels more French than English, more like a small village than someone's home. And it all felt endearingly crooked, built from small, ancient bricks, and with an air of slight crumbliness at every corner.

I could hear the whole party out on the top lawn. I went in slowly, noticing the bronze urns at the front, full of a blue-grey pansy with large, flat, cheery flowers, ones I associated more with a Hyde Park bedding scheme than with these grand, sombre pots at the entrance to Sissinghurst. Their colour almost matched that of a large clutch of rosemary bushes with particularly dark blue flowers (Sissinghurst's own hybrid, see p. 191) to their right and left, and the hanging bells of a small straggly vine of *Clematis alpina*, breaking the line of the arch overhead. This was the beginning of my exposure to Sissinghurst's painterly combinations – that blue, a genius contrast to the colour of the Elizabethan and Tudor bricks, is for ever seared into my mind.

The garden was by then – in the early 1980s – owned by the National Trust. Nigel, Vita and Harold's son, had given it to the Trust in 1967 in lieu of his mother's death duties, so that he could be sure their creation would be preserved in perpetuity. Pam Schwerdt and Sybille Kreutzberger had been the head gardeners from a couple of years before Vita's death in 1962 and they'd been taking care of and raising the horticultural level of the garden for the twenty-five-odd years since.

Adam and me, early on an April morning in the Spring Garden.

And now I've had the joy of living in this wonderful place. A few years after first seeing the garden I married Adam, grandson of Vita and Harold, and when his father Nigel became ill and died in 2004, we moved to Sissinghurst. No longer a doctor and now with two children, I had become a gardener, and as someone passionately interested in the beauty of what's around me, I'm lucky to have spent ten years of my life entwined with Vita and Sissinghurst. Her interiors, the rooms she made, are as rich, as stimulating and excitingly put together as her garden. In the morning I wake up in a bed brought by her from Knole, her nearby family home; I am surrounded by Chinese turquoise ceramic animals that belonged to Vita's mother. The light coming in from all three windows in our room radiates through amber flasks on the window ledges, which in Vita's childhood had stood in a window at Knole. There is the scent, on a spring morning, of the huge osmanthus trained on the wall below the windows – one of Vita's favourite plants (see p. 188), and as this fades it's replaced by the spicy fragrance of wisteria and the sweet smell of the rose 'Blossomtime', a variety loved by Vita for its good mildew resistance, frothy pink flowers and long season, with buds still covering it right into autumn.

I plunged into her books and the more I learnt about Vita, the more excited I felt. I loved her taste, her habit of covering tables with Persian carpets as well as having them on the floor, her lustrous deep-green china egg hanging in front of our huge open

A typical Vita interior – the Brew House, which she used as her workroom during the war. It's filled with many of her favourite things: a tapestry chair, a bronze hand on the high window ledge and a huge bowl of carved wooden fruit from a Mexican market.

fire to avert the evil eye, the turquoise Chinese lamps, the Duncan Grant painted box next to the Roman alabaster funeral urn in the middle of the chunky oak table, almost black with age. And all this before I'd walked out into the garden, with its powerful colours and textures 'rich as a fig broken open, soft as a ripened peach, flecked as an apricot, coral as a pomegranate, bloomy as a bunch of grapes', as she described her favourite varieties of old-fashioned rose.

My husband Adam became increasingly fired up by the idea of trying to enrich the whole Sissinghurst landscape. As he started to explore its history and all the related documents for the book he published in 2008, *Sissinghurst: An Unfinished History*, so our lives steadily filled with all the stories of what Sissinghurst had been in the past and during his own childhood. As time went on, I too increasingly revelled in Vita's writing and in the black and white photographs we have of Sissinghurst in Vita and Harold's day. Vita's words and those photographs show an exuberant place – a garden brimming and overflowing. As Vita says of herself, 'My liking for gardens to be lavish is an inherent part of my garden philosophy. I like generosity wherever I find it, whether in gardens or elsewhere. I hate to see things scrimp and scrubby.' 'Always exaggerate rather than stint,' she says later, 'masses are more effective than mingies.' Nothing was to be too tidy. 'Too severe a formality is almost as repellant as lack of any.' This was to garden in the maximalist, not minimalist, way.

For fifteen years, from the autumn of 1946 to 1961, in her workroom in the Elizabethan tower which presides over the whole of Sissinghurst, Vita wrote a gardening column for the *Observer*, mostly about plants – new and old – writing as if they were her friends with all their charm and idiosyncrasy. She didn't include much about her own garden, at least overtly, but everything she wrote in fact relates to Sissinghurst. She also contributed the odd foreword or introduction to gardening books of friends and some articles for *Country Life* and the Royal Horticultural Society magazine. This book draws on all these sources, as well as on her garden notebooks and the letters Harold and Vita wrote to each other after they moved here in 1930. Together they add up to a brilliantly vivid portrait of Vita's Sissinghurst.

In her four bound collections – *In Your Garden, In Your Garden Again, More for Your Garden* and *Even More for Your Garden,* which basically comprised her *Observer* articles with a few extras added, Vita organised her material month by month. I've used a different system, arranged according to the different themes in her gardening at Sissinghurst so that we might use them in thinking about our own gardens. I have started with a brief history – the parts relevant to Vita's obsession with Sissinghurst – followed by the story of how she and Harold found it, and the love affair between the place and the people. Then I move on to Harold's structuring of the garden, the skeletal design; then Vita's broad-brushstroke ideas for how to make it truly enveloping without too much maintenance; and on again into the finer detail – her favourite plants, which work on a more intimate scale.

There's lots of discussion here about flowers for cutting because Vita loved having an endless succession of small arrangements to scatter through her indoor life; and she gives advice for potted plants, interesting things to have on your desk or window ledge, particularly in the grey and wet of winter and early spring when the weather doesn't tempt you outside. There's practical information here too – for instance, growing lilies from seed (see p. 209) and how best to care for roses (see pp. 157 and 202). The last section of the book brings the history up to date, telling what has happened at Sissinghurst with Vita and Harold no longer there.

You might think that the garden writing of a woman in the 1930s, 40s and 50s would have little relevance now, that her aesthetic would not work today, that fashions would have changed too much, that garden design and the plants available would have moved on too far, but none of that is true. It is rousing and inspiring to go back and look at and read again about how she did things and what she thought, the plants she did and didn't choose.

The Big Room at Sissinghurst, created from the stables and designed for entertaining, which, in fact, they rarely did. This looks almost exactly the same now as it did when this photograph was taken in the 1950s.

Luckily for us, Vita is a chatty writer, light on her feet. From the moment I started reading her pieces, they became my favourite source of garden inspiration, for dipping into before I fell asleep or for reading in a great batch in one sitting.

Vita has strong loves and hates and she has a great turn of phrase. One of her favourite plants is the gentian *sino-ornata*, its brilliance of colour 'like the very best bit of blue sky landing by parachute on earth'; another is eremurus – the glorious foxtail lily, which looks 'like a cathedral spire flushed warm in the sunset'.

There are things she doesn't like such as privet and laurel, which are 'dark, dank, dusty and dull – how deadly dull', and standard roses – 'top-heavy with their great blooms on one thin leg like a crane' – and the month of August, 'this dull time, this heavy time, when everything has lost its youth and is overgrown and mature'. Furthermore, she 'hates, hates, hates' the rose '*American Pillar* and her sweetly pink companion *Perkins*' ('Dorothy Perkins'), 'which should be forever abolished from our gardens'.

She is accurate and sometimes funny in her descriptions. How true it is – now she's pointed it out – that the 'Silky-silvery seed-heads' of clematis 'remind me of Yorkshire terriers curled up in a ball'; that the flowers of *Magnolia grandiflora* look like 'great white pigeons settling among dark leaves'; the spikes of big gladiolus hybrids 'in those great peacock-tail displays look like swords dipped in all the hues of sunrise, sunset and storm'; and that we should all grow joke plants like the 'humble plant', *Mimosa pudica*, which collapses as if dead when you stroke it, only to jump up again when you turn your back. What Vita said about gardens and plants over half a century ago is just as true now, and it's hard to find it better said.

Vita and Harold filled a stack of leather-bound albums with

pictures of the garden as it evolved. This was before and after the war, helped by Jack Vass and his team of gardeners. Sissinghurst became famous quite quickly, the garden drawing many distinguished and talented people who wanted to see it at first hand, and some of the best photographs come from them. There are images by wonderful photographers such as A. E. Henson and Edwin Smith, who took the picture of her desk (see p. 46): still messy, covered in scraps of paper, notes, stamps, matches for her cigarettes, five little vases of flowers – the life of a woman still full of curiosity and adventure just a few weeks before she died. To this collection I've added up-to-date images of Sissinghurst at its best, and some new ones by two American friends, Stephen Orr and Ngoc Minh Ngo, and also by Jonathan Buckley, the photographer I have worked with on my books for years.

Vita's Tower, looking from the Orchard, photographed in May.

Fifty years after Vita's death, I wanted to collect together a sort of scrapbook of her garden writing, to tell the story of Sissinghurst in her own words, alongside this collection of photographs — many of which have never been seen — to re-create between these covers something of the garden she made.

SISSINGHURST SINCE THE SIXTEENTH CENTURY

1530	Sir John Baker buys Sissinghurst
1560s	Richard Baker builds the hunting palace
1573	Elizabeth I stays at Sissinghurst
	Richard Baker knighted
1756–63	French prisoners housed at Sissinghurst
1770s	Possible date of major fire
1796	Sissinghurst let to Cranbrook parish
1855	Let to George Neve
1892	Vita Sackville-West born
1903	Sold to the Cheeseman family
1926	Sold to the Wilmshurst family
1928	Put on the market again
1930	7 May: Vita Sackville-West and Harold Nicolson buy Sissinghurst. The design of the garden starts immediately. Two gardeners – George Hayter and son – plus Mr Copper, the handyman, help out
	Start to restore the upper lake to the south of the garden straight away
	December: Dam the nearby Hammer stream to make the lower lake (costing £125) – mainly Harold's project
1931	Finish the lake
	Clear the whole garden of rubbish

	Start putting in lots of hedge plants
	Vita writes poem 'Sissinghurst', dedicated to Virginia Woolf (see p. 35)
1932	Vita and Harold let Long Barn and move into Sissinghurst full time
1934	Plant six hundred *Lilium regale*
1935	Harold elected MP for Leicester West
1936	Victoria (Vita's mother) dies, so they have more money for the house and garden
	Another gardener, Mr Farley, is taken on
1938	First opening for National Gardens Scheme – only two days a year
1939	Jack Vass taken on as head gardener, but leaves to join the RAF in 1941
	During Second World War the Tower top serves as an observation point for the Observer Corps (spotting and reporting German air raids) and Vita moves to a study in the Brew House in the front range
1940	Garden open daily – Vita likes it, Harold does not
1946	Jack Vass returns and stays until 1957
1957–9	Ronald Platt becomes head gardener
1959	Pam Schwerdt and Sybille Kreutzberger become head gardeners
1962	2 June: Vita's death
1967	National Trust takes over
1968	1 May: Harold's death
1991	Sarah Cook becomes head gardener
2004	Alexis (Lex) Datta becomes head gardener
	23 September: death of Nigel Nicolson
2013	Troy Scott Smith becomes head gardener

Part 1

THE PEOPLE AND THE PLACE

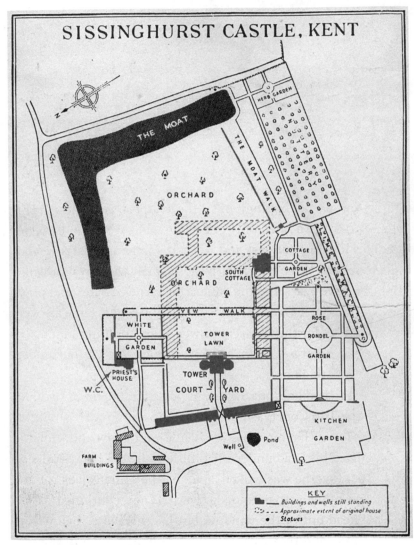

SISSINGHURST CASTLE, KENT

THE MOAT

THE MOAT WALK

HERB GARDEN

ORCHARD

COTTAGE GARDEN

ORCHARD

SOUTH COTTAGE

YEW WALK

WHITE GARDEN

TOWER LAWN

ROSE RONDEL GARDEN

PRIEST'S HOUSE

W.C.

TOWER COURT YARD

KITCHEN GARDEN

FARM BUILDINGS

Well

Pond

KEY
Buildings and walls still standing
Approximate extent of original house
● Statues

The map of the house and garden from a drawing by Harold; it was included in the first guide book, immediately after the war.

1

A BRIEF HISTORY

At night, our part of Sissinghurst – the southern arm of the front
range – looks like a liner, only one room wide, with windows on
both sides looking out east and west. It's long and narrow, and
studded over its three floors with those small windows glowing
with light. Five years ago the American garden-writer and photographer Stephen Orr came to stay for the night. He was over
from New York for the Chelsea Flower Show and I put him up in
what we call Juliet's – Adam's sister – room, the southernmost
room on the attic floor.

We went to bed late, but Steve was woken in the night by loud
voices in the Top Courtyard below his east window. He thought
Adam and I were having a middle-of-the-night row and, embar-
rassed, buried his head under the pillow and went back to sleep.
At half past four, he was woken again by the same voices shouting at each other across the courtyard. They continued as he
stuck his head out of the window, but had moved to below the
entrance arch; and they carried on, loud enough for him to hear
them out of his window on the other side. But there was no one
else staying at Sissinghurst then apart from the three of us – and

our children – and none of us was awake at that time of night, let alone shouting.

I love this story because it makes Sissinghurst so alive with its past. It's not a spooky place, but when it's quiet at night, it's easy to sense the atmosphere that was here in its short sixteenth-century heyday and feel Vita and Harold's presence from the 1930s, particularly in and around the South Cottage where they spent so much time.

It's that history, the layering of the different eras in Sissinghurst's life, that fed Vita's imagination on her arrival – the foundation for her great love affair with the place. It's inconceivable that she would have responded in the same way to a collection of walls and buildings that did not have this history seeping out of them. More so than Harold, who would probably have made his neoclassical garden scheme wherever they lived, the remains at Sissinghurst gave the link to the past that Vita felt as soon as she came here. There are three eras, the Elizabethan high point, followed by a long period of dilapidation, and then a Victorian moment of the best farming there has ever been. Each of these phases made its contribution to what Vita created here.

She did not love the twentieth century, but looked back to Elizabethan romance. Her heroes were Shakespeare and Sir Philip Sidney, and Knole, the house she was brought up in, redolent of the great age of Elizabethan glory. The fact that Sissinghurst had experienced such a similar rich, flamboyant moment made it perfect for her. In the sixteenth century there was a grand house, large enough to hold thirty-eight fireplaces (recorded in the seventeenth-century hearth tax) and stretching over three adjoining courtyards. It was built through the 1560s as a hunting palace at the centre of a newly made seven-hundred-acre deer park. Its

creator was Richard Baker, son of Sir John Baker who had prof-
ited from the dissolution of the monasteries. When Sir John
bought the place in 1530 there was a more modest medieval
manor house (of unknown date). As a would-be courtier and
Elizabethan gallant, Richard wanted something grander, fit for
entertaining the queen. With his eye on a knighthood, he was
aiming to lure Elizabeth and her court down from London.

A drawing by Francis Grose from the 1760s showing Sissinghurst at its fullest
extent.

We have a drawing by Francis Grose (1731–91), which Vita
had on her wall, showing the full extent of the house, sketched
two hundred years after it was built. The view is from the east –
from the back – beyond the corner of the moat. The new buildings were enclosed by a moat on three sides, with the Tower in
their centre (you can just see the pair of round roofs above the
main bulk of the house). The Tower is still there, almost exactly
as it was, except for a change in the shape of the turret roofs. The
main bulk of the Tower has one room filling the whole of the
central section and extending out into the southern turret on
each floor, the first of which Vita adopted as her writing room.
There is a staircase running up in the north turret, with three

floors above the arch and a flat roof platform. At this top level
there were two prospect towers, one on either side in each turret:
these were viewing galleries, and the main reason for the Tower's
construction. From here, the ladies could watch the hunt while
the men pursued their deer. Its height is just right for viewing
the whole newly formed park. These windowed rooms, decrepit
by the end of the eighteenth century, were removed a few
decades later to make the place safe.

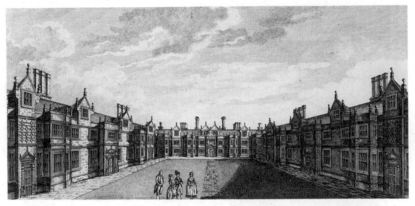

An engraving by Richard Godfrey (*c*.1787) of the main court at Sissinghurst in
its medieval heyday.

We have a print of another drawing, a copy of which is in
Vita's photo album, probably dating from the middle of the eighteenth century and published in Edward Hasted's history of
Kent, written in the 1780s. This shows the largest and grandest
court of the Elizabethan mansion – the buildings you would have
seen when you stood at the top of the steps at the base of the
Tower. Reminiscent of an Oxford or Cambridge University quad,

The Elizabethan wall and window on the Tower Lawn.

the middle courtyard had three decorated doorways on each side and one main entrance at the end. This linked onto the next court and the garden beyond.

When I stand on the wide top step at the foot of the Tower, I can feel the scale of the sixteenth-century palace. It always impresses me how far away to the right the original Elizabethan walls are, with their characteristic fine bricks, large windows and arched doors, and I imagine the rooms that would have stood behind them. Sissinghurst is now

South Cottage in 1930, before the extension was added to the northern side to house the flower room and Harold's bedroom above.

a relatively small house – or more a family of buildings – but the remnants of the original manor show how grand it once was.

What is now called the South Cottage contains the rooms that formed the right-hand far corner of this, the largest of the courtyards. There is one main room at ground level and another immediately above it. It has additions (built by Vita and Harold in the 1930s), but the original rooms give a clear idea of what the rest of the house would have looked and felt like. The downstairs is panelled now, with wide reclaimed-oak floorboards used for the walls as well as the floor, done when Vita and Harold's twentieth-century additions were made, so this room is more difficult to read, but the upstairs chamber is largely unchanged. This was Vita's bedroom, chosen by her for its bony Elizabethan grandeur; it has a large arched stone fireplace, covered over when Vita and Harold bought it, greying oak beams showing flecks of plaster, and wide oak floorboards.

Vita's bedroom in South Cottage, in the early 1960s (you can see a detail of the wooden settle and its cushions on p. 50). This room looks almost exactly the same today.

Of all the rooms in Sissinghurst, this room connects most immediately with its Elizabethan past. The original red bricks are a gentle colour, with lots of smoky pink-purple as a coating over the harsher terracotta, revealed in the odd brick that is softer and has worn away; and there's the occasional end-on tile shoved in. All the original walls have a creamy ancient lime mortar — soft and crumbly, wavering up and down and going broader then narrower along each seam. The bricks are fine, long, but narrow, their faces less than two-thirds the size of a modern brick, and many of them are pockmarked and irregular, cracked and holed over their entire surface. The 1930s changes tried to mimic the

The Priest's House se⁓ 1950s.
rose 'Flora' tumbl⁓
door – a Vita ⁓

⁓ower with the rambler
⁓ prunus tree by the front

look of the older walls – and it was done well – but they don't have the same irregularities and soft dustiness of the Elizabethan.

The Priest's House and the barn are other bits of the Elizabethan house that remain. The so-called Priest's House was built to the north of the main buildings as a banqueting house for guests to look out over the garden and park. One theory for its name is that because the Bakers were high-class crypto-Catholics in a part of Kent that was fiercely Protestant, the name Priest's House was given to this isolated building as a sort of sneer by the locals about 'them up there not being like us'.

June 1930. The Elizabethan barn and Victorian piggery, now the National Trust shop.

The Elizabethan barn is a handsome, hugely tall building, just one great space for storing the hay cut from the meadows around it, a landmark you can see from the north and east several miles away. It's a building on a magnificent scale, yet its bricks are the same narrow ones that form the Priest's House, the Tower, the South Cottage and the ruined palace walls.

Queen Elizabeth and her entire court did indeed come to stay, in August 1573, soon after the palace had been completed. They stayed only th... days, but Richard Baker's ambitions were fulfilled and he was ...ded a knighthood.

But the Bakers' ...t of glory – and Sissinghurst's fortunes – were both shor... side in the Civil War. I... The family ended up on the wrong Baker's grandson guilty of t... arliament found Sir Richard Things had already started

to slide before that, his wife producing four daughters and no
sons and each of them marrying people miles away – in
Gloucestershire and Sussex. Within eighty years of its building,
the palace at Sissinghurst was essentially deserted. Each daughter had inherited a quarter of the estate and it no longer
belonged to one family, but became an asset to be exploited or
ignored. Sissinghurst had been a sort of fantasy of beauty and
delight – a perfect house in a perfect landscape – used for short
visits and entertaining, but as family loyalties moved elsewhere
even that use dropped away.

Sissinghurst in 1760. An engraving by James Peak made from a drawing by one
of the English officers.

Parliament had imposed a huge fine on the royalist Bakers, and
a mortgage was arranged on the whole fifteen-thousand-acre
Sissinghurst estate to try and raise the funds. By 1756, the debts
were still mounting. The family's solicitors decided to pay some of
the mortgage by letting Sissinghurst to the government to house
French naval prisoners during the Seven Years War. From 1756 to

1763 there was a huge shifting population living in the *château*, and with the French word came the origins of the name, Sissinghurst Castle. There are no exact records for how many, but between one and three thousand prisoners were housed here at any one time.

Dated 1760, French prisoners-of-war are seen going about their daily chores on what is now the Tower Lawn. The Elizabethan palace is shown, enclosing the yard.

Given that number of people, the place must have been packed to the rafters, with the prisoners in appallingly crowded dormitories and cells. To distract themselves during the months and years of incarceration, some of them created objects they could sell to their guards, or to local people. There are still households around Sissinghurst that have these artefacts. Vita and Harold bought and collected a few. We have these now on our sitting room windowsill – some dominoes and a decorated wood-veneered vanity box made from mutton bone, some beautifully carved wooden dogs, a wine-bottle stopper and a primitive ship in full sail. The box is made with precise and careful craftsmanship, but from materials that cost nothing – here was someone trying to while away the days until he could go home, or make something of maximum value from minimal materials that he could sell. On the base of one of the dogs there's a label – 'Carved by the French prisoners at Sissinghurst Castle in Kent in the 18th cen[tury]'. All of this would have been thrilling to Vita; so many lives led within the walls of the place she now inhabited.

The most invaluable and accurate portrayal of this moment – almost certainly by one of the French prisoners – is a naive watercolour of Sissinghurst, painted in 1761 in ink and dye. The National Trust bought the painting recently and it now sits in the Big Room, on the ground floor of the north range of the house. It has a childlike perspective, the figures in it much bigger than true scale, but it is a brilliantly detailed depiction of the whole place at the time. There is the entrance range, with its main arch at its centre and two subsidiary arches to left and right, all still here. There's even the same pair of large oak doors in the entrance and the Tower arch, with a small wicket gate in the left-hand side, just as you see now. The Priest's House and three courtyards are here too, opening up beyond, and the Tower with its three floors and flat roof, extending above its grand entrance arch. You can see all three arms of the moat and the paths of the Elizabethan garden to the northwest of the house. This was the typical place to site a garden at the time. The plants and the design would then be seen in the most flattering soft light from the house windows, with no southern glare.

This painting was not found until well after Vita's death, but would have been a great thing for her to see, showing how

An ink and dye watercolour from 1761 of Sissinghurst, when it was used to house French prisoners during the Seven Years War. It shows, in faint outline, the Elizabethan garden layout, where Vita found her rose (see p. 16). Also shown are four 'night soil' carts, and the English guards in their sentry boxes with rifles and fixed bayonets.

unchanged many things are here since the eighteenth century and confirming what she suspected was the site of the Elizabethan garden, within the moat in Sissinghurst's northeast corner. When Vita arrived in 1930 the place was overgrown, with few plants remaining, but she did find one thing that excited her – a rich, dark, velvety rose with a magnificent scent. The rose was where the Elizabethan garden had been – now the Orchard. Vita hoped and believed it had been growing there ever since the garden's great sixteenth-century heyday. She named it the 'Sissinghurst Castle Rose' and took lots of cuttings to give away. It has since emerged that it is indeed a rose that may well have been grown in Elizabethan gardens – a Gallica variety, 'Rose des Maures'.

When the Seven Years War was over and the French prisoners were allowed to return home in 1763, Sissinghurst entered its next chapter. Accommodating so many people in such a confined space for those seven years had taken its toll, and by the end of this time the buildings were in a bad state. There is an inventory of the dilapidations of the house that record the buildings as '2/3 destroyed'.

Worse was to come. The drawing we have by Francis Grose, mentioned earlier (see p. 5), has two inscriptions on its reverse, the first where it came from – the Thomas Pennant and Earl of Denbigh Collection – the second, 'Sisinghurst [*sic*] House, near Cranbrook, Kent, now burnt'.

The fire probably happened towards the end of the eighteenth century, but no one knows exactly when, and this explains why so little of the Elizabethan palace remains by the time we see it again in a painting from the 1820s. This shows the Tower – its roofs now pointy, not round – with only the thatched South Cottage just visible behind it. How the South Cottage rooms survived the fire is

Sissinghurst in the mid-1820s. In 1796 the parish leased what remained of the building to use as a workhouse.

not clear, but the Tower, the front range and the Priest's House were all separate from the grand courtyards. If fire romped through these vandalised parts of the hunting palace, it would be possible for the separate buildings to escape.

Sissinghurst's disintegration, its melancholic dereliction, were part of its romance and beauty for Vita. If the palace had still been intact when she found it, it would have lacked the sense of lost glory and partial ruination she had been drawn to since she was a girl.

In 1796 the land at Sissinghurst and its remaining buildings were let to Cranbrook parish. It became the parish farm – the workhouse – where the unemployed were given work and housing. The farm did well – the land here is fertile – and it made a lot of money. We know that the parish hall of Cranbrook was built from the proceeds of Sissinghurst farm, nicknamed at the time the 'old cow' because you could always milk her.

The Cranbrook parish tenancy lasted until 1855, when the landlords (descended from the Bakers, but now called Cornwallis) decided to let it out to a gentry farmer, George Neve. Neve built a smart new farmhouse as soon as he arrived, while staying at Sissinghurst and renting the farm and buildings until 1903. He ran a good farm here, with a dairy herd, corn-fields, hop gardens and fruit orchards. The growing and drying of hops was very profitable at the time, so he built the large oast houses and the new dairy (which is now the coffee shop) to the west of the main buildings. He housed his workers in the remains of the castle and grew vegetables in among the ruins, but he him-self moved into his newly built farmhouse, now the Sissinghurst B and B.

This set the seal on the importance of Sissinghurst for Vita: land that had been beautifully managed and productive in the era of high-Victorian farming. She loved nothing more than the bur-geoning land, the animals, the men, the Virgilian landscape where human life and enterprise were bound in with the soil.

The entrance gateway in the 1820s, when Sissinghurst was rented by Cranbrook parish.

In 1903, having been in the family for nearly four hundred years, the Cornwallises finally sold Sissinghurst. It was first bought by a family called Cheeseman, who farmed here until 1926. They then sold it to the Wilmshursts. Old Mr Wilmshurst died and his son put the house and the estate on the market, but this was at the pit of the agricultural depression when vast acreages of England were for sale. It sat unsold for two years, and it is then – in 1930 – that Vita and Harold enter the Sissinghurst story. The three phases of its history – the resplendent Elizabethan palace; the period of decline and abandonment; then a resurgence in the value of the land and the work done on it – were all key to Vita's connection with the place. Together these made the almost perfect conditions for her vision of a garden.

The well-appointed Victorian farmhouse built by the Cornwallises' tenant, George Neve.

2

FINDING THE DREAM

Picture by Edie Lamont – one of Vita's lovers – given to Mary Stearns, the daughter of Vita's farm tenant. This painting shows clearly the Sissinghurst Vita wanted to create – loose, free and romantic, with the Tower floating above it – a haven from the rest of the world.

Born in 1892, Vita, the only child of Lord and Lady Sackville, was brought up in one of the largest houses in England, Knole, just outside Sevenoaks, twenty miles from Sissinghurst. She was passionate about Knole. With its picture-encrusted galleries, its vast attics and endless corridors, it was her solitary childhood playground and had a strong hold on her throughout her life.

King Edward VII at a Knole house party in 1898.

We have a photograph of a typical Knole house party, of 1898/9: Vita, then a little girl, is sitting at the front, with King Edward VII (sitting down to the left), her grandfather Lionel, Lord Sackville (standing in the centre), her mother Victoria seated to the left of the King, and her father – another Lionel – the dapper man standing right at the back behind her mother. Vita hated this Edwardian grandeur – her novel *The Edwardians* is about just that, how much she disliked this time – but she had a passion for its older underlayers – not the sheeny Edwardian pleasure house her mother

Vita, as a girl, with her father at Knole.

Vita in fancy dress in her early twenties.

loved and polished, but the Elizabethan and seventeenth-century romance of Knole, the way its grey stones seemed so deeply rooted in its park, its huge rambling-ness and a kind of romantic unknowability.

Vita spent most of her childhood exploring the outer reaches of Knole. It was not the garden that interested her – which was a formal, Victorian, soulless place with lines of stick-like, heavily pruned Hybrid Perpetual roses and not much else – but the house and the beautiful rolling ancient park full of oak and walnut trees in which she could imagine Queen Elizabeth and Philip Sidney pursuing the deer. She was a tomboy, possessing her own khaki and armour, and had one or two friends from Sevenoaks that she treated like lieutenants and soldiers of her own toy army. In her teens she fell in love with a pretty young girl her own age called Rosamund Grosvenor, which was more a romantic friendship than a sexual affair.

Vita lived at Knole until her marriage to Harold Nicolson – a brilliant and charming young diplomat – in the chapel there on 1 October 1913, when she was twenty-one and he five years older. Vita continued to stay there often when Harold was working away. Soon after their marriage, he was sent briefly to Constantinople. Vita joined him for his less than six-month posting. They returned to England in 1914, where their eldest son Ben was born, and lived mainly in Ebury Street in London, but in the spring of 1915 they decided to buy a house in the country too.

The wedding of Vita and Harold in the small private chapel at Knole, October 1913.

They chose a fourteenth-century cottage, Long Barn, only two miles from Knole, so Vita could then easily visit almost every day.

Only in her twenties did her understanding of her own sexuality deepen into the full-blown and wildly subversive love affairs which she continued to have through her thirties and forties. The most significant was with Violet Trefusis – a smart society girl and novelist – that in the years after the First World War and the

Harold (left), Vita, Rosamund Grosvenor and Vita's father, Lionel, in 1912.

birth of their second son Nigel very nearly destroyed Vita's marriage to Harold; but it was the experience which, having survived it, meant that Vita remained bonded to Harold for the rest of her life.

Both of them were chronically unfaithful to each other, he largely with upper-class young men, she with a series of beautiful young women writers; and in the 1920s with Virginia Woolf, for whom Vita represented a daring and threateningly adventurous plunge into a world of aristocratic fleshliness by which she was half attracted and half repulsed.

Vita's father died in 1928, but – as a woman – she could not inherit Knole. The house and estate passed to her Uncle Charlie and it became more difficult emotionally for her to go there. It was so close to Long Barn, where they had lived for fourteen years, and that was painful. On top of this, in 1929, Vita and Harold heard that the neighbouring farm had been sold and was to be developed with the addition of an intensive battery chicken farm. Neither of them liked the idea of this on their doorstep and both were keen to move.

The poet Dorothy – or Dotty – Wellesley, one of Vita's long-standing girlfriends, had heard of a house that might interest Vita from a friend, Mr Beale, a land agent from Tunbridge Wells.

An aerial photograph of Sissinghurst in 1932. The architectural structure is much the same today – the garden by the Priest's House has just been laid out (the new paths can be seen) but the north wall of the Top Courtyard has not yet been built.

The estate agent's particulars were mainly to do with Mr Neve's Victorian farmhouse, but at the end referred to 'picturesque ruins in grounds'. On 4 April 1930, Dotty drove Vita and Nigel to Sissinghurst to have a look.

Vita gives a fictional version of arriving here in her novel *Family History*, when the heroine Evelyn Jarrold is first taken to the home of her lover, Miles. They are coming by car at night: 'the lane widened, and the fan of light showed up a group of oast-houses

beside a great tiled barn; then it swung round on a long, low range of buildings with a pointed arch between two gables. Miles drove under the arch and pulled up. It was very dark and cold. The hard winter starlight revealed an untidy courtyard, enclosed by ruined walls, and opposite, an arrowy tower springing up to a lovely height with glinting windows.' At another moment in the novel she describes 'how the sunshine enriched the old brick walls

A 'snap' of the Tower at Sissinghurst, as Vita found it in 1930.

with a kind of patina that turned them pink'; and 'there was a peace within those high brick walls'.

Within minutes of arriving Vita was 'flat in love with Sissinghurst'. 'The place, when I first saw it on a spring day . . . caught instantly at my heart and my imagination. I fell in love at first sight ... It was Sleeping Beauty's Garden: but a garden crying out for rescue.' Standing in the middle of the vegetable patch looking up to the Tower, she turned to twelve-year-old Nigel and said, 'I think we shall be happy in this place.' He was much less sure, but there was no discouraging Vita, now set on the path of her long relationship with Sissinghurst.

Tomato plants growing in the Top Courtyard in the 1920s. The entrance arch is still blocked (see photograph on p. 36)

It fitted so well with her for many reasons. From the moment she arrived, she loved its general lack of smartness and its close relationship to the surrounding country. There was no ostentation – a dirty word – no pomposity, no lodge, no sweeping drive, no great gatehouse, just the few rough, decrepit buildings surrounded by her beloved Kentish Weald. She had great affection for the area around Sevenoaks: her childhood had been full of nutteries, apple and pear orchards and plenty of hop gardens, and Sissinghurst – not many miles away – felt just the same. All the more tempting, there was a nuttery included in the Sissinghurst site for sale.

She loved Sissinghurst's moat which, she said, 'provided a black mirror of quiet water in the distance', and its tower at the centre of the garden and visible from everywhere. Even as a child, Vita had dreamt of having her own tower, a solitary place in which she could write and reflect.

She loved the romance of the ruin and its crumbliness, the walls inviting a garden to be made within them, a garden that was not invented, for Sissinghurst was a real place in need of redemption. Vita and Harold had between them made a good garden at Long Barn but were both now ready to create something more ambitious. Vita had learnt a lot about plants in the last ten or fifteen years, and about the style in which she wanted to garden. On the first page of a notebook from Long Barn in 1916, she had written, 'when and how to plant lilac? When wild thyme? Wild sedums? What other good rock things, bushy? Good climbing roses.' In the following years she tried and tested many plants and combinations, and they had both become passionate and knowledgeable gardeners.

Vita never liked the brand-spanking-new, but rather things that had already clearly had a life, even if now slightly disintegrating (see the cushions on the bench in her bedroom on p. 50), and so this place – in its wrecked state – revealed itself more and more and by the minute as perfection. She liked the echoes of grandeur that she found here rather than grandeur itself. It's perfectly possible, walking through the garden today, to imagine those first few hours she spent here looking into all the hidden corners, exploring the damp buildings,

Sissinghurst when Vita and Harold arrived in 1930 – the view from the Tower looking towards the Elizabethan barn.

seeing from the top of the Tower the way Sissinghurst was deeply embedded in its own landscape, and almost feel a catch in the throat, the feeling of 'think what we could do here – we could make a poem of this place'.

When she researched the history, the bond tightened further. She found there had been a Knole and Sackville link with the people who had built Sissinghurst. Sir Richard Baker had a sister, Cicely, who was married to Thomas Sackville from Knole. Sir John Baker, Richard and Cicely's father, who bought Sissinghurst in about 1530, was therefore Vita's ancestor – her thirteenth great-grandfather – so there was even a genetic link between her family and this place she was now in. Lineage was one of Vita's obsessions, so Sissinghurst seemed the perfect compensation for her loss of Knole. From very early on, she flew the Sackville flag and staked her ancestral claim. There was no doubt this was her place – it was her estate, the acres around which she could stride like any Sackville squire from the previous five or six centuries, woman or not. Harold never owned a stick or a blade of grass here. He recognised and in some ways celebrated her dominance. When she died Harold commissioned Reynolds Stone,

Vita and her Tower. It was topped by the Sackville-West flag from the moment they arrived.

A series of photographs commissioned by Vita to illustrate *Country Notes*.

The oast house with hop sacks.

The hop garden.

The arch of the Elizabethan barn, looking southwards to the six kiln oast house.

A Sissinghurst gate: push the top bar and the rest folds.

the famous letterer, to carve a plaque: 'Here lived V. Sackville-West who made this garden.' There was no mention of him – not accurate, of course, as Harold was hugely important in the creation of the garden – but he made sure the point was strongly made.

The die was cast: the person and the place had found – and would restore – each other. On 4 April, Harold wrote in his diary: 'Vita telephones to say she has seen the ideal house – a place in Kent near Cranbrook.' On 5 April, the day after Vita saw it, Ben and Harold took the train down to Staplehurst to visit Sissinghurst, and on the 6th Vita and Harold went back again. Harold wrote in his diary, 'We walk round the fields to the brook and round by the wood. We come suddenly upon a nut walk and that settles it.'

Harold then wavered. In his entry for 13 April, a wet day on which they'd visited again, he writes, 'it all looks big broken down and sodden', and he tried to be momentarily sensible and say they could not afford it. He wrote to Vita on the 24th – half joking – that it was too expensive and needed too much done to make it habitable; and that 'for the £30,000 it would end up costing [equivalent to perhaps £3 million today], we could buy a beautiful place replete with park, garage, h and c, central heating, historical association, and two lodges r and l'. But he knew that Vita and Sissinghurst were now an inevitable partnership and he too rapidly fell for its charms. He says in the same letter, 'let's go ahead and buy it'. On 6 May 1930 her offer was accepted and she bought it with the adjoining Victorian farmhouse and the five-hundred-acre farm.

Their friends and children – to start with – thought they were crazy. As their friend the writer Raymond Mortimer wrote, 'we

A charcoal drawing by Carolus-Duran of Vita, aged fourteen, at Knole in July 1906.

all thought Sissinghurst a gloomy place in hideous flat country, with commonplace cottages and no view and couldn't think why they wanted it'. Mortimer – like the boys – loved his comfy weekends at Long Barn and was bemused, but Vita and Harold were raring to go.

As she says in her poem 'Sissinghurst', written in 1931 and dedicated to Virginia Woolf:

A tired swimmer in the waves of time
I throw my hands up: let the surface close:
Sink down through centuries to another clime,
And buried find the castle and the rose.
Buried in time and sleep,
So drowsy, overgrown,
That here the moss is green upon the stone,
And lichen stains the keep.
Here, tall and damask as a summer flower,
Rise the brick gable and the springing tower;
Invading Nature crawls
With ivied fingers over rosy walls ...
Wherein I find in chain
The castle, and the pasture, and the rose.

Vita had found a place in which they – and particularly she – would feel intensely at home. It was a forgotten place: its past, the sense all around her of the Elizabethan buildings; its present, the farm; and the garden she would make in it – its future.

Harold on his first-ever visit in spring 1930 – the entrance arch was blocked and the place was derelict.

3

SISSINGHURST'S DESIGN

Harold at the time he and Vita arrived at Sissinghurst.

It's well known that the garden at Sissinghurst was the joint creation of Vita and Harold. He had a genius for structural design,
making a series of axial vistas and enclosed 'rooms' that fitted
both expertly within the site they had found, and together as a
geometrically divided whole. Vita then filled those rooms with
her own particular planting style.

They bought Sissinghurst as much for the possibility of
making a garden in its Elizabethan ruins as for its being a house
in which they could live. A conventional house – with living,
eating and sleeping all under the same roof – was not one of their
priorities. Vita and Harold had previously had the idea of living
at Bodiam Castle, which had been on the market in 1925; their
vision of life there involved each of them living in one of the tur-
rets, one for Vita, one for Harold and one for each of their sons,
Ben and Nigel. The four of them could occasionally meet in the
open courtyard in the middle.

This is hardly what most of us think of as the basis for family
life – the children were fourteen and twelve in 1930 – but the
idea suited them and Sissinghurst fitted this vision well. Once
installed there, Harold spent the weekdays in London and the
boys were away at school, but when everyone was there, the
arrangement would allow for privacy and work and they could
all just meet each other for meals, a garden linking each building
into a home. They had the perfect empty canvas. Of all the gardens I've seen, only Ninfa, about forty miles southeast of Rome –
a garden also created in a ruin (and with a broad limestone
stream running through its heart) – comes anywhere near.

I can imagine them there through the first summer, a huge and
brilliant mutual project in front of them. As we know from
Portrait of a Marriage, Vita and Harold had been through hair-

raising times, but making a home here, creating some rooms and a garden, was something they could do together when their other work commitments – both their writing and Harold's political life – allowed. We all know how mutually bonding it is having a project on even a fraction of this daunting scale. They did not have enough money – at least, not until Vita's mother Victoria died in 1936 – but that was not going to hold them back, and within weeks they launched into the project with great gusto.

The plotting and planning of the garden started straight away. Harold drew up avenues and viewpoints, criss-crossing the ruined site. He was a descendant of Robert Adam, and proud of it, and was always in charge of the architectural improvements and the design of both their gardens. As Vita said in 1953, 'I could never have done it myself. Fortunately I had, through marriage, the ideal collaborator. Harold Nicolson should have been a garden-architect in another life. He has a natural taste for symmetry, and an ingenuity for forcing focal points or long-distance views where everything seemed against him, a capacity I totally lacked.'

He had had a practice run at Long Barn and was helped there in sketching the plan for the Dutch garden by Edwin Lutyens – a friend of Vita's mother – who came to visit for a day. Harold was clear what sort of garden he was going to lay out at Sissinghurst. His overall scheme for any garden design was this: 'The main axis of a garden should be indicated and indeed emphasized, by rectilinear perspectives, by lines of clipped hedges ending in terminals in the form of statues or stone benches. Opening from the main axis there should be small enclosed gardens, often constructed round a central pool, and containing some special species or variety of plant.'

Harold was as obsessed as Vita with their plans. They discussed what they both wanted. She confirms his vision as her vision in an article in 1953 in the *Journal of the Royal Horticultural Society*: 'a combination of long axial walks running north and south, east and west, usually with terminal points such as a statue or an archway, or a pair of sentinel poplars and the more intimate surprise of small geometrical gardens opening off them, rather as the rooms of an enormous house would open off the arterial corridors. There should be the strictest formality of design, with the maximum informality in planting.' The Sissinghurst garden would be like a house, but a house on the Knole scale. Just like moving from the library at Knole to the drawing room and into the Colonnade, that's how Sissinghurst's garden rooms were conceived – rooms opening off arterial corridors.

The new garden was naturally confined within the limits of the moat to the north and east side, and the front range of dilapidated buildings to the west. The third arm of the moat, in its Elizabethan heyday had at some point been filled in, probably in the sixteenth century, to make a garden wall. That was the beauty of the place – it was so obvious where it should begin and end, confined by its Elizabethan history. Harold used the inherited walls wherever he could, adding hedges and three new walls. In 1935 the north wall of the Top Courtyard was built. He also added a wall to divide the Priest's House garden from the Tower Lawn and at its centre included the arched Bishop's Gate with a plaque depicting three bishops. They had brought this marble back from their time in Constantinople, and Harold had it inserted in the brickwork. The final new wall, a very tall, straight line with a large semicircular niche at its centre, was built in the would-be Rose Garden. It was designed by the well-known restoration architect Albert Powys, and Vita in particular hated it from the start – too tall, the wrong brick, over-pointed, and too formal and smart to fit at Sissinghurst. That apart, the new walls added hugely to the garden's all-important sense of division and enclosure.

An aerial photograph taken in 1932. It shows the new wall by the Priest's House garden (later to become the White Garden), but the north wall is still to be built and there is, as yet, no Powys wall. Vegetables are growing in what became the Rose Garden.

None of Harold's linear, formal structure was going to be straightforward at Sissinghurst. Although the site was flat, it was not symmetrical. You can see his challenge very clearly in the 1932 aerial photograph and in any plan of the garden (see p. 2), showing that none of the spaces was a simple rectangle. The site is full of what Vita called 'minor crookedness'. As she said on describing her first few visits: 'The walls were not at all at right angles to one another: the courtyard was not rectangular but coffin shaped; the Tower was not opposite the main entrance', nor parallel with the front range. The Top Courtyard is not a true rectangle, the space between the Moat Walk and the Nuttery is not a rectangle either.

But Harold was up to the challenge. By means of rulers and graph paper, his design manages to skilfully camouflage the eccentricities of the place. As Anne Scott-James describes it in *Sissinghurst: The Making of a Garden*, 'paths had to be twisted, rectangles adjusted, circles bent, enclosures pushed this way and that, to achieve miracles of optical illusion'. The end result is that, standing above it on the Tower roof, you can see its awkwardnesses, but as you stand in the garden you're totally unaware of any anomaly.

In the first couple of years the whole scheme remained at the paper stage. Before anything could be actually planted, they had to clear vast amounts – centuries – of rubbish. There was an

Centuries of rubbish and lean-to cottages attached to the main buildings had to be cleared before gardening could begin. These are both views of the clutter in the Top Courtyard at the time of Harold and Vita's arrival.

Vita clearing ivy from the
Elizabethan walls, 1930.

The Lower Courtyard –
overgrown – with a greenhouse
in the southwest corner.

'appalling mess of rubbish to be cleared away before we could
undertake any planting at all'. Imagine the archaeology that
would have been undertaken nowadays; but most of the stuff was
to be dumped – rusty iron, 'old bedsteads, old plough-shares, old
cabbage stalks, old broken down earth closets, old matted wire
and mountains of sardine tins, all muddled up in a tangle of
bindweed, nettles and ground elder'.

More useful was the odd lump of stone, as well as sinks and bits
of fireplaces from the sixteenth-century ruins. All of these were
carefully preserved and many of them used later. The sinks were
made into trough gardens and put on brick plinths along the east
face of the western Top Courtyard wall; they resurrected the fireplace for the Big Room; and other chunks of stone were used to
create the Erechtheum – a temple-like pagoda – on the east side of
the Priest's House in 1933. This was the place where the family ate
outside when it was warm enough in the summer.

There was also the inevitable destructive first stage before they could get on with the creating, and they had two cottages and a lean-to demolished in the Top Courtyard, as well as a ramshackle greenhouse taken down from the right-hand Tower Lawn wall.

Almost every building needed work on walls, floors and roofs, and Harold, with the help of Powys, set about this in their first year, restoring and repointing the walls and the buildings to make somewhere good to live. They loved good, authentic – ideally local – materials but their restorations were basic: high finish was not their thing. Vita used to say frequently that Sissinghurst was '*not* a winter resort'. The lifestyle of trooping between one building and the next was 'idyllic in summer but demanded goodly amounts of English fortitude in the cold and wet'. The

Inside Long Barn – a classic Vita interior – full of things from Knole and her travels.

style of interiors they chose, with walls stripped to the brick and simple wooden floors, could also be very cold and draughty. Fitted carpets and plush cosiness was not their way.

Their first priority was to restore the Tower and make Vita's writing room on the first floor. The other floors were, to start with, used for storage. The Tower became the centre of Vita's life for the next thirty years, and her writing room is where she remains more present now than anywhere outside it. This was Vita's most private place, which Nigel said he visited only half a dozen times in his whole life when Vita was at Sissinghurst, and Harold went up there not much more. They would call from the

The family with their dog, Rebecca, in 1932, at the base of the Tower – the first place to be restored and made habitable.

Vita at her desk in 1932 in the newly renovated Tower.

bottom of the stairs if they needed her. Nigel tried to work up there after Vita died, but her presence was too strong and he retired back to his workroom in the south wing of the front range.

You can see lots of detail of Vita's desk, where she spent so much time, in the photograph by Edwin Smith (below), taken just after she died. As Adam wrote in his book *Sissinghurst: An Unfinished History*, everything in this room 'is rich and faded, a fraying of stuff that was once valuable and is now merely treasured. Nothing here was ever renewed. It

Edwin Smith's photograph of Vita's desk soon after her death in early summer 1962.

arrived and, as soon as it arrived, like a picked flower laid on a desk, it began to fade. Vita allowed her possessions to age, silks to wear, wood to darken, terracotta to chip and fail.' 'Her possessions must grow old with her,' Nigel wrote. 'She must be surrounded by evidence of time.' This was fundamental to her style, both inside and out.

Vita's workroom in the Tower – books, tapestries and a mirror from Knole on the wall.

A dilapidated old oak table.

There are signs of this all around the room: a chipped turquoise tile on which a vase can sit. And another, on the other table, a brown and amber medieval floor tile, made of English clay. There's a fire in the corner and the same corduroy sofa sitting in front of it, a sofa carried up there on her first day and never moved, with the same rather mean electric heater which she had on almost perpetually. There's Chinese amber, jade and amethyst trees and ceramic animals from Persia. Vita wanted everything in her room to be eclectic, worn yet rich, the whole interior feeling old as soon as it was made. One can forget that now, with everything muted by age, and the odd bright or rich splash of colour. It's not due to the weathering of the last seventy years: it was like that from the start, and purposefully created. She liked this look around her in all her rooms, and that's the sort of garden she wanted to create too, nothing shiny or new.

Ben in the early days when they were still camping out.

The South Cottage was next in the restoration programme, making Vita's bedroom and Harold's writing room, and then adding his bedroom after a couple of years. Vita's bedroom was covered in layers of Victorian wallpaper, completely obscuring the fireplace – imagine the joy when they found it – but she wanted the walls stripped back to bare brick, the floor to just boards, with rugs. This room is best with a roaring fire filling the hearth and lots of candles. That's how Vita loved it: we still have her candlesticks and candles in sconces on the walls. Then you can revel in imagining what it would have been like as a bedroom for one of Elizabeth's court, and for Vita nearly four centuries later. We have tried to keep her room as close as possible to how it was when she died, and have recently moved things back, which we know from photographs were there in her day.

Vita's bedroom in South Cottage, photographed by Edwin Smith just after she died. It still looks much like this today.

It has a powerful atmosphere. If you sit quietly there on your own, you can almost see an Elizabethan lady being dressed for dinner and, after her, Vita standing smoking by the fire. In its mixture of raw brick and old tarnished mirrors, richly embroidered, rather ragged seventeenth-century textiles and tapestries hanging against the brick, it has a strong characteristic feel. This is where you can sense the Vita aura.

The Nicolsons also restored the Priest's House; Ben and Nigel slept there for the first time in April 1931. This is constructed from the same narrow brick. Its first-floor chamber has a similar atmosphere and appearance to the bedroom in the South

A wooden settle with silk cushions, which sat by the fire in Vita's bedroom. This can be seen in the picture of her bedroom on p. 8.

Cottage, and it was here that Vita died early in the summer of 1962. Their kitchen was here, and if Vita was going to be brought meals in bed and be looked after by the cook – Mrs Staples and her daughters Pat and Jo – it was easier for all for Vita to be in this spare room, rather than everyone having to traipse across the garden carrying trays of food to the South Cottage, so she had to move.

There was deliberately no guest room at Sissinghurst. If people came to stay – which they rarely did – they would have been offered Ben's or Nigel's beds if they were not at home.

When they arrived, what was a stable in the front range was converted into the Big Room (now called the Library by the National Trust), their sitting room and their most public room for when they might entertain. They put in the big window to the north, and created the fireplace. Lots of the things here – the sconces and the furniture – came from Knole or were copies. Vita's mother had organised for the estate staff at Knole to give Vita and Harold copies of the seventeenth-century sconces from the Colonnade – one of Vita's favourite rooms – as their wedding present. They were hung here. The mirrors in the Big Room and the wig stands were also copies of seventeenth-century things at Knole. The fireplace was made from remnants of an Elizabethan one they found in the garden. Lots of the ceramics and glass here – and in her tower – were brought back from Constantinople, dating from the thirteenth and fourteenth centuries, adding to the overall aged, eclectic feel.

Vita and Harold kept their first home, Long Barn, until 1932 (when they let it), but they made working visits to Sissinghurst, usually staying at the George in Cranbrook or the Bull in Sissinghurst village. Their first night spent at Sissinghurst itself was early in October 1930, on two camp beds in the upper room of the Tower, putting up sheets of cardboard in the unglazed windows to keep the rain out. Harold did a hilarious BBC broadcast in November that year about the terrible night they had spent there, eating all his least favourite things – 'sardines, soup from a tablet, cheese wedges and tongue (tinned)'. By 9 April 1932, the buildings were nearly ready and they finally moved in.

The Herb Garden – the outermost garden room, enclosed on all four sides by yew hedges, fundamental to Sissinghurst's overall design.

Once the outdoor site had been cleared, Harold came into his own and set about the actual laying-out of the garden. He spent much time standing on top of the Tower thinking and rethinking, but by 1932 he had a complete plan that never altered.

There were two fundamentals to his design – long distant views, with secluded garden rooms opening off them. The hedge lines for the views were his first priority and were laid out during his weekends away from London, with Nigel often at the other end of his measuring tape. Everything was done by eye, home-made and handmade – no landscape architect, no surveys, no spirit levels, just the two of them with a pad of graph paper, a pencil, some bamboo canes and some string.

Nigel and Ben on the oak bench at the base of Vita's Tower in 1939.

As Vita wrote, and they both clearly thought: 'Hedges are always an important fea-ture in any garden, however small, however large. Hedges are the things that cut off one section of the garden from another; they play an essen-tial part in the general design.' They create surprise, containment, a sense of arr-ival, a narrative for anyone walking through the garden, and were fundamental to their initial design. From the start they planted box – throughout the Priest's House garden (now the White Garden) as well as in the vegetable patch (now the Rose Garden), and in the Lower Courtyard where we have photographs of young box plants, just put in.

The Yew Walk was planted in 1932, as was the yew Rondel (a sort of hedged circle, named by them after the drum of an oast house) in what was to become the Rose Garden, followed by the Lime Walk and the hornbeam hedge, all in the same year. They

An aerial view of Sissinghurst taken in the early 1960s, showing the abundant garden at its peak, and the importance to the garden's design of the yew hedges, as well as the 'inherited' walls and buildings.

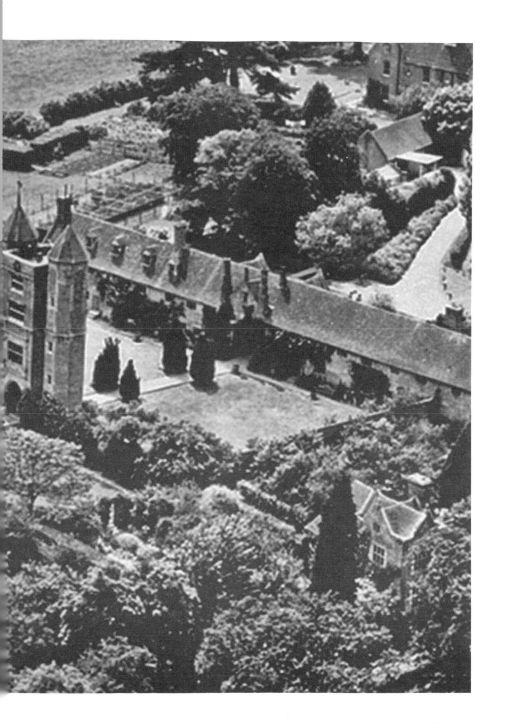

A *Country Life* photograph taken during the war.
Irish yews line the path from the entrance arch to
Vita's Tower. These were planted when they were
quite well grown to provide instant architecture for
the new garden.

both loved yew, beech, holly and hornbeam, although, in the end,
no beech was used at Sissinghurst.

As well as hedges, they both liked sentinel plants – topiary – not
elaborate shapes, but vertical lines to emphasise points in the
garden. These are equivalent to the chunky oak tables in all their
rooms, substantial, elegant, unfussy, essential in the rhythm of the
space. The Irish yews were planted in the Top Courtyard, also in
1932, and four Irish yews were added in a square at the centre of
the Cottage Garden two years later. If you stand in these two gardens now and imagine them without these great green pillars,
they'd be half the places they are. Their architectural presence

throughout winter as well as summer stops the gardens from being simple plateaux of plants and grass and makes them whole

The Moat Walk in 1931.

worlds in themselves, mini-landscapes with these crucial verticals breaking the plane.

With his structural planting, Harold created a series of five long-distance views, just as they'd planned. The first and main axis of the new garden had the Tower at its heart. It runs from the first point of arrival, through the entrance arch (reopened in 1931) and the Tower, then through a narrow gap in the yew hedge and down to the moat. Harold designed a wide York stone path from the entrance arch to the Tower in 1932. He also added the statue at the end of this view, of Dionysus, but it was not installed till after the war, in 1946. This is also the end point of another view running down the Moat Walk, with its wide grass path, from Sissinghurst

A postcard of Sissinghurst, showing the Yew Walk newly planted.

Crescent – a semicircular brick platform with a shaped box hedge on the east side of the Cottage Garden – to the moat's edge. The Moat Walk was turfed in 1932 and Sissinghurst Crescent built in the same year.

The third – and hugely important – axis is the Yew Walk, linked to a box-edged

The view from the Tower Lawn looking south to the Bacchante statue.

path to the south, which together bisect almost the whole garden from north to south, planted in 1932. To line up the double hedge for planting, Nigel stood at the southern end waving a flag, with Harold at the other shouting where to put it, to mark the correct central point.

The fourth viewpoint runs from the Priest's House garden (now the White Garden), through the Bishop's Gate and across the Lower Courtyard to finish in the Lime Walk at the Bacchante statue (a Bacchante is one of the dancing-girl followers of Dionysus – called Bacchus in Ancient Rome). This statue was formerly part of the Wallace Collection and a present from Vita's mother, and was very sadly stolen from the garden in spring 2013.

The Bacchante is also the start of the final viewpoint, down the lime and hornbeam avenue of the Lime Walk, and continuing into the Nuttery. The filberts there were planted in 1900 before the Nicolsons arrived, but Harold used the avenue of hazels and tied it in with his vista to extend the Lime Walk. The nut trees were thinned and pruned to link in with this avenue.

As Tony Lord says in his book *Gardening at Sissinghurst*, the 'apparent simplicity' of the overall layout ' is deceptive, leading some to suggest that there is little to the design, that the Nicolsons just threw up a few walls and hedges to complete existing enclosures and scattered a few statues'. He goes on: 'Consider as an example the axis from the White Garden to the head of the Lime Walk: this entire sequence is built up from one original feature that predated their arrival: the doorway at the south end of the Lower Courtyard. This determined the position of the Bishop's Gate and the wall that contains it, the *clairvoyee* at the farthest end of the White Garden, the Rondel and the statue at the end of the Lime Walk.' 'It is a tribute to [Harold Nicolson's] skill that visitors today find it so logical that it is hard to believe its enclosures and axes were not always there.' This difference between old and new is now brilliantly blurred.

Harold could then move on to the arrangement of the garden 'rooms', to create that sense of privacy that both he and Vita so much wanted. Privacy was key, he wrote: 'I admit that Versailles, Courances and Villandry are superb achievements of the architectural school of gardening. Yet a garden is intended for the pleasure of its owner and not for ostentation. Nobody could sit with his family on the parterre at Versailles and read the Sunday papers while sipping China tea.' Harold called the rooms a 'succession of privacies', each surrounded by walls or high hedges around an enclosure that is formal in shape – the Top Courtyard,

The Rondel, surrounded by the Rose Garden – displaying the contrast between the formal structure and lush abundance.

the Tower Lawn, the Rose Garden with its Rondel yew hedge, the Lime Walk, the Cottage Garden, the Herb Garden and the White Garden.

He had had a previous go at this idea – under the influence of Hidcote Manor's garden – at Long Barn, aiming to enclose each space in high hedges to give an element of surprise, each garden having an individual feel and peaking in a different season, yet melding into the overall feel.

Miniature box plants, just put into the Lower Courtyard, spring 1931.

At Sissinghurst, the paths were laid in the Cottage and Priest's House Gardens in 1931, and then the yew hedge between what was the vegetable garden and Cottage Garden was planted the next year. The central path of the Kitchen Garden was laid and box hedges put in there in 1933 as well as the to-be-monumental yew Rondel. In 1934 the yew hedges of the Herb Garden were also planted, but the garden was not made here till after the war.

Harold had finished the major plantings of trees and shrubs in six years, and everything then just needed to grow. In 1948, with the garden now mature, he stood back and assessed it – and whether they'd achieved what they wanted: 'Sissinghurst has a quality of mellowness, of retirement, of un-flaunting dignity, which is just what we wanted to achieve ... I think it is mainly due to the succession of privacies: the forecourt, the first arch, the main court, the tower arch, the lawn, the orchard. All a series of escapes from the world, giving the impression of cumulative escape.' On the overall scheme Vita and Harold almost always agreed, but there was the odd tension between

Vita planting climbers on the Lower Courtyard walls in 1932.

them and inevitably some disagreements. Sometimes her plants got in his way, and he was occasionally irritated by her romantic love for an incongruous tree or shrub which did not fit with his more austere design. When laying out the central path and the Rondel in the old kitchen garden, 'Vita refuses to abide by our decision or to remove the miserable little trees which stand in the way of my design,' reads Harold's diary entry for 27 September 1933. 'The romantic temperament as usual obstructing the classic.'

Harold also had a grander eye, more showy ambitions than Vita, who favoured the simple. Harold was keen on the idea of – and commissioned their architect Albert Powys to design – a covered loggia instead of the present wall at the north end of the Top Courtyard, and at one moment he even suggested niches along it for busts they'd had made of their friends. The levels of the Top Courtyard were difficult too, and when they were laying it out Harold suggested a nine-foot-wide terrace all the way along the top in front of the entrance range and with steps down to the lawn. Vita disagreed, arguing that a simple path of stone and then a sweep of green – reminiscent of the Green Court at Knole – were more fitting for the space.

In both cases Vita won. The Top Courtyard has a wonderful scale about it and a calm, better for its simplicity. As Jane Brown says about Sissinghurst, 'It has no long grass walks flanked by double borders, no pergola, no pools or fountains, no trellis walks or arbours and no topiary twists or triangles. There are no white-painted seats, no Versailles tubs ... no balustraded terrace or columned temple' as there were in so many other gardens at the time, part of the English classical revival; and this lack of ostentation, fiercely defended by Vita, is fundamental to its charm.

It's worth remembering that the set idea of how Vita and Harold divided their roles in the garden – Harold on structure and Vita on plants – doesn't allow room for the fact that Vita consulted Harold continually on planting, particularly in the earlier days, and that Harold was in charge of one of the most intensely planted areas at Sissinghurst, the Lime Walk.

You can see this team decision-making in a letter about the Long Barn garden in 1926 when Vita wanted to plant rhododendrons. 'I don't mind them in a big place round a lake,' Harold said. 'But I think they are as out of place at the cottage as a billiard table would be. I don't like putting in big things (as distinct from small flowers) – which are not indigenous; I am opposed to specimen trees.' He suggested cobnuts for the space instead of rhododendrons, with holly as the background. He wanted the garden there – and even more at Sissinghurst – to blend with the Kentish scene, and was a steady influence on Vita to achieve that end. There was a continual crossing over of ideas.

The Spring Garden (or Lime Walk), the avenue of pleached limes underplanted with spring flowers, is the most formal planting at Sissinghurst; as Anne Scott-James says, 'It is mathematically planned like a French garden.' Its flavour is a little different from the rest, but it's important to remember this was exclusively Harold's garden, and from 1933 he had his own gardener, Sidney Neve. Harold planned the planting carefully in the winter months, and we have the fabulously detailed planting plans from which he worked. Nigel reported that his father did nearly all the bulb planting there himself, and his diary has endless entries such as 'weeded Spring Garden'. This was his decompression chamber on his weekends away from work and from London, and he remained devoted to it all his life.

The garden designer Tom Stuart-Smith makes the point that at Sissinghurst, more than any other garden, the design reflected the two makers: the mix of formal with the odd surprise, the private verging on the reclusive, the straight lines softened by the flamboyant and the exaggerated; and the barely pruned roses equivalent to Vita's often eccentric garb – her black cloak and sombrero, for instance – next to the precision of the Lime Walk, based as it was on inch-by-inch maps and analysis.

All our gardens tend to do this, but you can read Vita and Harold and their marriage like a book from the photographs of the garden taken in the ten years or so before Vita's death, when they felt it was at its best. The garden at Sissinghurst belonged to both of them and its beauty is a friendly jostling of their skills and powers, a hybrid of precision and effusion – and the stronger for it.

Within five years of Vita and Harold's arrival, the garden's structure – its main trees and hedges – was in place. As time went on Vita's role became more important and Harold's receded. It's to Vita's planting that we now turn.

Part 2

VITA'S GARDEN THEMES

Sissinghurst at dawn, looking out of Juliet's bedroom window on the top floor of the south wing of the front range.

4

A Mixture of All Things

Vita had done a little rose and shrub planting in their first three years, but from 1934 she really began to pack the garden in her characteristically exuberant way. What had begun in the first couple of years as a few random favourites going in – such as the white rose 'Madame Alfred Carrière', planted on the South Cottage, and *Magnolia grandiflora* in the Top Courtyard – grew into large-scale planting, with massive orders such as six hundred *Lilium regale* bulbs put in in that one year, plus a huge shrub order from Hillier's nurseries – magnolias, prunus, viburnums, daphnes, sweet bay and lots of shrub roses.

She was mainly a plants person, someone who loved and wrote about individual varieties and new discoveries. But before she could get into that level of detail, she had to translate the vision she had for this place into the reality and come up with some sort of overall planting scheme. Vita seldom wrote about design, and if she did, would often just slip it in at the beginning or end of an article – very definitive, very sure that there was only one way of doing things. But it's these themes, her style characteristics, her ideas for how to fill a garden, which define her as an individual gardener who had a lasting influence on English garden design.

There are several themes that are prominent, some more startling in the photographs of the garden from the 1940s or 50s than they are today: she liked a full range of plants all mixed up in the borders together, as you'd see in a cottage garden, rather than the smart gardens of her day; she had a sophisticated take on colour which led her to make her three gardens – the White Garden, the Purple Border and the sunset-coloured Cottage Garden – within a narrow colour range; she liked every inch of each bed, every corner and every surface of her garden to be abundant and luxuriant. She was a big fan of the flowering shrub, low maintenance, easy plants with a substantial presence, to give the beds valuable architecture; and she loved scent, strong and delicious garden perfumes, right through the year. It's these themes, within its clever classical design, which make Sissinghurst the work of art it is.

In many ways the planting Vita did at Sissinghurst was similar to her garden writing. In her columns she deliberately plays a game, dropping a thread of glamorous or exotic poetry, or a reference to the classics or to Milton, and then immediately afterwards comes straight down to the mundane – good growing tips, how to propagate, even how to make a concrete path look like stone.

If you look at her gardening pieces, she often launches into a great thing, a grand idea – then collapses it with a joke or something she hates, or a piece of practicality (see her passages on *Coronilla glauca* (p. 184), myrtle (pp. 98–9) and *Rosa filipes* 'Kiftsgate' (p. 121)). Here's the good writer in a relaxed frame of mind, her style ranging from the poetic to the everyday, whisking up and down the octaves, never sticking safely to the stalwart middle range. It's that breadth and fusion that makes her writing so good and rich to read, repaying a visit again and again.

You'll also see this writing style in her garden. Her particular combination of qualities means that she achieves an atmosphere of great confidence – there's nothing tentative or anxious, but a full-on going-for-it engagement with the place. The garden is jam-packed with a mix of very different sorts of plants, normally kept well apart in the gardens of her day – and that's enlivening: high style, low style, big, delicate, careless and careful, all together.

Vita loved a riotous jumble, as you'd see in a good cottage garden, but she wanted a bit more structure than that. So she turned to William Robinson, 'who did more to alter the fashions of English gardening than any man of his time'. The now very

Vita in her twenties.

elderly garden designer had been experimenting in his own garden at Gravetye Manor in West Sussex since the 1880s.

The Edwardian gardens she'd been brought up with – at Knole, and the country houses she visited as a young woman – had long herbaceous beds, tiered from the front to the back, or carpet bedding: 'flower-garden planting made up of a few kinds of flowers which people were proud to put out in thousands and tens of thousands' in a highly ordered and structured way, as Vita wrote, quoting Robinson, in her collection of articles, *Country Notes*, published in 1939. Philip Sassoon at Port Lympne in Kent gave his gardener a full set of Asprey's enamelled cigarette boxes and asked him to model the borders on them – 'designs which may be quite all right on the surface of a carpet but not on the surface of the much enduring earth', Vita commented.

'There was hardly a country seat that was not marred by the idea of a garden as a conventional and patterned thing,' William Robinson wrote in 1883, Vita adding that 'the beds were regularly filled year after year with scarlet geraniums, pink begonias, discordant salvias, yellow calceolarias and greenhouse plants with variegated foliage. Nothing more hideous, unsuitable or unnatural could be imagined.'

Instinctively Vita knew that was not her thing. 'I have no great love for herbaceous borders or for the plants that usually fill them – coarse things with no delicacy or quality about them. I think the only justification for such borders is that they shall be perfectly planned, both in regard to colour and to grouping; perfectly staked; and perfectly weeded. How many people have the time or the labour?'

As Robinson wrote in *The English Flower Garden*, 'formality is often essential to the plan of a garden, but never to the arrangement of its flowers or shrubs'.

Victoria, Vita's mother, in her formal 'unnatural' rose garden at Knole, typical of gardens at that time.

Vita's planting at Sissinghurst in the 1950s.

'The real originality of Mr Robinsons's methods lay in his choice of what to grow and how to grow it,' Vita writes in *Country Notes*. In *The English Flower Garden* and *The Wild Garden*, both books read by Vita, Robinson moved away from swathes of bedding annuals and perennials to the idea of 'shrubs, pinks and pansies' all in together. He was inspired by 'the happy-go-lucky gardens of the poor cottagers, where no elaborate schemes had been adopted and flowers had been left to grow for themselves in a happy tangle'.

He went on to mix up all sorts of things together. Vita wrote: 'In his own square beds ... where he grew principally roses, he also grew clematis, whose purple clusters rose above low shrubs of silvery grey, and furthermore he covered the ground with pansies and even with low rock-plants, horrifying the rosarian whose conception of a rose garden had been one of savagely pruned bushes of uniform height, with bare ground in between.'

As Anne Scott-James says, he 'commended such garden ideas as straight lines; blossoming hedges (roses, sweet briar, honeysuckle); creepers and ramblers on a house to clothe the fabric; roses, not trained as standards but well grouped and underplanted; the loose planting of shrubs in a border; borders crammed with successions of hardy flowers and bulbs; cottage gardens; climbers rambling up trees, or festooning hedges or creeping through shrubs'. Almost all these ideas were adopted and translated by Vita at Sissinghurst. His style became her style.

Following Robinson, she'd put shrubs together with herbaceous perennials. She'd position wild British natives, her favourite 'wildlings', next to exotics she'd got to know during her visits to Italy and Greece and her travels with Harold to Turkey and Persia. She'd put simple cottage flowers with a sweetness to

Luxurious mixed borders in the Rose Garden at Sissinghurst in the 1950s.

them – wallflowers, poppies, large-flowered Roggli pansies, zinnias and dill – next to sophisticated foreigners – magnolias, abutilons, pomegranates and eremurus. Her garden would include a velvet Gallica rose with a wild honeysuckle left to climb through it and clamber up behind it on the wall; self-sown mulleins in a path, erupting through the purple skirts of an exotic indigofera; aubrieta – banned from smart gardens – in sweeping carpets frothing over the path at the feet of a great clump of her favourite imperial fritillary. Just like her writing, here was a hugely refined mishmash of so many different things, all combined in a luxuriant and glamorous way.

When knitting these groups of one thing, one style of plant, into another, she sometimes worked out her combinations, and sometimes left them a bit to chance and then tinkered with them, to fine-tune the colours and shapes of the design. When she was putting colours together, she tended to favour similar tones – like the blues of the rosemary, pansies and clematis at the entrance arch, preferring these calm, harmonious mixes to strong contrasts. She would sometimes think out these matches quite carefully, and give her readers a good tip for how to do the same:

'I have a gardening dodge which I find very useful. It concerns colour-schemes and plant-groupings. You know how quickly one forgets what one's garden has looked like during different weeks progressively throughout the year? One makes a mental note, or even a written note, and then the season changes and one forgets what one meant at the time. One has written "Plant something yellow near the yellow tulips," or "Plant something tall behind the lupins," and then autumn comes and plants have died down, and one scratches one's head trying to remember what on earth one intended by that.

'My system is more practical. I observe, for instance, a great pink, lacy crinoline of the May-flowering tamarisk, of which I put in two snippets years ago, and which now spreads the exuberance of its petticoats twenty feet wide over a neglected corner of the garden. What could I plant near it to enhance its colour? It must, of course, be something which will flower at the same time. So I try effects, picking flowers elsewhere, rather in the way that one makes a flower arrangement in the house, sticking them into the ground and then standing back to observe the harmony. The dusky, rosy *Iris Senlac* is just the right colour: I must split up my clumps as soon as they have finished flowering and make a group of those near the tamarisk for next May. The common pink columbine, almost a weed, would do well for under-planting, or some pink pansies, Crimson Queen, or the wine-red shades, as a carpet; and, for something really noble, the giant fox-tail lily, *Eremurus robustus*, eight to ten feet high. I cut, with reluctance, one precious spike from a distant group, and stick it in; it looks fine, like a cathedral spire flushed warm in the sunset. Undoubtedly I should have some *eremuri* next year with the plumy curtains of the tamarisk behind them, but the *eremuri* are too expensive and one cannot afford many of them.

'This is just one example. One has the illusion of being an artist painting a picture – putting in a dash of colour here, taking out another dash of colour there, until the whole composition is to one's liking, and at least one knows exactly what effect will be produced twelve months hence.'

Vita was also aware of balancing the rounded, bosomy shape with the odd tall spire. Then you'd get an interesting rhythm in a garden and prevent anything becoming too repetitive or dull. In July 1952 she writes in *In Your Garden Again*:

'You see, I believe that one ought always to regard a garden in terms of architecture as well as of colour. One has huge lumps of, let us say, the shrub roses making large voluminous bushes like a Victorian crinoline, or flinging themselves about in wild sprays; or, putting it another way, some plants make round fat bushes, and seem to demand a contrast in a tall sharp plant, say delphiniums, sticking up in a cathedral spire of bright blue amongst the roses instead of in the orthodox way at the back of a herbaceous border. It is all a question of shape. Architectural shape, demanding the pointed thin ones amongst the fat rounds, as a minaret rises above the dome of a mosque.

'Let me say here, for the small garden, that one might happily cause some spikes of the pink *Linaria Canon J. Went* to rise above a carpeting of low pansies or violas. This Linaria comes true from seed; sows itself everywhere like a welcome, not an unwelcome, weed; and is as pretty a thing as you could wish to have in quantities for picking for the house indoors.

'Another fine thing to make great steeples is *Yucca gloriosa*. This will tower in a vast heavy ivory pyramid in July, of a powerful architectural value. It does not flower every year, so you must have at least three plants in order to get a yearly blooming, and for this you need a certain amount of space. I did begin by saying that this article would be addressed to people with the larger type of garden; but if the smaller garden can spare even three yards of room in a corner, *Yucca gloriosa* will come as a fine surprise on the grand scale in July, and will carry out my contention that you want variety of shape and height to make an aesthetic composition instead of just an amorphous muddle. The Yucca, being a child of the desert in Mexico and some of the hotter parts of the United States, such as California, likes the

driest possible place and the sunniest, but on the whole accom-
modates itself very obligingly to our soil and climate.'

Vita when she met Harold.

She liked experimenting: Pam and Sybille have said that
even in the last two years of her life, when as employees of the
National Trust they overlapped with her in the garden, she'd
sometimes turn up with something new and walk round until
she found a good place to plant it. She was a firm believer in
the view that 'a good gardener makes experiments', that 'the
fun of gardening is nothing unless you take reckless risks'; but
you then have to be able to see and admit that your choices

were not always right – and if wrong, you needed to change them.

She knew creating a brilliant garden is always about refinement – looking critically as often as you can, making notes of what's good and what's bad and if necessary moving things around until you have it right. 'Gardening is largely a question of mixing one sort of plant with another sort of plant,' she says, 'and of seeing how they marry happily together; and if you see that they don't marry happily, then you must hoick one of them out and be quite ruthless about it.

'That is the only way to garden; and that is why I advise every gardener to go round his garden now – and make notes of what he thinks he ought to remove and of what he wants to plant later on.

'The true gardener must be brutal, and imaginative for the future.'

Once plants were in and well established: 'A bit of judicious cutting, snipping and chopping here and there will often make the whole difference. It may expose an aspect never noticed before, because overhanging branches had obscured it. It may reveal a coloured clump in the distance, hitherto hidden behind some overgrown bush of thorn or other unwanted rubbish. It is like being a landscape gardener on a small scale – and what gardener can afford to garden on the grand scale nowadays? It must also be like being a painter, giving the final touches to his canvas: putting just a dash of blue or yellow or red where it is wanted to complete the picture and to make it come together in a satisfactory whole.'

Both Vita and Harold and the gardeners since them have continually done this – refine, move, replant, until they were happy.

As the garden designer Mary Keen said to me recently, 'Some of her ideas might have ended in tears – the *Clematis flammula* or wisteria over a hedge, the more rampant roses up into smaller fruit trees – but that didn't matter. What mattered was that she had a brilliant vision and her own ideas.'

The garden she made in the 1930s and tended in the 40s and 50s had a billowing freedom, a joyous informality, a great romance, which could not have been more different from that rather prescriptive Edwardian style she had been surrounded by in her youth. Sissinghurst was a glamorous garden but with slightly unkempt hair; the grand and the simple, side by side, each somehow making the other more marvellous; some things quite carefully planned, but cleverly feeling relaxed, free and easy. That fitted so well with the place they'd found, those crumbling walls of a romantic ruin.

5

A SOPHISTICATED PALETTE

The statue of a vestal virgin by Toma Rosandić under a weeping silver
pear, surrounded by lambs' ears in the White Garden – *Stachys byzantina.*

Vita's vision for the White Garden, her Purple Border and the sunset-coloured Cottage Garden is perhaps her most lasting and copied garden legacy, not just at Sissinghurst, but around the world. When I asked the designer Dan Pearson what had influenced him most about the garden at Sissinghurst, he said it was the coloured rooms and particularly the hot colours of the Cottage Garden, which had inspired him in his Fire Garden at Home Farm (made famous by his TV series *A Year at Home Farm*).

Under the influence of garden designers such as William Robinson and Getrude Jekyll, the early twentieth century had begun to see gardens devoted to flowers of one colour or of one season, but Vita took this on another stage. She was clever with colour and had always had a sophisticated palette. As Harold said of her early days of gardening, 'Vita only likes flowers which are brown and difficult to grow.' She liked green flowers too – hellebores and euphorbias and the extraordinary green-flowered rose, which she grew in a pot next to the greenhouse. She had always been excited by unusual colour and had garden visions, like her dream of a verdigris garden, with flowers that were the blue-green of an old copper pot:

'It is agreeable sometimes to turn for a change from the dutifully practical aspects of gardening to the consideration of something strange, whether we can hope to grow it for ourselves or not. A wet January evening seemed just the time for such an indulgence of dreams, and in an instant I found my room (which hitherto had boasted only a few modest bulbs in bowls) filling up with flowers of the queerest colours, shapes, and habits. The first batch to appear, thus miraculously conjured out of the air, were all of that peculiar blue-green which one observes in verdigris on an old copper, in a peacock's feather, on the back of a beetle, or in the sea where the shallows meet the deep.

'First came a slender South African, *Ixia viridiflora*, with green flowers shot with cobalt blue and a purple splotch: this I had once grown in a very gritty pan in a cold greenhouse, and was pleased to see again. Then came the tiny sea-green Persian iris, only three inches high, which I had seen piercing its native desert but had never persuaded into producing a single flower here. Then came *Delphinium macrocentrum*, an East African, which I had never seen at all, but which is said to rival the Chilean *Puya alpestris* in colouring.

'*Puya alpestris* I knew. A ferocious-looking plant, and reluctant. Seven years had I cherished that thing in a pot, before it finally decided to flower. Then it threw up a spike and astonished everybody with its wicked-looking peacock trumpets and orange anthers, and side-shoots on which, apparently, humming-birds were supposed to perch and pollinate the flower. [This is still grown in the greenhouse and brought out in the summer when it's in flower.]

'And now here it was again, in my room, this time accompanied by the humming-birds which had been lamentably absent when I had flowered it after seven years. There were quite a lot of birds in my room by now, as well as flowers.'

She moves away from verdigris to exotic, cheerful thoughts for a grey January day: 'For *Strelitzia reginae* had also arrived, escorted by the little African sun-birds which perch and powder their breast-feathers with its pollen. It is rare for plants to choose birds as pollinators instead of insects; and here were two of them. *Strelitzia reginae* itself looked like a bird, a wild, crested, pointed bird, floating on an orange boat under spiky sails of blue and orange. Although it had been called regina after Queen Charlotte the consort of George III, I preferred it under its other name, the Bird of Paradise Flower.

'Then, as a change to homeliness, came clumps of the old primroses I had tried so hard to grow in careful mixtures of leaf-mould and loam, but here they were, flourishing happily between the cracks of the floorboards. Jack-in-the-Green, Prince Silverwings, Galligaskins, Tortoiseshell, Cloth of Gold; and as I saw them there in a wealth I had never been able to achieve, I remembered that the whole primula family was gregarious in its tastes and hated the loneliness of being one solitary, expensive little plant. They like huddling together, unlike the Lichens, which demand so little company that they will grow (in South America at any rate) strung out along the high isolation of tele-graph wires.

'There seemed indeed no end to the peculiarities of plants, whether they provided special perches for the convenience of their visitors, or turned carnivorous like the Pitcher-plants. Why was it that the Vine grew from left to right in the Northern hemisphere, but refused to grow otherwise than from right to left in the Southern? Why was the poppy called *Macounii* found only on one tiny Arctic island in the Behring Sea and nowhere else in the world? How had it come there in the first place? In a room now overcrowded with blooms of the imagination such speculations flowed easily, to the exclusion of similar speculations on the equally curious behaviour of men.

'The walls of the room melted away, giving place to a garden such as the Emperors of China once enjoyed, vast in extent, varied in landscape, a garden in which everything throve and the treasures of the earth were collected in beauty and brotherhood. But a log fell in the fire: a voice said: "This is the B.B.C. Home Service; here is the news," and I awoke.'

It's from this instinct – love of the odd and the brave – that her ideas for a carefully composed and restricted palette grew. At Long Barn, she had made and loved a white and yellow garden. Once at Sissinghurst, this became a unifying theme. As she noted in *In Your Garden*, for January 1950:

'It is amusing to make one-colour gardens. They need not necessarily be large, and they need not necessarily be enclosed, though the enclosure of a dark hedge is, of course, ideal. Failing this, any secluded corner will do, or even a strip of border running under a wall, perhaps the wall of the house. The site chosen must depend upon the general lay-out, the size of the garden, and the opportunities offered. And if you think that one colour would be monotonous, you can have a two- or even a three-colour, provided the colours are happily married, which is sometimes easier of achievement in the vegetable than in the human world. You can have, for instance, the blues and the purples, or the yellows and the bronzes, with their attendant mauves and orange, respectively. Personal taste alone will dictate what you choose.'

The idea for the Purple Border came first, all the flowers in a range around Vita's favourite colour: 'I must allow myself a purple patch. It isn't purple at all: it is blue. Blue as the Mediterranean on a calm day; blue as the smoke rising in autumn bonfires from our autumnal woods; blue seen through the young green of chestnut or beech; blue as the star-cabochon sapphire given to a bride on her wedding-day; hyacinth-scented beyond all these, just a blue-bell wood, an ordinary thing, a thing we take for granted.'

Once the wall on the north side of the Top Courtyard was complete in 1933, Vita was able to start planting and create a long border full of blue, purple and crimson. It was such a success – and still is – that Tony Lord wrote a chapter in his book *Best Borders* about this bed. Especially towards the end of the summer, it gives you a typical Sissinghurst blast of rich and effusive colour, not crazily gaudy but carefully held inside the boundaries of Vita's treasured purple.

The Cottage Garden came next in 1934/5, with a difficult range of colours – oranges, yellows, scarlets and deep reds which many gardeners steer well clear of, but here they were combined in a brave and sophisticated way. Harold influenced the making of this garden and there was always debate about whose initial idea it was for the sunset range of colour. He claimed it, but so did Vita. He had seen a garden in Mexico full of all the brilliant hues – magenta, scarlet, yellow and orange – thick with tropical creepers, morning glory, jacaranda and hibiscus.

Whether inspired by Harold or Vita, together they created a garden within the strict enclosure of the yew and holly hedge of the Cottage Garden: 'a symphony of all the wild sunset colours, a sort of western sky after a stormy day,' as Vita described it in 1952. 'The sunset colours are not always very good mixers in a garden, happily though they may consort in the heavens. In a garden they should, I think, be kept apart from the pinks, and be given, if possible, a place to themselves. I know that few gardens nowadays can afford this extravagance of separate space, but I can still imagine a hedged-off enclosure where nothing but the glow of blood-orange-and-yellow roses should have its own way.'

She added four years later: 'In a small square garden enclosed by holly hedges, I have been making notes of some plants in flower just now. They are all in the same range of colour – yellow, red, and orange – which explains why people often call it the sunset garden. At its best, it glows and flames. The dark hedges enhance the effect. Ideally, the hedges ought to be draped in ropes and curtains of the scarlet *Tropaeolum speciosum*, the Flame Flower so rampant in the North; but this must be a Scottish Nationalist by conviction, for it will have little to say to Sassenach persuasions.'

Harold's study overlooked this garden, and he wrote several times about how much pleasure it gave him. In a letter to Vita in August 1940: 'The Cottage Garden is ablaze with yellow and orange and red. A real triumph of gardening.' He sat out there almost every day when he was at Sissinghurst, far away from work in London. He had a chair on the doorstep, in which he used to sit in the summer early afternoon and have a sleep.

Finally and most famously came the White Garden. This had started out life as Vita's first rose garden, housing her ever expanding collection of old shrub roses. It was always an important garden, en route from the Priest's House – where they ate – to both their workrooms and the South Cottage. As Vita discovered more and more beautiful Gallica, Moss and Bourbon roses, she decided to move the whole lot into the garden on the southern edge of the site, which was until 1937 devoted to growing vegetables, fruit and herbs.

It was then that her gradually evolving idea of having a white garden – or more accurately a grey, green and white garden – came to fruition, a development and a tightening of her monochrome colour theme.

The arch from the Rose Garden to the Tower Lawn, box hedges enclosing eremurus, which Vita loved. This is the place she first tried out her White Garden idea, but it was too shady and damp and she wanted more space.

She first had the idea during the war. In December 1939, the Lion Pond was drained – it had always leaked – and Vita thought of planting in that small corner of the Lower Courtyard 'all white flowers, with some clumps of very pale pink. White clematis, white lavender, white agapanthus, white double primroses, white anemones, white camellias, white lilies including *giganteum* in one corner, and the pale peach-coloured *Primula pulverulenta*.' They realised quickly it could not work, because that corner had too much shade, and many of the white plants she wanted to include were sun-lovers. The idea of a whole garden devoted to this range of colours then took shape:

'I am trying to make a grey, green, and white garden. This is an experiment which I ardently hope may be successful, though I doubt it. One's best ideas seldom play up in practice to one's expectations, especially in gardening, where everything looks so well on paper and in the catalogues, but fails so lamentably in ful-filment after you have tucked your plants into the soil. Still, one hopes.

'My grey, green, and white garden will have the advantage of a high yew hedge behind it, a wall along one side, a strip of box edging along another side, and a path of old brick along the fourth side. It is, in fact, nothing more than a fairly large bed, which has now been divided into halves by a short path of grey flagstones terminating in a rough wooden seat. When you sit on this seat, you will be turning your back to the yew hedge, and from there I hope you will survey a low sea of grey clumps of foliage, pierced here and there with tall white flowers. I visual-ize the white trumpets of dozens of Regale lilies, grown three years ago from seed, coming up through the grey of southern-wood and artemisia and cotton-lavender, with grey-and-white edging plants such as *Dianthus Mrs. Sinkins* and the silvery mats of *Stachys Lanata*, more familiar and so much nicer under its English names of Rabbits' Ears or Saviour's Flannel. There will be white pansies, and white peonies, and white irises with their grey leaves … at least, I hope there will be all these things. I don't want to boast in advance about my grey, green, and white garden. It may be a terrible failure. I wanted only to suggest that such experiments are worth trying, and that you can adapt them to your own taste and your own opportunities.

'All the same, I cannot help hoping that the great ghostly barn-owl will sweep silently across a pale garden, next summer, in the twilight – the pale garden that I am now planting, under the first flakes of snow.'

These themes of so effectively concentrating the colour palette not just once, but three times, in one garden is masterly, confident, strong – a sign of her masculine dimension, an ability to impose her view on the world and key to the beauty of the Sissinghurst garden.

6

CRAM, CRAM, CRAM

Harold, Nigel (left) and Ben after some of the first planting on
the walls, August 1931.

In her planting, the filling and flowering up of her spaces, Vita had a clear and individual style. It is 'Cram, cram, cram, every chink and cranny,' she wrote on 15 May 1955. You have plants popping up in the paths: you have plants trained over almost every square inch of wall; and where there's a gap, Vita encourages plants to grow *in* the walls. As she says of herself, 'My liking for gardens to be lavish is an inherent part of my garden philosophy. I like generosity wherever I find it, whether in gardens or elsewhere. I hate to see things scrimp and scrubby. Even the smallest garden can be prodigal within its own limitations ... Always exaggerate rather than stint. Masses are more effective than mingies.'

You'll see this clearly in the photographs of both Long Barn and Sissinghurst from the 1930s until the 1960s, a great profusion, a shagginess, a relaxedness, a softness to almost every hard surface, path, wall or step, as well as all the borders filled to over-brimming. As Anne Scott-James puts it, 'She planned for rich planting and thick underplanting ... the whole garden to be furnished with a lavish hand.' Lavish is only partly it – it's also about embroidery and lace and nearly an old-ladyish sort of delicacy.

Go for it, overwhelm with plants, was a keystone of Vita's Sissinghurst. Don't plant just one of something – seven or nine, or even six hundred would be better if you can find the money and the room. She liked exaggeration: 'big groups, big masses; I am sure that it is more effective to plant 12 tulips together than to split them into 2 groups of 6'.

Pam and Sybille, in their continuing development of the garden in the 1960s, 70s and 80s, took this one step further. They would create a strong group of five or seven of one plant on one side of the path and then repeat it in a lesser group on the other. What Vita and then the gardeners were avoiding was the staccato look of dotting singly or in tiny groups, which gave a fussy feel. 'The more I see of other people's gardens the more convinced do I become of the value of good grouping and shapely training,' she declared in *In Your Garden Again*. 'These remarks must necessarily apply most forcibly to gardens of a certain size, where sufficient space is available for large clumps or for large specimens of individual plants, but even in a small garden the spotty effect can be avoided by massing instead of dotting plants here and there.'

COVER THE WALLS

I think Sissinghurst – more than any garden I have seen – uses the vertical as much as the horizontal, every surface brimming over.

Looking from the Tower to the climber-swagged front range and the table with the bowl for the shilling entrance fee.

This is obviously due partly to the number of walls they inherited from the ruined Elizabethan palace. As Vita said very early on, in a letter to Harold in 1930, 'I see that we are going to have heaps of wall space for climbing things.' But Vita really went for it, planting the soft-coloured terracotta with hundreds of climbers: roses, clematis, hydrangeas, wisterias. She wanted 'a tumble of roses and honeysuckle, figs and vines. It was a romantic place, and, within the austerity of Harold Nicolson's straight lines, must be romantically treated.'

As she says, 'Climbers are among the most useful plants in any garden. They take up little ground space, and they can be employed for many purposes: to clothe a boring fence, to scramble over a dead tree, to frame an archway, to drape a wall, to disguise a shed, or to climb lightly into a pergola. They demand comparatively little attention, once they have taken hold of their support, maybe a yearly pruning or a kindly rescue if they have come adrift in a gale'. This theme has been built on by the gardeners at Sissinghurst ever since.

She'd put lots of climbers and wall shrubs against the house at Long Barn, and wanted even more here. She admitted she had more walls to cover than most of us, but 'any garden, however small, has a house in it, and that house has walls. This is a very important fact to be remembered. Often I hear people say, "How lucky you are to have these old walls; you can grow anything against them," and then, when I point out that every house means at least four walls – north, south, east, and west – they say, "I never thought of that." Against the north and west sides you can grow magnolias or camellias; on the east side, which catches the morning sun, you can grow practically any of the hardy shrubs or climbers, from the beautiful ornamental quinces, commonly, though incorrectly, called Japonicas (the right name is Cydonia, or even more correctly, Chaenomeles), to the more robust varieties of *Ceanothus*, powdery-blue, or a blue fringing on purple. On the south side the choice is even larger – a vine, for instance, will soon cover a wide, high space, and in a reasonable summer will ripen its bunches of small, sweet grapes (I recommend Royal Muscadine, if you can get it); or, if you want a purely decorative effect, the fast-growing *Solanum crispum*, which is a potato though you might not think it, will reach to the eaves of the house and will flower in deep mauve for at least two months in early summer.'

The appearance of structural woody climbers – figs, wisterias and osmanthus, pruned flat against the shelter of the red brick and around the windows – is fundamental to the character of Sissinghurst, but Vita did not just leave it at this. She had lots of other things, and a particular passion for climbing and rambler roses, but all these were given only the lightest prune. This was partly because she hated to destroy the bird's nests, which were almost always in them, but partly because she loved the swathes. Harold complained in a letter: 'I suppose one must take for granted this birds'-nest passion ... I will have to resign myself to my home being an omelet most of the spring and a guano dump the rest of the time.' She liked the wayward natural growth of yews, not wanting them tightly clipped. She loved shrub roses billowing or even tangling over your head; tall roses – like 'Nevada' – tower up right at the edge of the path, columns of shrubs almost obscuring them. Roses were to her a 'wildly blossoming shrub' and that's how they should be grown.

SPRING

For spring Vita planted azara and osmanthus on west-facing walls, their scent in April one of the characteristic smells of the Sissinghurst garden and deliciously strong on a warm day.

Actinidia kolomikta on the west side of the Powys wall.

For its elegant Neapolitan ice-cream, triple-coloured leaves she added actinidia, tucked in a sheltered west-facing corner on the south range, below one of our bedroom windows. It's a slow grower, but an exotic thing: 'If you want something which will never exceed 8 to 10 feet let me recommend *Actinidia Kolomikta* as a plant to set against a wall facing east or west. The small white flowers are insignificant and may be disregarded; the beauty lies in the leaves, which are triple-coloured, green and pink and white, so gay and decorative and unusual as to provoke friends and visitors into asking what it is.'

Akebia is another one, a quick-growing, rampant climber with the delicious and unusual smell of an old-fashioned boiled sweet. I remember seeing this on the main house at Glyndebourne, drawn by its smell that was being thrown twenty yards away. I'd never seen it before, but immediately planted it in my own garden and now – in spring – its scent adds to the medley drifting in through the windows on a warmish day.

As Vita says, '[Akebias] are not often seen, but they should be. They are strong growers, semi-evergreen, with shamrock-like leaves and curiously coloured flowers. The flowers of *A. trifoliata* are brown, and the flowers of *A. quinata* are of a dusty violet, which might best be described by that neglected adjective, *gridelin*. Both kinds are hardy, and in a mild climate or after a hot sunny summer will produce fruits the size of a duck's egg, if you will imagine a duck's egg in plum-colour, with a plum's beautiful bloom before it has got rubbed off in the marketing. These fruits have the advantage that their seeds will germinate 100 per cent if you sow them in a pot; at any rate, that has been my experience.' On Vita's advice, my mother still has an *Akebia quinata* with an *Actinidia kolomikta* growing up a wall next to a Judas tree.

Vita particularly relished the jewel-like flowers of the ornamental quince, and this was one of the first plants she put in as soon as the restoration work was completed on the Big Room walls. I like looking at that plant, the same one that was there seventy years ago and still looking strong and healthy. In *In Your Garden Again*, Vita notes in October 1951:

'The ornamental quinces should not be forgotten. They may take a little while to get going, but, once they have made a start, they are there for ever, increasing in size and luxuriance from year to year. They need little attention, and will grow almost anywhere, in sun or shade. Although they are usually seen trained against a wall, notably on old farmhouses and cottages, it is not necessary to give them this protection, for they will do equally well grown as loose bushes in the open or in a border, and, indeed, it seems to me that their beauty is enhanced by this liberty offered to their arching sprays. Their fruits, which in autumn are as handsome as their flowers, make excellent jelly; in fact, there is everything to be said in favour of this well-mannered, easy-going, obliging and pleasantly old-fashioned plant . . .

'There are many varieties. There is the old red one, C[ydonia] lagenaria, hard to surpass in richness of colour, beautiful against a grey wall or a whitewashed wall, horrible against modern red brick. There is *C. nivalis*, pure white, safely lovely against any background. There is *C. Moerloosei*, or the Apple-blossom quince, whose name is enough to suggest its shell-pink colouring. There is *Knaphill Scarlet*, not scarlet at all but coral-red; it goes on flowering at odd moments throughout the summer long after its true flowering season is done. There is *C. cathayensis*, with small flowers succeeded by the biggest green fruits you ever saw – a sight in themselves.'

Beside the japonica Vita planted evergreen myrtle, its leaves so deliciously fragrant when crushed and its black berries so tangy it is not surprising that they are used as flavouring – like juniper's – with meat. Vita could crumple up a leaf when going in and out of the Big Room and that is why it's planted there:

'I have a myrtle growing on a wall. It is only the common myrtle, *Myrtus communis*, but I think you would have to travel far afield to find a lovelier shrub for July and August flowering. The small, pointed, dark-green leaves are smothered at this time of year by a mass of white flowers with quivering centres of the palest green-yellow, so delicate in their white and gold that it appears as though a cloud of butterflies had alighted on the dark shrub.

'The myrtle is a plant full of romantic associations in mythology and poetry, the sacred emblem of Venus and of love, though why Milton called it brown I never could understand, unless he was referring to the fact that the leaves, which are by way of being ever-green, do turn brown in frosty weather or under a cold wind. Even if it gets cut down in winter there is nothing to worry about, for it springs up again, at any rate in the South of England. In the north it might be grateful for a covering of ashes or fir branches over the roots. It strikes very easily from cuttings, and a plant in a pot is a pretty thing to possess, especially if it can be stood near the house-door, where the aromatic leaves may be pinched as you go in and out. In very mild counties, such as Cornwall, it should not require the protection of a wall, but may be grown as a bush or small tree in the open, or even, which I think should be most charming of all, into a small grove suggestive of Greece and her nymphs.

'The flowers are followed by little inky berries, which in their turn are quite decorative, and would probably grow if you sowed a handful of them.' Like the japonica, this is the same plant put in by Vita in the early 1930s, and I always do as she says, pinching the leaves as I pass.

SUMMER

For summer wall shrubs and climbers, Vita's favourites were of course the roses. There were so many outstanding ones to choose from and they fitted perfectly – if pruned quite loosely – with her idea of embroidered exuberance, wands arching over-head as well as looping up and over all her walls. 'How wide is the scope, whether we plant against a wall, or over a bank, or up a pillar, or even an archway, or in that most graceful fashion of

Roses tumbling off the top of a wall, only lightly pruned.

sending the long strands up into an old tree, there to soar and dangle, loose and untrammelled,' she mused.

VITA'S FAVOURITES

'Albertine'

This is a lovely soft pink rose which Vita mentions as rare among the rambling wichuraianas, in that it's not prone to mildew even when trained on a wall. 'Albertine' is planted to the right of the Tower steps, where it merges with 'Paul's Lemon Pillar', both planted by Vita in the 1930s. There used to be two or three 'Albertines' in the Lower Courtyard, but – a slightly tender rose – all but one were lost in the severe winter of 1962/3.

'Albertine' roses and 'Paul's Lemon Pillar' with potted plants.

'Allen Chandler'
This is the rose planted on the entrance arch in the Top
Courtyard, planted by Vita in the 30s – 'A magnificent red, only
semi-double, which carries some bloom all through the summer.
Not, I think, a rose for a house of new brick, but superb on grey
stone, or on white-wash, or indeed any colour-wash.'

'Lawrence Johnstone'
'A splendid very deep yellow,' Vita enthuses, 'better than the very
best butter, and so vigorous as to cover 12 ft. of wall within two
seasons. It does not seem to be nearly so well known as it ought to
be, even under its old name *Hidcote Yellow*, although it dates back
to 1925 and received an Award of Merit from the R.H.S. in 1948.
The bud, of a beautifully pointed shape, opens into a loose, nearly-
single flower which does not lose its colour up to the very moment
when it drops. Eventually it will attain a height of 50 ft., but if you
cannot afford the space for so rampant a grower, you have a sister
seedling in *Le Rêve*, indistinguishable as to flower and leaf, but more
restrained as to growth. It must, however, be said that the first
explosion of bloom is not usually succeeded by many subsequent
flowers.' This was planted on the South Cottage and is still there.

'Madame Alfred Carrière'
This was the first rose planted by Vita at Sissinghurst in 1930,
before the deeds were even signed, and it quickly covered most
of the south face of the South Cottage and in Vita and Harold's
day was left to 'render invisible' most of the front of the house
and trained around her bedroom window to pour scent into the
house for months at a stretch. It is still there, and now has a huge
trunk wider than my husband's thigh.

Rosa 'Madame Alfred Carrière' climbing all over South Cottage.

'If you want a white rose, flushed pink, very vigorous and seldom without flowers,' she writes, 'try *Mme Alfred Carrière.* Smaller than Paul's rose [see p. 105], and with no pretensions to a marmoreal shape, *Madame Alfred* has the advantage of a sweet, true-rose scent, and will grow to the eaves of any reasonably pro-portioned house. It's best on a sunny wall but tolerant of a west or even a north aspect. I should like to see every Airey house [a pre-fabricated house built after the Second World War] in this country rendered invisible behind this curtain of white and green.'

'Mermaid'

'Perhaps too well known to be mentioned, but should never be forgotten, partly for the sake of the pale-yellow flowers, opening flat and single, and partly because of the late flowering season, which begins after most other climbers are past their best. I must add that *Mermaid* should be regarded with caution by dwellers in cold districts.' This turned out to be all too true at Sissinghurst, where Vita planted it on the east-facing wall of the front range. In the severe winter of 1985 it was cut right to the ground and had to be removed. It has been replanted in the Top Courtyard on the east-facing wall to the left of the arch.

Rosa mulliganii on the rose frame in the White Garden, designed by Nigel using paperclips on his desk.

Mulliganii

This is the rose planted at the centre of the White Garden, long thought to be the rose *longicuspis.* There used to be four, planted to grow up the central path lined with almond trees, but the rose is so rampant, the almonds were starved of light and died. Three of the *mulliganii* were then removed and the remaining one trained over the central arbour of the White Garden in the 1970s. This is now struggling and recently a new one has been planted to gradually take its place.

'New Dawn'
This is grown against the wall of the Tower Lawn, where it is only lightly pruned. Its stiffer branches and non-rampant growth mean that its most vigorous stems need only shortening slightly. 'Among other wichuraianas, of a stiffer character than the ramblers, the *New Dawn* is to my mind one of the best, very free-flowering throughout the summer, of a delicate but definite rose-pink.'

'Paul's Lemon Pillar'
This was planted in two places by Vita at Sissinghurst, against the south-facing wall of the Rose Garden next to the gate into the Top Courtyard, and towards the southwest corner of the Tower Lawn.

'Another favourite white rose of mine,' says Vita, 'is *Paul's Lemon Pillar*. It should not be called white. A painter might see it as greenish, suffused with sulphur-yellow, and its great merit lies not only in the vigour of its growth and wealth of flowering, but also in the perfection of its form. The shapeliness of each bud has a sculptural quality which suggests curled shavings of marble, if one may imagine marble made of the softest ivory suede. The full-grown flower is scarcely less beautiful; and when the first explosion of bloom is over, a carpet of thick white petals covers the ground, so dense as to look as though it had been

'Paul's Lemon Pillar' merging with 'Albertine' roses on the Lower Courtyard wall.

deliberately laid ... One of the most perfectly shaped roses I know, and of so subtle a colour that one does not know whether to call it ivory or sulphur or iceberg green.'

PRUNING THE CLIMBING ROSES

Vita liked her climbing roses only lightly pruned, as noted earlier. She loved to see their great tresses climbing up into trees, providing shaggy moustaches and eyebrows to the buildings. They were given only a scant tidy-up in the winter, the dead wood removed, the most rampant growth neatened, but they were never hard shorn. What you got with this pattern of pruning was a great luxuriance of tangled growth each summer, the roses

Rosa mulliganii pruned hard on its frame in the White Garden.

standing out a good two feet from the walls in places, but you got fewer flowers than if they had been pruned more systematically.

The gardeners' policy since Pam and Sybille's time is to take the roses back to a tight frame. The climbing-rose pruning season at Sissinghurst now starts in November. First, the gardeners cut off most of that year's growth. This keeps the framework clear and prevents the plant from becoming too woody. Next, large woody stems are taken out – almost to the base – to encourage new shoots. These will flower the following year. The remaining branches are reattached to the wall, stem by stem, starting from the middle of the plant, working outwards, with the pruned tip of each branch bent down and attached to the branch below. That's the key thing – bending each stem down.

Climbers such as 'Paul's Lemon Pillar' are a bit more reluctant to comply with this treatment than ramblers like 'Albertine' and the *Rosa mulliganii* on the frame in the centre of the White Garden, which are very bendy and easy to train.

MORE OF VITA'S FAVOURITE SUMMER WALL SHRUBS AND CLIMBERS

One of the most significant and large-scale wall plants at Sissinghurst is *Magnolia grandiflora* with its vast, canoe-shaped leaves all year round, their copper backs just glimpsed as they flicker in the wind. Vita put in two soon after their arrival – one at the entrance and one in the Top Courtyard – and unusually for magnolias, they flower intermittently right through the summer.

'The flowers . . . look like great white pigeons settling among dark leaves,' she noted in 1950. 'This is an excellent plant for covering an ugly wall-space, being evergreen and fairly rapid of growth. It is not always easy to know what to put against a new red-brick wall; pinks and reds are apt to swear, and to intensify the already-too-hot colour; but the cool green of the magnolia's glossy leaves and the utter purity of its bloom make it a safe thing to put against any background, however trying. Besides, the flower in itself is of such splendid beauty. I have just been looking into the heart of one. The texture of the petals is of a dense cream; they should not be called white; they are ivory, if you can imagine ivory and cream stirred into a thick paste, with all the softness and smoothness of youthful human flesh; and the scent, reminiscent of lemon, was overpowering.

Magnolia grandiflora.

'There is a theory that magnolias do best under the protection of a north or west wall, and this is true of the spring-flowering kinds, which are only too liable to damage from morning sunshine after a frosty night, when you may come out after breakfast to find nothing but a lamentable tatter of brown suede; but *grandiflora*, flowering in July and August, needs no such consideration. In fact, it seems to do better on a sunny exposure, judging by the two plants I have in my garden. I tried an experiment, as usual. One of them is against a shady west wall, and never carries more than half a dozen buds; the other, on a glaring southeast wall, normally carries twenty to thirty. The reason, clearly, is that the summer sun is necessary to ripen the wood on which the flowers will be borne. [Vita's two original plants are still here at Sissinghurst, one on the west wall of the entrance courtyard, one on a south-facing wall on the top lawn, and the difference in flowering is still apparent.] What they don't like is drought when they are young, i.e. before their roots have had time to go far in search of moisture; but as they will quickly indicate their disapproval by beginning to drop their yellowing leaves, you can be on your guard with a can of water, or several cans, from the rain-water butt.

'Goliath is the best variety. Wires should be stretched along the wall on vine-eyes for convenience of future tying. This will save a lot of trouble in the long run, for the magnolia should eventually fill a space at least twenty feet wide by twenty feet high or more, reaching right up to the eaves of the house. The time may come when you reach out of your bedroom window to pick a great ghostly flower in the summer moonlight, and then you will be sorry if you find it has broken away from the wall and is fluttering on a loose branch, a half-captive pigeon trying desperately to escape.'

'Goliath' is excellent for a garden on the Sissinghurst scale, as it tends to be very broad-spreading, while there is another cultivar, 'Harold Poole', which is smaller in all its parts and so would fit in a smaller garden. 'Samuel Sommer' has the largest flowers of all, which can be over a foot across, yet it's not a

massive grower and is said to be particularly hardy. It's ideal for
those with smaller gardens.

There were relatively few clematis at Sissinghurst until Pam
and Sybille arrived in 1959. Sybille remembers going with
Vita to Christopher Lloyd's garden and nursery at Great Dixter
in East Sussex to help her select a few. They gradually put in
more and more, favouring particularly the late-flowering viticel-
las, which were resistant to the destructive fungus, clematis wilt.

'However popular, however ubiquitous, the clematis must
remain among the best hardy climbers in our gardens,' Vita
writes. 'Consider first their beauty, which may be either flamboyant or delicate. Consider their long flowering period, from
April till November. Consider also that they are easy to grow; do
not object to lime in the soil; are readily propagated, especially
by layering; are very attractive even when not in flower, with
their silky-silvery seed heads, which always remind me of
Yorkshire terriers curled into a ball; offer an immense variety
both of species and hybrids; and may be used in many different
ways, for growing over sheds, fences, pergolas, hedges, old trees,
or up the walls of houses. The perfect climber? Almost, but there
are two snags which worry most people.

'There is the problem of pruning. This, I admit, is complicated
if you want to go into details, but as a rough working rule it is
safe to say that those kinds which flower in the spring and early
summer need pruning just after they have flowered, whereas the
later flowering kinds (i.e., those that flower on the shoots they
have made during the current season) should be pruned in the
early spring.

'The second worry is *wilt*. You may prefer to call it *Ascochyta
Clematidina*, but the result is the same, that your most promising

plant will suddenly, without the slightest warning, be discovered hanging like miserable wet string. The cause is known to be a fungus, but the cure, which would be more useful to know, is unknown. The only comfort is that the plant will probably shoot up again from the root; you should, of course, cut the collapsed strands down to the ground to prevent any spread of the disease. It is important, also, to obtain plants on their own roots, for they are far less liable to attack ... Slugs, caterpillars, mice, and rabbits are all fond of young clematis, but that is just one of the normal troubles of gardening. Wilt is the real speciality of the clematis.

'There is much more to be said about this beautiful plant but space only to say that it likes shade at its roots, and don't let it get too dry.'

Clematis 'Perle d'Azur' on the Powys wall.

The clematis 'Perle d'Azur' is one of the iconic plants of Sissinghurst, growing on the semicircular wall in the Rose Garden. This was planted after Vita's day, by Pam and Sybille. It forms a majestic mauve backcloth to the Rose Garden for many weeks in late summer. This is no mean feat – it is very elaborately trained to achieve such drama. The wall is covered with six-inch netting above the clematis. The plant is cut back hard in late autumn and every ten days in May and June, then carefully spread out over the wall as it grows, with new growth tied in as you might do for your tomatoes or sweet peas. The gardeners use paper-covered wire twists so as to be more gentle to the stems, and attach the new stems to the wire behind with these.

There have also been lots of clematis on the wall along the back of the Purple Border, six or seven merging into a great curtain of crimson and purple, varieties chosen to overlap but flower in succession to give the maximum weeks of interest to this high-summer border. There is an ingenious system of wiring that goes over the top of the wall, bridging one side and the other with sheep netting. When the clematis reaches the top, rather than being blown around like a huge sail and then collapsing back on itself, it clings to the wire, which then carries it from the Top Courtyard side into the garden known as Delos.

SUMMER AND AUTUMN

Vita was also very fond of four other slightly tender wall plants, which added a bit of exoticism to her walls. The first was the shrub *Abutilon megapotamicum*, which she picked as one of her favourite plants in her short book, *Some Flowers*, published in 1937. She decribes it at length:

'This curious Brazilian with the formidable name is usually offered as a half-hardy or greenhouse plant, but experience shows that it will withstand as many degrees of frost as it is likely to meet with in the southern counties. It is well worth trying against a south wall, for apart from the unusual character of its flowers it has several points to recommend it. For one thing it occupies but little space, seldom growing more than four

Abutilon megapotamicum.

feet high, so that even if you should happen to lose it you will not be left with a big blank gap. For another, it has the convenient habit of layering itself of its own accord, so that by merely separating the rooted layers and putting them into the safety of a cold frame, you need never be without a supply of substitutes. For another, it is apt to flower at times when you least expect it, which always provides an amusing surprise ...

'It is a thing to train up against a sunny south wall, and if you should happen to have a whitewashed wall or even a wall of grey stone, it will show up to special advantage against it ... It is on the tender side, not liking too many degrees of frost, so should be covered over in winter ...

'You should ... grow it where you are constantly likely to pass and can glance at it daily to see what it is doing. It is not one of those showy climbers which you can see from the other side of the garden, but requires to be looked at as closely as though you were short-sighted. You can only do so in the open, for if you cut it to bring into the house it will be dead within the hour, which is unsatisfactory both for it and for you. But sitting on the grass at the foot of the wall where it grows, you can stare up into the queer hanging bells and forget what the people round you are saying. It is not an easy flower to describe – no flower is, but the Abutilon is particularly difficult. In despair I turned up its botanically official description: "Ls. lanc, 3, toothed. Fls. 1½, sepals red, petals yellow, stamens long and drooping (like a fuchsia)".

'Now in the whole of that laconic though comprehensive specification there were only three words which could help me at all: *like a fuchsia*. Of course I had thought of that already; anybody would. The flower of the Abutilon *is* like a fuchsia, both in size and in shape, though not in colour. But it is really a ballet dancer, something out of *Prince Igor*. "Sepals red, petals yellow" is translated for me into a tight-fitting red bodice with a yellow petticoat springing out below it in flares, a neat little figure, rotating on the point of the stamens as on the point of the toes. One should, in fact, be able to spin it like a top.' This abutilon has recently been planted in a very prominent position to cover the front of the South Cottage, sharing the south-facing wall there with *Rosa* 'Madame Alfred Carrière'.

Her next recommendation is for campsis (known then as bignonia), a very luscious plant with large, deep burnt-orange trumpet flowers which you see much more commonly on the Continent than in gardens here. This may get cut to the ground in a hard winter, but usually re-emerges just as well the following spring and can romp its way up over the top of a barn roof in no time:

'They are so showy and so decorative ... Their big orange-red trumpets make a noise like a brass band in the summer garden. They are things with a rather complicated botanical history, often changing their names. *Bignonia grandiflora* is now known as *Campsis grandiflora* (it went through a phase of calling itself Tecoma) and *Bignonia radicans* is now *Campsis radicans.* The best variety of it is Mme Galen; and as it has rather smaller flowers than *grandiflora*, a friend of mine calls it Little-nonia, a poor joke that will not appeal to serious gardeners, but may be helpful to the amateurs who wish to remember the difference.

'They all want a sunny wall, and should be pruned back like a vine, that is, cut right hard back to a second "eye" or bud, during the dormant season between November and January. Like a vine, again, they will strike from cuttings taken at an eye and pushed firmly into sandy soil.' Campsis was, and still is, planted on the moat wall where it tumbles from the orchard side, the flowers almost echoing the colour of the brighter bricks.

Cobaea scandens on the Erechtheum.

Vita also enjoyed the exotic-looking cup-and-saucer plant, *Cobaea scandens*, and planted this on the east-facing wall of the south range in the Top Courtyard and on the Erechtheum, where it is still planted every year today. It reaches not eight to ten foot high, as Vita suggests below, but thirty, right up to our daughter Molly's bathroom window on the second floor.

Vita tells her readers: 'An interesting and unusual plant which should find a place is *Cobaea scandens*, which sounds more attractive under its English name of cups-and-saucers. This is a climber, and an exceedingly rapid one, for it will scramble eight to ten feet high in the course of a single summer. Unfortunately it must be regarded as an annual in most parts of this country, and a half-hardy annual at that, for although it might be possible with some protection to coax it through a mild winter, it is far better to renew it every year from seed sown under glass in February or March. Pricked off into small pots in the same way as you would do for tomatoes, it can then be gradually hardened off and planted out towards the end of May. In the very mild counties it would probably survive as a perennial.

'It likes a rich, light soil, plenty of water while it is growing, and a sunny aspect. The ideal place for it is a trellis nailed against a wall, or a position at the foot of a hedge, when people will be much puzzled as to what kind of a hedge this can be, bearing such curious short-stemmed flowers, like a Canterbury Bell with tendrils. Unlike the Canterbury Bell, however, the flowers amuse themselves by changing their colour. They start coming out as a creamy white; then they turn apple-green, then they develop a slight mauve blush, and end up a deep purple. A bowl of the mixture, in its three stages, is a pretty sight, and may be picked right up to the end of October.' I find these last a few more days in water if you sear the stem ends (see pp. 345–6).

Similar in feel to the cup-and-saucer plant and also useful for picking and floating in a shallow bowl for a table, Vita liked the Passion flower, *Passiflora caerulea*, 'which is hardier than sometimes supposed, springing up from its roots again yearly, even if it has been cut down to the ground by frost and has apparently given up all attempt to live. Its strangely constructed flowers are not very effective at a distance, but marvellous to look into, with the nails and the crown of thorns from which it derives its name. It should be grown against a warm wall, though even in so favoured a situation I fear it is unlikely to produce its orange fruits in this country.' Later, she added: 'I must go back on this remark. Plants on two cottages near where I live, in Kent, produce a truly heavy crop of fruits. I could not think what they were till I stopped to investigate. The curious thing is that both plants are facing due east, and can scarcely receive any sun at all.'

And a last word: 'There is a white variety called Constance Elliott. I prefer the pale blue one myself; but each to his own taste.'

VITA'S TOP SHRUBS AND CLIMBERS

FOR A SOUTH WALL

Abutilon megapotamicum
Indigoferas
Solanum crispum var. *autumnalis*, 'so useful in August – a trifle tender, perhaps, wanting a warm south wall'
Solanum jasminoides, white, 'another August flowerer, a most graceful climber, also a trifle tender but well worth trying in southern counties'
Vine 'Royal Muscadine'

FOR A NORTH WALL

> *Clematis flammula*
> *Garrya elliptica*
> *Kerria japonica*
> Morello cherry
> Winter jasmine

FOR A NORTH OR WEST WALL

> Camellias
> Magnolias
> Osmanthus
> Wisteria

FOR AN EAST WALL

> Hardier ceanothus
> Japonica (ornamental quince)

COVER THE TREES

When I ask my mother how Vita influenced my parents' garden most of all, she remembers Vita's passion for growing climbers and particular roses up into trees. She still has several roses grown like that in their garden in the village of Shepreth, just outside Cambridge, a garden mainly planted in the late 1950s, when through her *Observer* columns Vita's influence was most felt. There is 'Madame Alfred Carrière' up a Bramley apple tree,

'Albéric Barbier' up a rhus, 'Crimson Conquest' up a white-flow-ered lilac and 'Wickwar' up a euonymus by the house.

Vita liked to decorate the trees, and is well known for using the apple and pear trees in the Sissinghurst Orchard and the almonds in the centre of the new White Garden as climbing frames for clematis and roses, sometimes at the cost of the tree beneath the rampant canopy. The soft pink rose 'Flora' is the one remaining, clambering right to the top of a soft prunus outside the door of the Priest's House. She recommends ivy and vines too – of the right varieties – as well as *Clematis montana* and the tricolour-leaved actinidia (see also p. 96):

'We do not make nearly enough use of the upper storeys. The ground floor is just the ground, the good flat earth we cram with all the plants we want to grow. We also grow some climbers, which reach to the first-floor windows, and we may grow some other climbers over a pergola, but our inventiveness usually stops short at that. What we tend to forget is that nature pro-vides some far higher reaches into which we can shoot long festoons whose beauty gains from the transparency of dangling in mid-air. What I mean, briefly, is things in trees ...

'There is no need to stick to ivy. The gadding vine will do as well. The enormous shield-shaped leaves of *Vitis coignetiae*, turn-ing a deep pink in autumn, amaze us with their rich cornelian in the upper air, exquisitely veined and rosy as the pricked ears of an Alsatian dog. Then, if you prefer June–July colour to October colour, there is that curious vigorous climber, *Actinidia kolomikta*, which starts off with a wholly green leaf, then develops white streaks and a pink tip, and puzzles people who mistake its colour-ing habits for some new form of disease. Cats like it: and so do I, although I don't like cats.'

Vita also suggests a vigorous climber such as *Clematis montana* for a large tree. '[It] should soon clothe it to the top; this small-flowered clematis can be had in its white form, or in the pink variety, *rubra*. The so-called Russian vine, *Polygonum bald-schuanicum*, most rapid of climbers, will go to a height of 20 ft. or more, and is attractive with its feathery plumes of a creamy white. It should scarcely be necessary to emphasize the value of the wisterias for similar purpose.

'One advantage of this use of climbers for a small garden is the saving of ground space. The soil, however, should be richly made up in the first instance, as the tree-roots will rob it grossly, and will also absorb most of the moisture, so see to it that a newly planted climber does not lack water during its first season, before it has had time to become established and is sending out its own roots far enough or deep enough to get beyond the worst of the parched area.'

VITA'S TOP TREE-CLIMBING ROSES

All three of these roses were planted by Vita in the Orchard and two are still there, but not on trees.

'Félicité et Perpétue'
'Commemorating two young women who suffered martyrdom at Carthage in A.D. 205', Vita recommends this for growing on a tree. On a wall it can get mildew, but on a tree 'it will grow at least 20 ft. high into the branches, very appropriately, since St. Perpetua was vouchsafed the vision of a wonderful ladder reaching up to heaven'. Vita planted this in the Orchard to climb into a pear tree.

The tree has died and a new rose has been planted, but this one is rather too tidily trained over a chestnut frame.

Rosa filipes 'Kiftsgate'

'If you want a very vigorous climber, making an incredible length of growth in one season, do try to obtain *Rosa filipes*,' Vita urges. 'It is ideal for growing into an old tree, which it will quickly drape with pale-green dangling trails and clusters of small white yellow-centred flowers. I can only describe the general effect as lacy, with myriads of little golden eyes looking down at you from amongst the lace. This sounds like a fanciful description, of the kind I abhor in other writers on horticultural subjects, but really there are times when one is reduced to such low depths in the struggle to convey the impression one has oneself derived, on some perfect summer evening when everything is breathless, and one just sits, and gazes, and tries to sum up what one is seeing, mixed in with the sounds of a summer night – the young owls hissing in their nest over the cowshed, the bray of a donkey, the plop of an acorn into the pool.

'*Filipes* means thread-like, or with thread-like stems, so perhaps my comparison to lace is not so fanciful, after all. Certainly the reticulation of the long strands overhead, clumped with the white clusters, faintly sweet-scented, always makes me think of some frock of faded green, trimmed with Point d'Alençon – or is it Point de Venise that I mean?'

'Madame Plantier'

'I am astonished, and even alarmed, by the growth which certain roses will make in the course of a few years. There is one called

Madame Plantier, which we planted at the foot of a worthless old apple tree, vaguely hoping that it might cover a few feet of the trunk. Now it is 15 feet high with a girth of 15 yards, tapering towards the top like the waist of a Victorian beauty and pouring down in a vast crinoline stitched all over with its white sweet-scented clusters of flower.

'*Madame Plantier* dates back, in fact, to 1835,' Vita continues, 'just two years before Queen Victoria came to the throne, so she and the Queen may be said to have grown up together towards the crinolines of their maturity. Queen Victoria is dead, but *Madame Plantier* still very much alive. I go out to look at her in the moonlight: she gleams, a pear-shaped ghost, contriving to look both matronly and virginal. She has to be tied up round her tree, in long strands, otherwise she would make only a big straggly bush. We have found that the best method is to fix a sort of tripod of bean-poles against the tree and tie the strands to that.'

This was another rose planted in the Orchard to climb into a tree, but Pam and Sybille felt it to be too rampant. It quickly smothered the old apple tree, and itself grew rapidly so huge that it became difficult and very time-consuming to prune. It has collapsed now into a mound of nothing but rose, the remains of the tree buried underneath.

COVER THE GROUND

To achieve the feeling of maximum fullness, Vita crams things at ground level, as well as overhead:

'The more I prowl round my garden at this time of year, especially during that stolen hour of half-dusk between tea and

Every patch of ground is covered in the Cottage Garden, 1962.

supper, the more do I become convinced that a great secret of good gardening lies in covering every patch of the ground with some suitable carpeter. Much as I love the chocolate look of the earth in winter, when spring comes back I always feel that I have not done enough, not nearly enough, to plant up the odd corners with little low things that will crawl about, keeping weeds away, and tuck themselves into chinks that would otherwise be devoid of interest or prettiness.

'The violets, for instance – I would not despise even our native *Viola odorata* of the banks and hedgerows, either in its blue or its white form, so well deserving the adjective *odorata*. And how it spreads, wherever it is happy, so why not let it roam and range as it listeth? (I defy any foreigner to pronounce that word.) There are other violets, more choice than our wildling; the little pink *Coeur d'Alsace*, or *Viola labradorica* [still at Sissinghurst, as a carpeter], for instance, which from a few thin roots planted last year is now making huge clumps and bumps of purplish leaf and wine-coloured flower, and is sowing itself all over the place wherever it is wanted or not wanted. It is never not wanted, for it can be lifted and removed to another place, where it will spread at its good will.

'There are many other carpeters beside the violets, some for sunny places and some for shade. For sunny places the thymes are perhaps unequalled, but the sunny places are never difficult to fill. Shady corners are more likely to worry the gardener trying to follow my advice of cram, cram, cram every chink and cranny. *Arenaria balearica* loves a dark, damp home, especially if it can be allowed to crawl adhesively over mossy stones. On a dark green mat it produces masses of what must be one of the tiniest flowers, pure white, starry; an easy-going jewel for the right situation. *Cotula squalida* is much nicer than its name: it is like a miniature fern, and it will spread widely and will help to keep the weeds away.

'The *Acaenas* will likewise spread widely, and should do well in shade; they have bronzy-coloured leaves and crawl neatly over their territory. The list of carpeters is endless, and I wish I had enough space to amplify these few suggestions. The one thing I feel sure of is that every odd corner should be packed with something permanent, something of interest and beauty, something tucking itself into something else in the natural way of plants when they sow themselves and combine as we never could combine them with all our skill and knowledge.'

COVER THE PATHS

Apart from the walls, the paths and steps were the main hard structures in each of the garden rooms. They were designed by Harold and laid in the first two or three years after their arrival.

'Tramplees' swathing the steps at the northern end of the White Garden.

They could not always afford the vast expanses of York stone called for, and so in the less prominent paths, away from the entrance and the formal axes and vistas, they sometimes used a mix of materials.

In the Cottage Garden, Harold designed a scheme using brick with stone; in the Rose Garden, the main path was grass, and the side paths were left as grass, as they had been when this was the kitchen garden; in the Lime Walk the paths were made not just from concrete, but the surprising thing was that they were coloured, a mix of red, yellow and green. That is one of the few mystifying decisions Harold made, the colours luckily fading quite quickly, and the concrete has now been replaced by York stone.

Harold often designed wide sweeps of paths in the knowledge that Vita would soon be covering them with plants, both in between the stones and creeping in from the sides. Vita sets down her thoughts on the subject:

'The first essential [for planting in paths] is that it shall be something which does not mind being walked upon. There was once a play called *Boots and Doormats*, which divided people into two categories: those who liked to trample and those who enjoy being trampled. To-day, in modern jargon, I suppose they would be called tramplers and tramplees; I prefer boots and doormats as an expression of this fundamental truth. Many big boots will walk down a paved path, and there are some meek doormats prepared to put up with such gruff treatment. The creeping thymes really enjoy being walked on, and will crawl and crawl, spreading gradually into rivulets and pools of green, like water slowly trickling, increasing in volume as it goes, until they have filled up all the cracks and crevices. The thymes are the true standby for anybody who wants to carpet a paved path.

'There are other tramplees also. *Pennyroyal* does not mind what you do with it, and will give out its minty scent all the better for being bruised underfoot. *Cotula squalida* ... has tiny fern-like leaves, cowering very close down; no flower, but very resistant to hard wear and very easy to grow. All the *Acaenas* are useful;

Paths and steps almost invisible under carpets of plants at Long Barn.

Acaena Buchananii, a silver-green, or *Acaena microphylla*, bronze in colour. A pity that such tiny things should have such formidable names, but they are neither difficult to obtain nor to establish.'

You can see this in the garden at Long Barn, where all the hard surfaces were almost covered by curtains of rock roses, smaller species of roses, cistus, azaleas and rosemary, swathing the stone or brick from each side. This was a theme which Vita carried on at Sissinghurst and something that contributed hugely to the overall abundant feel of almost every part of the garden. Edwin Smith captures it brilliantly in his photograph of the Cottage Garden, taken in 1962 (see p. 123).

Vita goes further, suggesting 'filling up the cracks' in the path or steps 'with good soil or compost, and sow[ing] seeds quite recklessly. I should not mind how ordinary my candidates were, Royal Blue forget-me-not, pansies, wallflowers, Indian pinks, alyssum Violet Queen, because I should pull up 95 per cent later on, leaving only single specimens here and there. It is not, after all, a flower-bed that we are trying to create. If, however, you think it is a waste of opportunity to sow such ordinary things, there are plenty of low-growing plants of a choicer kind, especially those which dislike excessive damp at the root throughout the winter: this covering of stone would protect them from that. The old-fashioned pinks would make charming tufts: *Dad's Favourite*, or *Inchmery*, or *Little Jock*, or *Susan*, or *Thomas*. The Allwoodii, with their suggestion of chintz and of patchwork quilts, should also succeed under such conditions.'

SELF-SOWING AND PRETEND SELF-SOWING

Allowing self-sowing of favourite annuals and biennials was another essential thread, and very much part of Vita's cram-cram-cram design. She liked the random appearance of things, which often cropped up in plant combinations that were much better than one would have thought of oneself, as well as the freedom this gave to the feel of a garden – aubrieta, lupins, dill, poppies and thyme all left in the cracks in the paths and steps, or in the edges of the beds, as they came up.

She also liked the abundance self-sowing gave you, the miraculous appearance suddenly of many hundreds of Californian poppies in the cracks of the Lime Walk paths, which she banned the gardeners from weeding out, and she writes about walking round the garden with canes to mark things that popped up, volunteering themselves, which she wanted left just where they were.

Vita also loved to encourage a few select wild flowers to make their home in the garden. Not of course the brutes such as nettles and docks, but she liked to see daisies 'enamelling' the lawn. Columbines were always left to seed themselves and the dark-foliaged *Viola labradorica*, mentioned earlier, was allowed where it would. Both Vita and Harold hated gardens to be over-tamed or over-trimmed. As Anne Scott-James commented, 'To Vita, Sissinghurst always remained the Sleeping Beauty's castle, and though she was willing to clear a tangle of a hundred slumbering years she did not want the garden scrubbed clean. It was to be hospitable to wildlings.'

She took this one step further and actually planted seedlings of rosemary and wallflowers into the cracks in the Tower steps and the Moat Walk wall in a random way to make them look as if they were self-sown. There are lots of wild ivy-leaved toadflax in the Sissinghurst walls and some clumps of the yellow-flowered wild corydalis, but Vita wanted to add greater variety.

At Long Barn, on a sloping site, Vita and Harold had created great lengths of terraced walls so as to level it, and inserted Cheddar pinks, lavender, aubrietas, cistus and even species tulips into them, an idea she'd got from the terraced olive groves in southern Spain, adding these things to the walls as they were being built and then hoping they'd self-sow.

'How envious one feels of the terraced hillsides of the south,' she writes, 'for there are few more delightful or satisfactory forms of gardening than dry-wall gardening. Plants can run their roots right back into the cool soil between stones, finding every drop of moisture even in a dry season, and can open their faces to the sun on the wall-front. I write these words in Spain, wishing that I could bring home even one length of the rough walling, probably many hundreds of years old ...

'English people who live in a stone country such as the Cotswolds or the Lake District are fortunate in that they may be able to assemble sufficient stones at little cost. The important thing to remember is that the wall-front should be on a batten, i.e. sloping slightly backwards from the base to the top, and that each stone should be tilted back as it is laid in place, packed with good soil, for you must remember that the soil can never be renewed short of taking the whole wall to pieces. If you can plant as you go, layer by layer, so much the better, for then the roots can be spread out flat instead of ramming them in later on, cramped, constricted, and uncomfortable. This method also enables you to vary the soil according to the requirements of its occupant: peat, or grit, can be added or withheld at will.

'The top of the wall is full of possibilities. (I am assuming that your dry-wall is a retaining wall, built against a bank.) Not only can you fill it with things like *lithospermum* or pinks, or that pretty little rosy gypsophila called *fratensis*, to hang down in beards, on the wall-face, but a number of small bulbs will also enjoy the good drainage and will blow at eye-level where their delicate beauty can best be appreciated.

'I can think of many small subjects for such a kingdom. The Lady-tulip, *Tulipa clusiana*, striped pink-and-white like a boiled sweet from the village shop, might survive for many more seasons than is usual in a flat bed. The little Greek tulip *orphanidea* would also be happy, in fact all the bulbs which in their native countries are accustomed to stony drought all through the summer. The dwarf irises would give colour in the spring, and their grey-green leaves would look tidy all the year round. Ixias, so graceful, for a later flowering. Lavender *stoechas*, which is all over these Spanish hills, should not damp off as it is apt to do in an ordinary border. This lavender would form agreeable clumps between the bulbs; fairly dwarf, it makes a change from the usual lavenders, such as the deep purple *nana atropurpurea*. Clip them close, when the flower-spike is going over, to keep them neat and rounded.'

There could not be this range of plants crammed into the walls as if self-sown at Sissinghurst, because the brick-built – rather than stone – walls would not allow it, but it is still very much a theme in the planting style, particularly noticeable on the Moat Walk wall. When the wall was restored in the 1990s the gardeners felt it had been done too perfectly, without any planting holes left. So they carefully picked out small pockets in the brickwork into which they could then plant things.

Every year the perennial wallflower, *Erysimum* 'Bowles Mauve', is added in small plugs. These are done as cuttings rooted into Jiffy pots, which can then be pressed into the holes, supplementing those that are still there from the year before. For every two, only one takes, and then survives for about four years. I'm sure Vita would very much approve.

7

Flowering Shrubs

Magnolias framing the view from the White Garden, looking through the
Bishop's Gate.

Vita's view, certainly as time went on, was that once you have the 'bones' of your garden, the walls and hedges, in place, you then need to fill them out in a carefully balanced way, the first layer of flesh almost as planned as the bones themselves. She needed to think about introducing large-scale plants which would give a real sense of architecture, adding another layer to Harold's design.

In the 1950s Vita wrote about her regrets that she had not got on with more structural planting straight away at Sissinghurst, but as the years went by, more and more large plants were added to the borders, things that would give 'a sense of substance and solidity', a topography, some ups and downs, a shape and a rhythm, as well as that all-important feeling of fullness which would carry through even into the winter:

'It is a truly satisfactory thing to see a garden well schemed and wisely planted. Well schemed are the operative words. Every garden, large or small, ought to be planned from the outset, getting its bones, its skeleton, into the shape that it will preserve all through the year even after the flowers have faded and died away. Then, when all colour has gone, is the moment to revise, to make notes for additions, and even to take the mattock for removals. This is gardening on the large scale, not in details. There can be no rules in so fluid and personal a pursuit, but it is safe to say that a sense of substance and solidity can be achieved only by the presence of an occasional mass breaking the more airy companies of the little flowers.

'What this mass shall consist of must depend upon many things: upon the soil, the aspect, the colour of neighbouring plants, and above all upon the taste of the owner ... The possibilities of variation are manifold, but on the main point one must remain adamant: the alternation between colour and solidity, decoration and architecture, frivolity and seriousness. Every good garden, large or small, must have some architectural quality about it; and, apart from the all-important question of the general lay-out, including hedges, the best way to achieve this imperative effect is by massive lumps of planting.'

Vita wanted her 'massive lumps' to come from shrubs, particularly flowering forms. 'The alternative' to the herbaceous border, she wrote in October 1951, 'is a border largely composed of flowering shrubs, including the big bush roses … it is possible to design one which will (more or less) look after itself once it has become established.' This was increasingly important. With the memories of recent war and the challenges that Vita faced with only one gardener there to help at that time, to have a flower garden that didn't need intensive maintenance was at the forefront of her mind.

Many of the plants she cherished and planted at Sissinghurst are now well known – shrubs and small trees such as *Prunus subhirtella* 'Autumnalis', *Hoheria lyallii*, *Hydrangea paniculata* 'Grandiflora', and the pretty early-flowering almond. These were rarer, more obscure and much less readily available in the days when she was championing them – her 'faithful friends', as she called them. Many of these still remain the best today, though shrubs such as hoheria are surprisingly rarely planted even now.

It was with plants such as these that you could get a massed effect with minimal maintenance: 'The main thing, it seems to me, is to have a foundation of large, tough, un-troublesome plants with intervening spaces for the occupation of annuals, bulbs, or anything that takes your fancy.'

She puts their case again and again:

'Those gardeners who desire the maximum of reward with the

minimum of labour would be well advised to concentrate upon the flowering shrubs and flowering trees. How deeply I regret that fifteen years ago, when I was forming my own garden, I did not plant these desirable objects in sufficient quantity. They would by now be large adults instead of the scrubby, spindly infants I contemplate with impatience as the seasons come round.

'That error is one from which I would wish to save my fellow-gardeners, so, taking this opportunity, I implore them to secure trees and bushes from whatever nurseryman can supply them: they will give far less trouble than the orthodox herbaceous flower. They will demand no annual division, many of them will require no pruning; in fact, all that many of them will ask of you is to watch them grow yearly into a greater splendour, and what more could be exacted of any plant?'

She adds at a later date: 'The initial outlay would seem extravagant, but at least it would not have to be repeated, and the effect would improve with every year.'

Vita – as in all her gardening – was a great experimenter, always wanting to try out new things and ready to uproot them if they failed to impress. She was advised on potentially interesting shrubs by Norah Lindsay, the renowned between-the-wars garden designer, and Collingwood (often called 'Cherry') Ingram, an expert on the prunus family, who lived in Benenden, only a village away. Both had a great influence on what was chosen and planted all through the garden; there would be a process of filtering, with things coming in, some then staying, others being ripped out, or moved from one place to another.

Through this filtering, Vita ended up with some lifelong favourites, many of which she wrote about in her *Observer* columns. As we have seen, there are other shrubs and climbers she liked for positioning against the many walls, but it's the flow-ering shrubs in the following list to which she turned as the main decorative shapes for her flower beds.

VITA'S TOP SHRUBS AND TREES

WINTER

Many of the best winter-flowering shrubs, such as hamamelis, mahonias, wintersweet, are scented (see pp. 181–3) – Vita loved

Camellia 'Alba Simplex'.

these for picking too, so they have their own section (see p. 175) – but she also included camellias in her early structural planting.

She liked the single *Camellia* 'Alba Simplex', which she planted in the White Garden and the south-west corner of the Top Courtyard where it still is today. This is the most ele-gant variety, with very dark green, shiny foliage. I also grow it and love it for its sim-plicity compared to so many camellias that have a slightly plastic texture and an artificial-looking pink or red colour. 'Alba Simplex' is pure white around a golden centre packed with anthers and pollen.

Vita also grew the pink 'Donation', planted in the Tower beds in the Top Courtyard, and had this as a pot plant, grown in her cold greenhouse. She could then bring it in in the early spring to cheer up a dingy corner.

SPRING

Our bedroom window looks east, so that on a good spring morning we look out first thing at a sun rising behind the trees in the garden. There are several magnolias here, and in a year when there are no late frosts they glow in that first sunlight as if laden with lit candles, their branches peering over the garden walls. So often magnolias are full of promise in that first emergence of their buds, but then get nailed – literally browned off in the cold spring weather; but when they don't, they tower over the garden as its most flamboyant spring climax.

Of course, trees grow, and so if a magnolia does well it becomes more magnificent with every passing year. These particular ones, mostly put in by Vita in Delos and the Lower Courtyard, are now huge, like hot-air balloons of flowers, giving a massive third dimension to the garden.

Magnolias were one of her favourite garden trees – Vita would love to see them now.

'Many people hesitate to plant that most noble of flowering trees, the magnolia,' she writes, 'under the impression that they will never live long enough or remain for long enough in the same place to see it flower. It is true that some kinds of magnolia are not suitable for a short-term tenancy. *Magnolia campbellii*, for instance, may demand twenty-five years before it pays any dividend on its

original cost. [It also grows to about a hundred foot!] But this is
not true of some other kinds.

'The Yulan tree, *M. denudata*, produces a few of its creamy
chalices within a year or two of planting, and increases in size
and fertility until it is one hundred years old or more. I planted
one twenty years ago, and it has long since achieved a height of
20 ft. and a spread of 15 ft. So you see. Its only serious enemy,
very serious indeed, is a March frost which may turn its candid
purity to a leathery khaki brown. Sometimes it escapes; one must
take the risk; it is worth taking.

'It is best planted in April or May, and the vital thing to remember is that it must never be allowed to suffer from drought before
it has become established. Once firmly settled into its new home,
it can be left to look after itself. Avoid planting it in a frost pocket,
or in a position where it will be exposed to the rays of a warm sun
after a frosty night: under the lee of a north or west wall is probably the ideal situation, or within the shelter of a shrubbery.

' ... people who for reasons of limited space feel unwilling to
take the risk, in spite of the immense reward in a favourable
season, would be better advised to plant the later-flowering
Magnolia Soulangeana, less pure in its whiteness, for the outside
of the petals is stained with pink or purple; or *Magnolia Lennei*,
which is frankly rosy, but very beautiful with its huge pink gob-
lets, and seldom suffers from frost unless it has extremely bad
luck at the end of April.

'*M. stellata*, which also flowers in extreme youth, is perhaps the
most familiar of all the magnolias to be seen in the amateur gardener's garden. To my way of thinking, it is by no means one of
the most beautiful, being ragged and tattered-looking, but a well-
grown bush is certainly effective, seen at a distance.'

Magnolia soulangeana 'Lennei'.

Vita's dismissal of *stellata* is a bit tough, as it's the one a lot of people like best. It's the classic for a small town garden with its widely spaced, spidery-petalled flowers, and makes a compact plant, shrubbier than most. It's also one of the earliest to bloom and its flowers are more resistant to frost, so they often look good for most of the spring. All magnolias have wonderful buds, like furry mice sitting on the branch. You can really see – and feel – them with any of the *stellata* forms.

She continues: '*M. salicifolia* is one of the easiest and hardiest, and its flowers are less susceptible to frost than either the Yulan or *M. stellata* ... Or, if you want something really sumptuous, there is the claret-coloured *M. liliiflora nigra*, which in my experience flowers continuously for nearly two months, May and June; it is a good plant for small gardens, as it grows neither too high nor too wide, and I have never known it fail to flower copiously every year.' Vita planted the deep, rich *M. liliiflora* 'Nigra' in the southeast corner of the Tower Lawn. The *liliiflora* has been replanted recently, but it's now filling out.

'I have not even mentioned that the magnolia is easygoing as to soil,' she adds. '[It] likes some peat or leaf-mould but does not exact it; appreciates a rich mulch from time to time; is rather brittle and thus prefers a sheltered to a windy position; and should be transplanted in spring (March) rather than in autumn.'

On a smaller scale, Vita favoured for spring other flowering shrubs including corylopsis, deutzias and kolkwitzias. *Corylopsis*

Deutzia longiflora – a classic late-spring flowering shrub that Vita loved.

pauciflora is a delicate thing, with pagoda-like primrose-yellow flowers. She describes it as 'a little shrub, not more than four or five feet high and about the same in width, gracefully hung with pale yellow flowers along the leafless twigs, March to April, a darling of prettiness.

Corylopsis spicata is much the same, but grows rather taller, up to six feet, and is, if anything, more frost-resistant. They are not particular as to soil, but they do like a sheltered position, if you can give it them, say with a backing of other wind-breaking shrubs against the prevailing wind.

'Sparrows ... peck the buds off, so put a bit of old fruit-netting over the plant in October or November when the buds are forming. Sparrows are doing the same to my Winter-Sweet this year [1952], as never before; sheer mischief; an avian form of juvenile delinquency; so take the hint and protect the buds with netting before it is too late.'

She also liked *Halesia carolina*, the snowdrop tree, and was given one by a friend. As with lots of her larger-scale plant presents, she planted it in the Orchard where it did well for years, but it has now succumbed to honey fungus. (A new one has recently been planted by the South Cottage back door). 'This is a very pretty flowering tree, seldom seen; it is hung with white, bell-shaped blossoms, among pale green leaves, all along the branches. It can be grown as a bush in the open, or trained against a wall. There is a better version of it called *Halesia monticola*, but if you cannot obtain this from your nurseryman *Halesia Carolina* will do as well.'

For later in the spring, as well as deutzias and kolkwitzias Vita grew dipeltas, their branches all packed thickly with blossom. She had a deutzia in the Rose Garden and one in the White Garden in the early days, which she could use for picking. As she says, they need a sheltered spot or their blossom may brown in a late frost overnight, just as it's emerging. They are 'graceful and arching, May–June flowerers, four to six feet, ideal for the small garden where space is a consideration. They are easy, not even resenting a little lime in the soil, but beware of pruning them if you do not wish to lose the next year's bloom. The most you should do is to cut off the faded sprays and, naturally, take out any dead wood. The only thing to be said against them is that a late frost will damage the flower, and that is a risk which can well be taken. *Deutzia gracilis rosea*, rosy as its name implies; *D. pulchra*, white; *D. scabra Pride of Rochester*, pinkish white, rather taller, should make a pretty group. They are not very expensive.'

This flowered at much the same time as *Kolkwitzia amabilis* and *Dipelta floribunda*, which Vita kept in a duo together in the Rose Garden: 'two very pretty May–June flowering shrubs not difficult to grow, but for some reason not very commonly seen. They go well together, both being of the same shade of a delicate shell-pink and both belonging to the same botanical family

(Caprifoliaceae), which includes the more familiar Weigelas and the honeysuckles, with small trumpet-shaped flowers dangling from graceful sprays.

'*Kolkwitzia* comes into flower a little later than *Dipelta*, and thus provides a useful succession in the same colouring; in other words, a combination of the two would ensure a cloud of pale pink over a considerable number of weeks. It ought to be planted in front of the *Dipelta*, as it tends to make a more rounded bush, whereas the *Dipelta* grows taller and looser, and flops enough to require a few tall stakes. Both come from China, and each deserves the other's adjective, as well as their own, for they are both amiable and floriferous.' There are none now at Sissinghurst but Troy, the head gardener, is thinking of reinstating a *Kolkwitzia* somewhere.

SUMMER

Vita's favourite summer-flowering shrubs were undoubtedly roses. She was famously passionate about the old-fashioned Gallica, Bourbon and Moss types, as well as a few elegant and larger-growing species and varieties, among them *Rosa moyesii* (see p. 150) and its descendant 'Nevada'. Writing about the old-fashioned roses, she says, 'What incomparable lavishness they give ... There is nothing scrimpy or stingy about them. They have a generosity which is as desirable in plants as in people.' The joy of a rose, she goes on, is in a June or early July evening, 'when for once in a while we are allowed a deep warm sloping sunlight; how rare and how precious [such evenings] are. They ought to be accompanied by fireflies, wild gold flakes in the air, but in this island we have to make do with tethered flowers

Rosa 'Nevada' photographed by Edwin Smith at Sissinghurst.

instead. Amongst these, the huge lax bushes of the old roses must take an honoured place.'

She loved roses, of course for their scent (see pp. 199–200), and climbing roses for draping the elegant Sissinghurst walls, but it was the shrub roses that Vita added in great numbers to her newly made Purple Border and Cottage Garden, and en masse to her Rose Garden. She had built up such a large collection since arriving at Sissinghurst, getting some from the old-fashioned rose specialist Edward Bunyard – as well as from Constance Spry and the nurserywoman Hilda Murrell, who helped her with the design and plant choice for the White Garden – that she'd outgrown her first rose garden, made outside the Priest's House. Vita needed more space, and moved everything to a new site in what had been the vegetable garden on the southern edge of the garden.

Vita's favourite roses were the ones with velvet textures to their petals and a richness and grandeur to their colours, roses that 'swept me quite unexpectedly back to those dusky mysterious hours in an Oriental storehouse,' she remembers, 'where the rugs and carpets of Isfahan and Bokhara and Samarkand were unrolled in their dim but sumptuous colouring and richness of texture for our slow delight. Rich they were, rich as a fig broken open, soft as a ripened peach, flecked as an apricot, coral as a pomegranate, bloomy as a bunch of grapes. It is of these that the old roses remind me.'

Those old-fashioned shrub roses, 'the Gallicas, the Damasks, the Centifolias or Cabbage, the Musks, the China, the Rose of Provins . . . all more romantic the one than the other', had a deep glamour, a fading grandeur, just like all the favourite plants she chose and just like her interiors – her writing room and her bedroom. They were 'the gipsies of the rose-tribe. They resent restraint; they like to express themselves in all their vigour freely as the fancy takes them, free as the dog-rose in the hedgerows. I know they are not to everybody's taste, and I know that it isn't everybody who has room for them in a small garden, but all the same I love them much and would sacrifice much space to them.'

Vita hated Hybrid Teas, and was not keen on most of the Hybrid Perpetuals, except for one or two such as 'Ulrich Brunner' (see p. 155). She felt the new varieties lacked 'the subtlety to be found in some of these traditional roses which might well be picked off a medieval tapestry or a piece of Stuart needlework. Indeed, I think you should approach them as though they were textiles rather than flowers. The velvet vermilion of petals, the stamens of quivering gold, the slaty purple of *Cardinal Richelieu*, the loose dark red and gold of *Alain Blanchard*; I could go on for ever, but always I should come back to the idea of embroidery and of velvet and of the damask with which some of them share their name. They have a quality of their own.

'They usually smell better than their modern successors,' she

Roses underplanted with bearded iris in Vita's Rose Garden during the war.

went on. 'People complain that the modern rose has lost in smell what it has gained in other ways, and although their accusation is not always justified there is still a good deal of truth in it. No such charge can be brought against the Musk, the

Cabbage, the Damask, or the Moss. They load the air with the true rose scent ... Have I pleaded in vain?

'This charm may be partly sentimental, and certainly there are several things to be said against the old roses: their flowering time is short; they are untidy growers, difficult to stake or to keep in order; they demand hours of snipping if we are to keep them free from dead and dying heads, as we must do if they are to display their full beauty unmarred by a mass of brown, sodden petals. But in spite of these drawbacks a collection of the old roses gives a great and increasing pleasure. As in one's friends, one learns to overlook their faults and love their virtues.'

Roses gave Vita the all-important masses in the mixed borders, as well as being the glorious high point in her new Rose Garden. Created in 1937, this looked good almost straight away, and Vita managed to maintain it herself, with the help of one gardener and the occasional pruning skills of Harold, right through the war. The garden was so jam-packed that by 1959 – when Pam and Sybille arrived – if one rose bush failed from poor health or old age, they didn't bother to replace it. They were sure that a bit more air in between the plants would do them good.

At its peak, on a late June evening in the Rose Garden, you still feel like you've walked into a bowl of potpourri – or not quite potpourri because it's something fresher, juicier and more vegetable than that. From the flat severity of the York stone paths roses undulate in every direction, some tall and columnar, others quiet and petite, with the odd massive virtual tents of flowers – three bushes trained into one. They are all in full bloom at much the same time, and particularly at dawn and dusk, when there's greater moisture in the air, their abundance and scent stop you dead.

That's just what Vita wanted.

VITA'S TOP SHRUB ROSES

'Drunk on roses, I look round and wonder which to recommend.'

Rosa alba 'Great Maiden's Blush'
Vita writes: '[*Rosa alba*] sounds as though it were invariably a white rose. Make no mistake. The adjective is misleading ... the *alba* roses include many forms which are not white but pink ... *Great Maiden's Blush* [is] a very pretty and innocent-looking pink and white debutante ... she holds her flowers longer than most. This is a very beautiful old rose, many-petalled, of an exquisite shell-pink clustering among the grey-green foliage, extremely sweet-scented, and for every reason perfect for filling a squat bowl indoors. In the garden she is not squat at all, growing 6 to 7 ft high and wide in proportion, thus demanding a good deal of room, perhaps too much in a small border but lovely and reliable to fill a stray corner ... The *albas* ... tolerate difficult situations, thriving in soil penetrated by the roots of trees (such as in woodland walks); they are resistant to mildew; and they can either be pruned or left un-pruned, according to the taste of the grower, the space available, and the time that can be devoted to them.'

Rosa gallica 'Complicata'
This rose, as Vita says in *More for Your Garden*, has a 'graceful untidiness', which is just what Vita's style is all about. It's 'a perfect rose-pink' with 'enormous single flowers borne all the length of the very long sprays. I cannot think why it should be called

Rosa 'Complicata'.

complicata, for it has a simplicity and purity of line which might come straight out of a Chinese drawing. This is a real treasure, if you can give it room to toss itself about as it likes; and whether you lightly stake it upright or allow it to trail must depend upon how you feel about it. Personally I think that its graceful untidiness is part of its charm, but whatever you do with it you can depend upon it to fill any corner with its renewed surprise in June.' There is still a *Rosa complicata* in the garden, and more are being added.

Rosa 'Grandmaster'

This one is a 'hybrid musk ... which would associate well as a bush planted in front of either *Lawrence Johnstone* or *Le Rêve* [see climbers, p. 000]. This is an exquisite thing, a great improvement on the other hybrid musk, *Buff Beauty*, though that in all conscience is lovely enough. *Grandmaster* is nearly single, salmon-coloured on the outside and a very pale gold within, scentless, alas, which one does not expect of a musk, but that fault must be overlooked for the extreme beauty of the bush spattered all over as it were with large golden butterflies. These shrubby roses are invaluable, giving so little trouble and filling so wide an area at so little cost.'

Rosa moyesii

This is a very important rose at Sissinghurst, and one that Vita picked out to write about in *Some Flowers*. She used it to extend the colour in her Purple Border out from blue and purple and towards some rich pinks and dusky reds, including this one. There are two plants in the Top Courtyard, both put there by Vita and still healthy and vigorous growers. That's a pretty good testament to this species.

'This is a Chinese rose, and looks it,' she writes. 'If ever a plant reflected all that we had ever felt about the delicacy, lyricism, and design of a Chinese drawing, *Rosa Moyesii* is that plant. We might well expect to meet her on a Chinese printed paper-lining to a tea-chest of the time of Charles II, when wall-papers first came to England, with a green parrot out of all proportion, perching on her slender branches. There would be no need for the artist to stylise her, for Nature has already stylised her enough. Instead, we meet her more often springing out of our English lawns, or overhanging our English streams, yet *Rosa Moyesii* remains for ever China. With that strange adaptability of true genius she never looks out of place. She adapts herself as happily to cosy England as to the rocks and highlands of Asia.

'"Go, lovely rose." She goes indeed, and quickly. Three weeks at most sees her through her yearly explosion of beauty. But her beauty is such that she must be grown for the sake of those three weeks in June. During that time her branches will tumble with the large, single, rose-red flower of her being. It is of an indescribable colour. I hold a flower of it here in my hand now, and find myself defeated in description. It is like the colour I imagine Petra to be, if one caught it at just the right moment of sunset. It is like some colours in a rug from Isfahan. It is like the dyed leather sheath of an Arab knife – and this I do know for certain, for I am matching one against the other, the dagger-sheath against the flower. [This knife is still in Vita's desk drawer.] It is like all those dusky rose-red things which abide in the mind as a part of the world of escape and romance.

'Then even when the flowers are gone the great graceful branches are sufficiently lovely in themselves. Consider that within three or four years a single bush will grow some twelve feet high and will cover an area six to eight feet wide; long waving wands of leaves delicately set and of an exquisite pattern, detaching themselves against the sky or the hedge or the wall, wherever you happen to have set it. Never make the mistake of trying to train it tight against a wall: it likes to grow free, and to throw itself loosely into the fountains of perfect shape it knows so well how to achieve. Do not, by the way, make the mistake either of industriously cutting off the dead heads, in the hope of inducing a second flowering. You will not get your second flowering and you will only deprive yourself of the second crop which it is preparing to give you: the crop of long bottle-shaped, scarlet hips of the autumn. Preserve them at all costs, these sealing-wax fruits which will hang brighter than the berries of the holly ... We already have the variety called Geranium, of stockier growth, and the beautiful white Nevada, which is not a chance seedling but a deliberate cross.'

Rosa mundi (correctly, *R. gallica* 'Versicolor')
This is still grown, lightly staked, in the Rose Garden.

'Striped and splotched and blotted,' Vita writes again in *Some Flowers*, 'this fine old rose explodes into florescence in June, giving endless variations of her markings. You never know what form

Rosa gallica 'Versicolor'.

these markings are going to take. Sometimes they come in red orderly stripes, sometimes in splashes, sometimes in mere stains and splotches, but always various, decorative, and interesting. They remind one of red cherry juice generously stirred into a bowl of cream. A bush of *Rosa Mundi* in full flowering is worth looking at. It is not worth cutting for the house unless you have the leisure to renew your flower-vases every day, for in water it will not last. Even out of doors, blooming on its own bush, it does not last for very long. It is a short-lived delight, but during the short period of its blooming it makes up in quantity what it lacks in durability ...

'Perhaps all the foregoing makes it sound rather unsatisfactory and not worthwhile. On the contrary, it is very much worthwhile indeed. For one thing, you can stick it in any odd corner, and indeed you will be wise to do so, unless you have a huge garden where you can afford blank gaps during a large part of the year. You can also grow it as a hedge, and let it ramp away.

'A word as to pruning ... *Rosa Mundi* needs all weak shoots to be cut out after the flowering time is over, and in the spring the remaining shoots should be shortened to within half a dozen buds.'

Rosa 'Mutabilis', or *Rosa* 'Turkestanica'

Mutabilis means 'liable to change' in Latin, a characteristic of this rose, which opens pink and gradually fades to a sort of apricot. You'll see both colours on a bush at one time. As with many of the China roses (such as 'Comtesse du Cayla', which Vita also loved and picked for the house (see p. 329)), this flowers lightly for almost six months. It's hugely useful and looks wonderful against red brick. In August 1952 Vita writes: 'This makes an amusing bush, five to six feet high and correspondingly wide, covered throughout the summer with single flowers in different colours, yellow, dusky red, and coppery, all out at the same time. It is perhaps a trifle tender, and thus a sheltered corner will suit this particular harlequin.'

Rosa 'Nevada'

This was one of Vita's favourite roses which she had planted right at the edge of the path in Delos, so she could see it with the Tower standing behind it in the background.

'This is not a climber,' she notes in *In Your Garden*, 'but a shrubby type, forming an arching bush up to seven or eight feet in height, smothered with great single white flowers with a centre of golden stamens. One of its parents was the Chinese species rose *Moyesii*, which created a sensation when it first appeared and has now become well known ... The grievance against *Moyesii* is that it flowers only once, in June; but *Nevada*, unlike *Moyesii*, has the advantage of flowering at least twice during the summer, in June and again in August, with an extra trickle of odd flowers right into the autumn. One becomes confused among the multitude of roses, I know, but *Nevada* is really so magnificent that you cannot afford to overlook her. A

snowstorm in summer, as her name implies. And so little
bother. No pruning; no staking; no tying. And nearly as thornless as dear old *Zéphyrine Drouhin*. No scent, I am afraid; she is
for the eye, not for the nose.'

Rosa 'Tuscany'

'Tuscany' is the epitome of the sort of rose that Vita delighted
in. It's plush velvet in all its parts – it has deep crimson petals
with a whorl of golden anthers at their heart, and a sweet,
intense, classic rose perfume. It's quite a healthy rose too – I've
had it in my organic rose trial in a partially shaded spot now for
five years, and it does not get blackspot. There are still several
bushes of this in the Rose Garden.

'Tuscany opens flat (being only semi-double),' Vita says, 'thus
revealing the quivering and dusty gold of its central perfection ... It is more like the heraldic Tudor rose than any other.
The petals, of the darkest crimson, curl slightly inwards and the
anthers, which are of a rich yellow, shiver and jingle loosely
together if one shakes the flower.

'The velvet rose. What a combination of words! One almost
suffocates in their soft depths, as though one sank into a bed of
rose-petals, all thorns ideally stripped away. No photograph can
give any idea of what it is really like. Photographs make it look
merely funereal – too black, almost a study in widow's crêpe.
They make the flower and the leaf appear both of the same dark
colour, which is unfair to so exquisite a thing.

'As like *Rosa Mundi*, Tuscany is a Gallica, it needs the same
kind of pruning; it will never make a very tall bush, and your
effort should be to keep it shapely – not a very easy task, for
it tends to grow spindly shoots, which must be rigorously cut

out. Humus and potash benefit the flowers and the leaves respectively.'

Rosa 'William Lobb' – the Moss rose
Another classic Vita rose with extraordinary colouring – properly purple, then fading a little like a tapestry or embroidered cushion. It also has excellent scent:

'As they reach the stage where some of the flowers are passing while others are still coming out, they look as though some rich ecclesiastical vestment had been flung over them. The dull carnation of the fresh flowers accords so perfectly with the slaty lilac of the old, and the bunches cluster in such profusion, that the whole bush becomes a cloth of colour, sumptuous, as though stained with blood and wine. If they are to be grown in a border, I think they should be given some grey-leaved plant in front of them, such as *Stachys lanata* (more familiarly, Rabbits' Ears), for the soft grey accentuates their own musty hues, but ideally speaking, I should like to see a small paved garden with grey stone walls given up to them entirely, with perhaps a dash of the old rose prettily called Veilchenblau (violet-blue) climbing the walls and a few clumps of the crimson clove carnation at their feet.'

Rosa 'Ulrich Brunner'
In Vita's view this is one of the best Hybrid Perpetuals, useful for prolonging the season and lasting well in water. It was one of the first roses the gardener Jack Vass experimented on with his new rose-training technique (see pp. 156–9). 'Ulrich Brunner' is 'stiff-stemmed, almost thornless, cherry-red in colour, very prolific indeed, a real cut-and-come-again ... *Ulrich Brunner, Frau Karl*

Druschki, and the Dicksons, Hugh and George, are very suitable for this kind of training. The hybrid perpetuals can also be used as wall plants; not nearly so tall as true climbers and ramblers, they are quite tall enough for, say, a space under a ground floor window; or they may be grown on post-and-wire as espaliers outlining a path.'

TRAINING SHRUB ROSES

What looks like unbridled profusion in the Sissinghurst roses relies on meticulous work behind the scenes early in the year, when precision horticulture guarantees that wonderful roman-

Shrub roses trained on to hazel benders, in the characteristic Sissinghurst way.

tic effect. It's well worth visiting the garden at the beginning of the growing season, when the bare bones – the beautiful, intricate webs of rose stems without their leaves – are clearly visible, so you can see how the gardeners do it. This rose-training system originated at Cliveden in Buckinghamshire with the Astors' head gardener Jack Vass, who moved to Sissinghurst in 1939. Other National Trust properties now send their gardeners to Sissinghurst to learn the ingenious technique. We know how devoted Vita was to her roses, but it was Jack Vass who started to grow them in this exceptional way.

All roses can be encouraged to produce more flowering side-shoots if their stems are trained as nearly horizontal as possible. If you put every stem of a rose plant under pressure, bending and stressing it, the rose will flower more prolifically. The plant's bio-chemistry is telling the bush it's on its way out and so needs to make as many flowers as possible.

They should be pruned before they come into leaf to prevent leaf buds and shoots from being damaged as their stems are manipulated, so do this in the winter or early spring. Depending on their habit, shrub roses are trained in one of three ways.

First, the tall, rangy bushes with stiffer branches – such as 'Charles de Mills', 'Ispahan', 'Gloire de France', 'Cardinal de Richelieu' and 'Camayeux' – are twirled up a frame of four chestnut or hazel poles. Every pruned tip is bent and attached to a length below.

Second, the big leggy shrubs, which put out great, pliable, triffid arms that are easy to tie down and train, are bent on to hazel hoops arranged around the skirts of the plant. Roses with this lax habit include 'Constance Spry', 'Fantin-Latour', 'Zéphirine Drouhin', 'Madame Isaac Pereire', 'Coupe d'Hébé', 'Henri Martin' and 'Souvenir du Docteur Jamain'.

In *Even More for Your Garden*, Vita comments in September 1957: 'These strong growers lend themselves to various ways of treatment. They can be left to reach their free height of 7 to 8 ft., but then they wobble about over eye-level and you can't see them properly, with the sun in your eyes, also they get shaken by summer gales. A better but more laborious system is to tie them down to benders, by which I mean flexible wands of hazel with each end poked firmly into the ground and the rose-shoots tied down at intervals, making a sort of half-hoop.

This entails a lot of time and trouble, but is satisfactory if you can do it; also it means that the rose breaks at each joint, so that you get a very generous *floraison*, a lovely word I should like to see imported from the French into our language. If you decide to grow hybrid perpetuals on this system of pegging them down, you ought to feed them richly, with organic manure if you can get it, or with compost if you make it, but anyhow with something that will compensate for the tremendous effort they will put out from being encouraged to break all along their shoots. You can't ask everything of a plant, any more than you can exact everything of a human being, without giving some reward in return. Even the performing seal gets an extra herring.'

Under Pam and Sybille the technique was refined. All the old and diseased wood is removed and then, stem by stem, last year's wood is bent over and tied onto the hazel hoop. You start at the outside of the plant and tie that in first, then move towards the middle, using the plant's own branches to build up the web and – in the case of 'Constance Spry' and 'Henri Martin' – create a fantastic height, one layer domed and attached to the one below. Without any sign of a flower, this looks magnificent as soon as it's complete, and in a couple of months each stem, curved almost to ground level, will flower abundantly.

The third method of training shrub roses applies to the contained, well behaved, less prolific varieties ('Petite de Hollande', 'Madame Knorr', 'Chapeau de Napoléon' (or *Rosa × centifolia* 'Cristata') and those that produce branches too stiff to bend ('Felicia' and the newish David Austin rose, 'William Shakespeare 2000'), and these are tackled slightly differently. They are pruned hard, then each bush is attached with twine to a single stake cut to about the height of the pruned bush. Without the stake, even these would topple under the weight of their summer growth.

OTHER SUMMER-FLOWERING SHRUBS

Roses were the dominant flowering shrubs for Vita's summer garden, and rightly so, but she had a few other beauties, good recommendations still worth taking seriously today.

In her new White Garden she planted the huge, crinkly white-bloomed romneya, or Californian tree poppy, a flowering but not woody shrub, more like an evergreen perennial – and it's still there. It takes a while to get established, but after three or four years will flower prolifically and will last for decades. My mother grows lots of it in her garden outside Cambridge and it's been there now for almost fifty years. Vita describes it in *In Your Garden*:

'A beautiful thing in flower in July is the Californian tree-poppy. It is not exactly an herbaceous plant; you can call it a sub-shrub if you like; whatever you call it will make no difference to its beauty.

'With grey-green glaucous leaves, it produces its wide, loose, white-and-gold flowers on slender stems five or six feet in height. The petals are like crumpled tissue paper; the anthers quiver in a golden swarm at the centre. It is very lovely and delicate.

'I don't mean delicate as to its constitution, except perhaps in very bleak districts. Once you get it established it will run about all over the place, being what is known as a root-runner, and may

Romneya coulteri.

even come up in such unlikely and undesirable positions as the middle of a path. I know one which has wriggled its way under a brick wall and come up manfully on the other side. The initial difficulty is to get it established, because it hates being disturbed and transplanted, and the best way to cheat it of this reluctance is to grow it from root cuttings in pots. This will entail begging a root cutting from a friend or an obliging nurseryman. You can then tip it out of its pot into a complaisant hole in the place where you want it to grow, and hope that it will not notice what has happened to it. Plants, poor innocents, are easily deceived . . .

'It likes a sunny place and not too rich a soil. It will get cut down in winter most likely, but this does not matter, because it will spring up again, and in any case it does not appear to flower on the old wood, so the previous season's growth is no loss. In fact, you will probably find it advisable to cut it down yourself in the spring, if the winter frosts have not already done it for you.'

She offers another suggestion:

'A good companion to the tree-poppy is the tall, twelve-foot shrub which keeps on changing its name. When I first knew and grew it, it called itself *Plagianthus Lyallii*. Now it prefers to call itself *Hoheria lanceolata* [now correctly called *Hoheria lyalli* (see following page)]. Let it, for all I care. So far as I am concerned, it is the thing to grow behind the tree-poppy, which it will out-top and will complement with the same colouring of the pale green leaves and the smaller white flowers, in a candid white and green and gold bridal effect more suitable, one would think, to April than to July. Doubts have been cast upon its hardiness, but I have one here (in Kent) which has weathered a particularly draughty corner where, in optimistic ignorance, I planted it years ago. There is no denying, however, that it is happier with some shelter by a wall or a hedge.'

Hoheria lyallii has ivory-coloured flowers, beautiful singles like

Hoheria lyalii, one of Vita's favourite summer shrubs with beautiful saucer-like flowers, similar to cherry blossom.

one of the Japanese cherries, only each flower is almost twice the size. They feel like spring blossom but come in summer, their flowers a fine contrast to their bright apple-green leaves. There's almost no lovelier jug of flowers to have in a great cloud at the end of summer. As Vita says, 'I can't think why people don't grow *Hoheria lyallii* often, if they have a sheltered corner and want a tall 10-ft. shrub that flowers in that awkward time between late June and early July, smothered in white-and-gold flowers of the mallow family, to which the hollyhock also belongs, and sows itself in such profusion that you could have a whole forest of it if you had the leisure to prick out the seedlings and the space to replant them.

'It really is a lovely thing, astonishing me every year with its profusion. I forget about it; and then there it is again with its flowers coming in their masses suggesting philadelphus, for which it might easily be mistaken, but even more comely than any philadelphus, I think, thanks to the far prettier and paler leaf.

'It has other advantages. It doesn't dislike a limy soil, always an important consideration for people who garden on chalk and can't grow any of the lime-haters. It doesn't like rich feeding, which tends to make it produce leaf rather than flower. This means an economy in compost or organic manures or inorganic fertilizers which could be better expended elsewhere. Bees love it. It is busy with bees, making their midsummer noise as you pass by.'

She also loved the 'false acacia', *Robinia pseudoacacia*, another small tree which was – and still is – little grown in England. She would have come across it, as she says, in her travels to the Mediterranean, where it's still a common tree lining many small squares and side streets. It's a delicate, fine-looking thing which does not throw too much shade, so it's ideal for a small country or town garden and its flowers have a delicious orange blossom scent. In France they dip them in batter and serve them – scattered with sugar – as a pudding.

These trees 'abound in France and Italy,' she remarks, 'but are equally at home with us. There are few summer-flowering trees prettier than they, when they hang out their pale, sweet-scented tassels, and few faster of growth for people in a hurry. I have planted them no taller than a walking-stick, and within a contemptible number of years they have taken on the semblance of an established inhabitant, with sizeable trunks and a rugged bark and a spreading head, graceful and fringy. If they have a fault, it is that their boughs are brittle, that they make a good deal of dead wood, and, I suspect, are not very long-lived, especially if the main trunk has forked, splitting the tree into halves. This a height of twenty-five feet, but in this country it apparently limits itself to something between six and eight feet; and quite enough, too, for the average garden. Do not confuse it with *H. hortensis*, the one which sometimes comes sky-blue but more often a dirty pink, and which is the one usually seen banked up in Edwardian opulence against the grandstand of our more fashionable race-courses. *H. paniculata grandiflora*, in spite of its resounding name, is less offensively sumptuous and has a far subtler personality.

'It reveals, for instance, a sense of humour, and even of fantasy in the colouring it adopts throughout its various stages. It starts off by flowering white; then turns into the pink I have already described as looking like pink lilac. Then it turns greenish, a sort of sea-green, so you never know where you are with it, as you never know where you are with some human personalities, but that makes them all the more interesting. Candidly white one moment; prettily pink the next; and virulently green in the last resort ... As I was leaning over the gate, looking at this last pink-green inflorescence, the tenant of the cottage observed me and came up. Yes, he said, it has been in flower for the last three months. It changes its colour as the months go by, he said.'

There have been lots of new varieties of *H. paniculata* since Vita's day and they are much underrated – widely grown in France and Germany, but little known here. They are big (about three feet by three feet if pruned), but not too big, so go well at the back of a herbaceous border, or underplanting and interlinking with taller shrubs. They are also excellent at an entrance or as a marker at the beginning or end of a bed, and are particularly lovely mixed with shrubs with variegated leaves. They look good throughout the summer, reach their flowery peak in the autumn and have good winter interest, only needing to be cut back in March or April.

I particularly like *Hydrangea paniculata* 'Limelight' . This opens the cleanest, brightest, acid green, with a brilliant architectural chiselled flower form, unfurling to cups in a green-washed cream. Then the flowers fully flatten and turn pure ivory, before being washed with rich pink, the last stage before they gracefully brown and dry on the stem. It's an amazing succession which lasts from August until January, or even longer if the flowers are not thrashed around too much by the wind and rain.

'*Hydrangea aspera* 'Kawakamii' group.

Vita goes on to say: '*Hydrangea aspera* is good too and there are some decorative forms called *villosa* and *Sargentiana*. A bush, pouring over a paved path or covering the angle of a flight of steps, is a rich and rewarding sight in August, when everything becomes heavy and dark and lumpish.' It's true – any *H. aspera* is gorgeous, but a newly found form called 'Kawakamii', in particular, is an amazing performer. It has no sensitivity to pH, so its flowers keep their lovely colour whatever the profile of your soil. It goes on flowering very long and late, retaining its delicate beauty and wonderful overall shape. With just one plant you get a complex multi-storey effect, perfect for filling a corner in any partly shaded or soil drawn up to a depth of three or four inches; and in case of extremely hard weather an old sack can temporarily be thrown over them. Their arching sprays are graceful; I like the ecclesiastical effect of their red and purple amongst the dark green of their foliage; and, of course, when you have nothing else to do you can go round popping the buds.

'The most familiar is probably *Fuchsia magellanica Riccartonii,* which will flower from July to October. *F. gracilis* I like less; it is a spindly-looking thing, and *F. magellanica Thompsonii* is a better version of it. *F. Mrs. Popple,* cherry-red and violet; *Mme Cornelissen,* red and white; and *Margaret,* red and violet, are all to be recommended.

'They ... like a sunny place in rather rich soil with good drainage. You can increase them by cuttings inserted under a hand-light [a glass cloche] or a frame in spring.'

Vita's final recommendation, not for their flowers but for their seedpods and brilliant autumn leaves, are the coluteas, plants that many people are snooty about, feeling they're common as muck and not worth growing.

Often anti-snob about these things, Vita had a line in such garden plants, and she was keen on these particular ones. My parents – possibly under her influence – also grew one of the coluteas, and as a child I loved popping the swollen banana-shaped seedpods, blown up taut like a balloon. Here's what Vita says about them:

'Two shrubs or little trees with an amazingly long flowering period – *Colutea arborescens* and *Colutea media,* the Bladder Sennas. They have been flowering profusely for most of the summer, and were still very decorative in the middle of October. Of the two I prefer the latter. *C. arborescens* has yellow flowers; but although *media* (with bronze flowers) is perhaps the more showy, they go

very prettily together, seeming to complement one another in
their different colouring. Graceful of growth with their long
sprays of acacia-like foliage, amusingly hung with the bladders
of seed-pods looking as though they would pop with a small
bang, like a blown-up paper bag, if you burst them between your
hands ... which give them their English name, the bright small
flowers suggest swarms of winged insects. *C. arborescens* amuses
me, because it carries its flowers and its seed-pods at the same
time. In one garden where I saw it the pods were turning pink,
very pretty amongst the flowers.

'They are of the easiest possible cultivation, doing best in a
sunny place, and having a particular value in that they may be used
to clothe a dry bank where few other things would thrive, nor do
they object to an impoverished stony soil. They are easy to propagate, either by cuttings or by seed, and they may be kept shapely
by pruning in February, within a couple of inches of the old wood.

'I know that highbrow gardeners do not consider them as very
choice. Does that matter? To my mind they are delicately elegant, and anything which will keep on blooming right into
mid-October has my gratitude.

'By the way, they are *not* the kind of which you can make
senna-tea. Children may thus regard them without suspicion and
will need little encouragement to pop the seedpods. It is as satisfactory as popping fuchsias.'

PLACING AND PRUNING

The shrubs and roses were often placed right by the path, rather
than further back in the border, and then minimally and loosely

Vita wanted her garden to mimic a Dutch flower painting, as she wrote in *The Land*, like a 'Dutchman's canvas crammed to absurdity'.

pruned – all contributing to the 'cram, cram, cram' of Vita's garden look. This is one of the most noticeable things about the photographs of the early garden: within the yew hedges, or the brick-wall edges of the garden 'rooms', were living divisions, decorative curtains splitting the space into cosier corners, areas which would work on an intimate, human scale.

Vita felt firmly that, once the massed plantings or large individual shrubs were well established, it was important to shape and prune them, but not too much. So as to be safe and not over-prune, she tells us in *More for Your Garden*, do this when they're going at full tilt in the summer, not at normal pruning time in autumn or winter. 'By this time of the year, most of our plants have grown into their full summer masses, and this is the moment when the discerning gardener goes round not only with his notebook but also with his secateurs and with that invaluable instrument on a pole 8 ft. long, terminated by a parrot's beak, which will hook down and sever any unwanted twig as easily as crooking your finger.' If you wait till winter, it's difficult to see or remember the effect you want, and then it's all too easy to wantonly hack away.

Plants in Vita's borders, as Anne Scott-James writes, 'are mixed with joyous informality and allowed freedom to grow naturally, with a minimum of stakes, secateurs and shears'. Some would say this tipped too far into messy chaos and I'm sure that's true at times, but the art of 'fine carelessness' was Vita's way. She was following a long tradition. Consider this quote describing a wedding masque in 1606: 'The men were clad in Crimson, and the women in white. They had every one a white plume of the richest herons' feathers, and were so rich in jewels upon their heads as was most glorious ... As citizens of Arcadia, they had their hair "carelessly (but yet with more art than if more affected) bound under the circle of a rare and rich coronet". Naturalness was virtue.'

It's not naturalness, of course, but highly contrived art, an understanding that beauty lives on the border between the wild and the controlled. It's just this sort of look that Vita was cultivating in her garden, a question of taking a risk, experimenting with something that might just be too much, but that also might give a kind of pleasure that the over-controlled can never even approach.

'Fine carelessness' is a carefully calibrated phrase. And it takes some doing.

8

SCENTS

Mahonia lomariifolia, one of Vita's favourite families for winter scent.

Heavy, heady scents were another of Vita's passions, and she spurs us on to prioritise planting as many things as possible that will add this other string to our garden's bow. And it will give us a perfume reservoir which we can also bring inside. The important thing is the reminder that we should try to include one or two scented flowers in our gardens for every week of the year.

She had been brought up on the particular perfume of the Knole potpourri, a recipe followed there since the eighteenth century. It involved the 'drying of double violets, rose leaves, lavender, Myrtle flowers, verbena, bay leaves, rosemary, musk and geranium, which were stored in jars with bay salt and many spices', Vita explains in her book *Knole and the Sackvilles*, published in 1922. She periodically made a batch to scent her writing room and bedroom. As she says, one of the things that is so seductive about perfumed plants is that they behave so unpredictably. One moment, or one evening, they are exuding perfumes like a Sultan's harem – and the next, there's no hint, not the merest puff, of scent.

'This whole question of scent in plants is one which I do not understand, though no doubt a scientific explanation is available. The warmth of the sun and the humidity of rain and dew account for much, as we all know from observation and experience, but there must be other factors unrevealed to the ignoramus. Why, for instance, does the balsam poplar waft its scent a hundred yards distant sometimes and at other times remain so obstinately scentless and sniff-less as to be imperceptible on the closest approach? These things retain their mystery for me, and I am not sure that I want the answer. A little mystery is precious to preserve.'

On New Year's Day, 1956, she noted: 'We know that we owe

our pleasure in flower-scent to certain essential oils contained in cells which release their content by some process not fully understood. The essential oils are what we call attars, one of the few words for which the English language has to thank the Persian. (Attar of roses will be the most familiar to most people.) The chemical composition of these attars has been analysed, and you would be surprised to learn what everyday substances we should encounter if we were to take some favourite petals to pieces, alcohol for instance, vinegar, benzine; but I am no chemist and should blunder into some shocking howlers were I to pursue the subject. I profess to be nothing more than the average gardener, enjoying such useless but charming bits of information as that some butterflies and moths exude the same scent as the flowers they visit; that white flowers are the most numerous among the scented kinds, followed by red, yellow, and purple in that order, with blue a very bad fifth; that flowers fertilized by birds have no scent at all, birds being without a sense of smell; that dark-haired people have the most highly developed sense, whereas albinos are generally lacking it altogether; that some flowers smell different in the morning from in the evening; and, finally, that the flower-like scent so often observed emanating from the dead bodies of saintly persons may be due to the same breaking-down or release of essential oils in the first stages of decomposition. This supposedly mystical fragrance is usually said to suggest roses or violets.'

Before we get stuck into each season and the recommendations that Vita has for each of them, it's interesting to hear which were her overall favourites, the really powerful wafting things, the plants she would perhaps have taken for their scent alone if banished to a desert island. This is what she tells us in *More for Your Garden*:

'The first thing to say about scents in the open is that there are relatively few plants whose scent will hang on the air in such a way as to make you sniff in inquiry as you walk past. Many things smell good when you push your nose into them, or crush them, or bring them into a warm room, but what we are thinking about is the garden path as we stroll, something that will really hit you in surprise. I think my choice would be:

'An edging of Cheddar pinks.
A hedge of hybrid musk roses, especially *Penelope.*
Some bushes of the rugosa rose, *Blanc double de Coubert.*
Azaleas.
A hedge of sweetbriar.
The Balsam poplar when it first unfolds its sticky leaves.
Lilium auratum, as a luxury.

'I know everyone will disagree and everyone will have other ideas of his own. I quite expect a spate of suggestions about the things I have left out, for in the region of the five senses, the sense of smell (and the allied sense of taste) is highly controversial. Some people love the scent of phlox: to me, it suggests pigsties, not that I dislike pigsties, being country-born, and well accustomed to them. Much depends also on the keenness of the nose, and also on the fact that not all scented plants give off their scent all the time. They may vary with the temperature, with the degree of moisture in the air, and even with the time of day. This capriciousness makes them perhaps more precious. One may catch an unexpected whiff as one passes a bush of winter sweet or witch hazel, not to be detected an hour ago, or of that vanilla-scented little tree, *Azara microphylla.* And the scent of box in the sun, and of box-clippings as you crush them underfoot. And of a bed of warm wallflowers. And the night-scented stock, that lack-lustre annual which comes into its own after twilight.

'But perhaps there is nothing to equal the woodland acres of our native bluebell, smoke-blue as an autumn bonfire, heavy in scent as a summer rose, yet young as the spring which is its season.'

WINTER SCENT

January and February are the gloomiest months of the year, and scented flowering shrubs one of the few beacons of delight we can guarantee in our gardens. There are a good handful with truly powerful scents, precious things from which you will catch an unexpected whiff as you hurry by and from which you can cut regular sprigs to bring inside.

Vita loved hamamelis – witch hazel – it was one of her key plants for winter and for picking a small sprig for her desk. It is quite slow-growing, so either buy it big or plant it well in rich soil when you first move to a new garden, so that you can reap the benefits when it reaches a decent enough size. Then it won't feel too vandalistic to pick.

Hamamelis × intermedia.

'Hamamelis mollis is perhaps more familiar to many people when they meet it in a bottle under the name Witch Hazel or Hazeline, but to the gardener it means a small shrubby tree, covered in the early part of the year with curly spider-like flowers on its naked branches. There is a particular charm about all trees which carry their flowers before their leaves, such as the almond or the judas: they have a cleanness of design, undisturbed by tufts of green; they allow us to observe the fine tracery of the twigs, while at the same time offering us some colour to look at. The Witch Hazel is certainly a tree which everyone should grow, for its merits are many, and if it has a fault I have yet to discover it, except that it is a slow starter.

'Mollis, a Chinaman, is the best of the family, which includes also two Americans (Virginiana and vernalis) and a Jap (*Japonica*), and arborea, which is the tallest of all but whose flowers are inferior to those of *mollis*. Mollis is perfectly hardy and even the flowers do not wilt in a heavy frost. It likes a sunny place, where it has room to develop and although it will not revenge itself upon you by perishing outright in a poor soil but will struggle manfully even against the stickiest clay, it will also show its gratitude for a good loam with some leaf-mould mixed in. Another of its virtues is that it starts flowering at a very tender age, so that there is none of that long weary wait of years until the plant has reached a certain size before embarking on the business which made us desire it. From the very first it is possible to pick it for indoors, and there are few things more welcome at the churlish time of the year when it occurs. New Year's Day may see it open; perhaps even Christmas Day. The queer, wriggly, yellow petals with the wine-stained calyx at their base will last for quite ten days in water, especially if you bring it indoors while still just in the bud, and will smell far more delicious than you would believe possible if you had only caught it out in the cold winter air. So delicious is it, that the owner of one small new tree begins to long for the day when he can cut big generous branches instead of the few twigs which is all that he can get at first. Every one of these twigs, however, will be doing its best, and flowering on all its little length.'

Hamamelis – in all its guises – stands near the top of the late-winter perfume lists, and there are some new hybrids since Vita's day. One of the best for scent is *Hamamelis* × *intermedia* 'Aurora', with copper-yellow flowers, and *Hamamelis* × *intermedia* 'Aphrodite', with slightly crimped, creamy orange-red flowers. Both grow into vase-shaped shrubs over time and are lovely for autumn colour. There is another new one, *Hamamelis* 'Dishi' which is also spectacular in autumn.

As well as choosing the right variety, the key to the good use of hamamelis is position. You need to get the low winter sun shining through the spidery flowers. These are distinctly two-toned in 'Dishi', orange-red in the middle and shading to gold at the tips. With the light at the right angle they really glow, and the scent is glorious.

That's true of the elegant hamamelis, but not of another of Vita's favourites for winter, wintersweet, *Chimonanthus fragrans*. This is not a looker and is only really suitable for a large garden, but it has a hugely powerful, intensely sweet scent. What Vita encourages is to tuck this into an out-of-the-way sunny corner. From there it can pour out its scent across hedges and over walls, so as you walk in and out of their fragrant cloud, you are looking around trying to spot the plant that is the perfume factory. That's the precious thing – catching an unexpected whiff as one passes by, as well as the sprigs you can regularly cut to bring inside.

Chimonanthus won't flower well for five or six years but is well worth the wait. Even in cold weather, you won't believe the intensity of fragrance. Vita loved to pick boughs of it as soon as it came into flower: 'It is extremely sweet-scented, even in the cold open air, long sprigs loaded with the strange maroon-and-yellow flowers can be cut all through January and February; it lasts for two or three weeks in water, especially if you smash the stems with a hammer, a hint which applies to all hard-wooded growth.' Better still, sear the stem end in boiling water for thirty seconds – this makes the flowers last even longer.

She continues: 'The Winter-sweet will eventually reach to a height of ten feet or more; it is happiest grown against a wall for protection, but I have seen it growing into a big bush in the open in a garden in Kent – not my garden, alas!' If you pick it once it's well established, you won't then need to worry much about pruning.

There are several mahonias planted by Vita at Sissinghurst – she loved them for their lily-of-the-valley-scented flowers in January and February. We have one of the ones she planted beside our back door, and I pick a few sprigs when I want something delicate and pretty, with wonderful scent, to scatter in small glasses all around our sitting room or to put beside someone's bed.

As she says, '*Mahonia japonica* … is a shrub highly recommendable if you have the right place for it. This does not mean that it is fussy as to soil. It likes a good loam, but does not object to some lime. What it really dislikes is a cold wind from the north or east, and who could agree more? We have those frightful months when knives from the north and east cut through us, and we shiver and shudder and wonder if we have caught a chill. We can go indoors and get warm again, but our plants have to stand out in the cold, and do their best for us. We ought to be grateful to them, and I do feel grateful to the lily-of-the-valley-scented barberry that will endure some degrees of frost and will give me its yellow racemes of flower in January or February. It must have been very exciting for the plant-collector Robert Fortune, when he first discovered this treasure in Chusan Island so long ago as 1848. Now, it is a commonplace in our gardens.

'It has the great advantage of being evergreen. It has the disadvantage of resenting transplantation. This means you must get it from a good nurseryman who will send it with a huge ball of soil, so that it scarcely notices that it has been dug up; but once you have got it established you will find that it pays a good dividend, year after year, in increasing value of scented racemes to pick for indoors.'

For deep winter, on a smaller scale, you also want at least one coronilla and a clump of sarcococcas. The sarcococca Vita discusses only in passing, but these are brilliant for a more restricted shady space, and there are some excellent new ones since Vita's day. I love *S. ruscifolia* 'Dragon Gate', which was collected by the gardener and broadcaster Roy Lancaster in China. It has a much smaller leaf than even *S. hookeriana* var. *humilis* and grows into a very compact little shrub, but still with the same wonderful scented flowers. Use it to fill a shady space where many other plants wouldn't thrive.

Coronilla glauca is another which doesn't look much but is a winter scent giant, and Vita loved it for its presence when most needed in the first few months of the year.

'Easter Day,' Vita commented in 1957. 'It seems odd to look back to Christmas Day, but there is a gay little butter-yellow shrub in my garden which has been flowering continuously between those two great feasts of the Church, a sort of hyphen linking the Birth and the Resurrection which is more than can be said for most shrubs, so I think it deserves a write-up, as these recommendations are colloquially called, and a tribute of gratitude for the pleasure it has given me in its persistence throughout the dreary months.

'The shrub I mean is called *Coronilla glauca*.

'There are several sorts of coronilla. I know I shall be told that *Coronilla emerus* is the hardier, but on the whole I should advise *glauca*. I know I shall be told that it isn't quite hardy. I know it isn't supposed to be, but all I can say is that it came through the frightening frosts of February 1956, with no protection, and if a supposedly tender shrub can survive that test, it qualifies for at least a trial in the Home Counties and the south-west, though perhaps not in the Midlands, East Anglia, or the north. I must admit also that I planted it in a narrow border under the south-facing wall of the house, where it got the maximum of shelter against cold north winds or east winds; and there it still is, flowering exuberantly away, one of the most delightful surprises and successes I ever had.

'I must add another word in praise of this rarely planted shrub. It has its own sense of humour. Sometimes it gives off so strong a scent as to delude me into thinking that I caught the scent of some neighbouring wall-flowers; then I discovered that the coronilla is powerfully fragrant by day and scentless by night.'

Vita loved to pick the odd sprig of daphne for a mini-bunch, and she had pots of the daphnes *collina* and *tangutica* in her cold greenhouse for bringing inside when they were in flower, but we have many more cultivars available to us now than in Vita's day. If you were dispatched to the moon and allowed to take two or three scents with you, daphnes would have to be one. Their fragrance is spicy, definitely eastern with a little citrus, but without the overtones of honey or sugar. It's strong, but not cloying, a plant perfume you're unlikely to tire of – one of the best in the world and miraculous for being around at the dullest garden time.

Daphne bholua is perhaps the best of all, and we now have several varieties to choose from. There's *Daphne bholua* 'Jacqueline Postill', which is relatively short-lived (ten to fifteen years is typical), but in that time flowers its heart out while giving off an incredible scent. It's very hardy and ideal for small gardens, content in a pot (although pots need to be protected in cold weather to avoid damage if the root system freezes solid), and will fill your garden with its cinnamony-lemon fragrance for a good six weeks. There is also a less well known 'Darjeeling' form. 'Darjeeling' flowers very early, definitely in January, but it can be in flower by Christmas in a sheltered spot.

Mimosa (*Acacia dealbata*) was another Vita special, particularly for picking. But as she says, 'It's no good picking it until the flowers are fully out ... You must wait until the clusters are as fluffy and yellow as ducklings.' She recommends growing it as a pot plant until it gets too big, and then risk transferring it outside, particularly in the warmer counties of Britain. At Sissinghurst she grew it in a sheltered corner, 'wrapping its trunk and lower branches in trousers of sacking for the winter'. I wish I'd done that with mine, which I lost last winter.

If you have a greenhouse, a good-sized pot of mimosa could be kept there as a stalwart February mood lifter, and the same applies to *Jasminum polyanthum*, the white-flowering jasmine (see p. 267). You can leave its pot safe in the cold greenhouse and now and then pick a six-inch sprig, which will often have more than twenty buds and flowers plus a scent twenty times as powerful as the summer-flowering jasmine, *J. officinale.*

SPRING SCENT

At Sissinghurst spring is a season of scent. Osmanthus and azara come out early, to pick up the baton as the mahonias and hamamelis tire. Then comes the wafting sweetness of the wall-flowers, in large drifts against the south-facing wall of the Cottage Garden, followed by the spicy, exotic perfume of the white wisteria on the Moat Walk.

Vita wrote at length about the balsam poplar mentioned earlier: 'The Balsam poplar has now unfolded its very sticky leaf-buds and is scenting the air. It surprises me that this deliciously scented tree should not be more widely grown. It is not too large for even a small garden, and if only our road planners and village beautifiers would plant it in avenues along our new roads, or in clumps round our old village greens, every motorist would surely stop with an inquiring sniff. Smells are as difficult to describe as colours, but I should describe this one as a sweet, strong resin, powerful enough to reach for yards around in the open air and almost too strong to put in a vase in your room.

'Do not allow yourself to be fobbed off, as I foolishly was, by anyone telling you that *Populus candicans* is as good as *Populus balsamifera*. It isn't. You must insist on getting *P. balsamifera*, alternately known as *tacamahac*, which I take to be a Red Indian name, for the tree is a native of the United States and Canada.

'*P. trichocarpa* is also said to be very powerfully scented. If you can get cuttings from a friend's garden it will save your pocket, for all poplars root very readily from cuttings and will even throw out white worm-like roots in a glass of water. Like all poplars, the balsam-scented tribe grows very rapidly.'

In early spring, *Azara microphylla* fills the air with scent from small insignificant flowers amongst evergreen leaves. 'A very pleasing little shrub or small tree,' Vita tells us, 'not often seen in gardens, and has been in flower since the middle of March. It is not at all showy, and most people would pass it by without noticing, unless they happened to catch a whiff of the scent. It is pure vanilla ... I would hesitate to recommend it except to gardeners who want something their neighbour probably hasn't got; but, after all, it is for those gardeners that I write these articles. Gardeners who want something different from the usual, and yet something easy to grow. *Azara microphylla* is quite easy to grow. It is an evergreen; it has neat little shiny leaves that look as though they had been varnished; and it has this tiny yellow flower which is now spreading its scent over my writing table and into the whole of my room. I sit and sniff. Wafts of vanilla come to me as I write.

'*Azara microphylla* is a native of Chile ... Some authorities say that it is not hardy here in Britain except in the favoured climate of Devon or Cornwall. I don't believe this. I have got it thriving where I live in Kent, and I have seen a twenty-foot-high tree of it in the rather colder climate of Gloucestershire. So I would say: plant it and risk it.

'It likes to be planted in leaf-mould. It would do well trained on to a wall with a north or west aspect; by which I mean that the early morning sun would not get at it after a frosty night. This is always an important point to remember when you are planting things affected by frost and by the warm morning sun which comes as too great a shock after the chill of the night. Plants must be let down gently. The transition must not be too quick ... The borderline tenderness of Azara make it safest to plant in the shelter of a wall.'

There is a more recent introduction, *Azara petiolaris*, which smells like *microphylla* but has a more interesting leaf, which is larger, shiny and with a slight crinkling to its edge.

'Another [wall] shrub I would like to recommend is *Osmanthus Delavayi* ... found by one Father Delavay in Yunnan, southwest China, some sixty years ago. This, also, like the *Azara microphylla*, has dark green box-like leaves and a scented flower, white, not yellow. It flowers in March and April, and you can cut it and cut it, and the more you cut it the better it grows. It is well worth the attention of gardeners who want something away from the ordinary,' Vita concludes.

You need to take care where you plant *Osmanthus delavayi* too – its flowers can be easily browned in early sun after frost. One that Vita put in still thrives at Sissinghurst on the Big Room wall, and there's another on the south wing of the front range, clipped around the upstairs windows. And just as she says, west-facing, the flowers never seem to get frosted, and they fill that side of the house, and our bedroom, with spectacular perfume. These should be only very lightly pruned – just dead-headed and tidied – immediately after flowering.

As Vita would say, you've also got to have a good collection of rosemaries. Rosemary played a particular part in her gardening imagination – as something that had strong Elizabethan and Shakespearean associations; but it was also a plant of the fragrant Mediterranean south, and thus a joining up of her love of England with her love of the foreign. She championed the plant, as, odd though it may seem to us, people in the 1940s hardly seemed to know what it was:

'It surprises me always when people fail to recognize the common rosemary. "What is that?" they say, looking at the great dark-green bushes that sprawl so generously over the paths at the entrance to the place where I live. I should have thought that rosemary was one of our most common plants, if only for the sake of its sentimental associations. It was said to have the peculiar property of strengthening the memory, and thus became a symbol of fidelity for lovers. "A sprig of it hath a dumb language," said Sir Thomas More; and another legend connects it with the age of Our Lord, thirty-three years, after which it stops growing in height but never in width. A romantic plant, yet so oddly, it seems, unknown.'

It's well worth seeking out a better than ordinary colour form. Vita loved the darker-blue-flowered Corsican rosemary (*R. angustifolius* 'Corsicus'), with 'bright blue flowers, almost gentian blue', and a more feathery type of leaf than the usual, as well as the ceanothus-blue 'Tuscan Blue'.

'There are several different forms of the rosemary,' Vita writes in *In Your Garden Again* in September 1951. 'There is the ordinary bushy type, *Rosmarinus officinalis*, which can be grown either as a bush or clipped into shape as a hedge. I don't like it so well as a hedge, because the constant clipping means the loss of the flowers which are half its beauty, but all the same it makes a dense neat hedge if you want one. Do not cut back into the old wood. Then there is the Corsican rosemary, *R. angustifolius Corsicus* with a more feathery growth of leaf and bright blue flowers, almost gentian blue; it is less tough-looking than the common rosemary, and perhaps not quite so hardy, but so lovely a thing that it well deserves a sheltered corner. It hates cold winds ... and there is Tuscan Blue, which, as its introducer Mr. Arnold-Forster remarks, is used for hedges in Tuscany where they are "conspicuous from a distance owing to their ceanothus blue". His recipe for making it flower well in our country is to shorten the long spikes. I have seen it growing magnificently in Cornwall, trained flat against a wall to a height of quite 10 ft., and I fancy that that would be the safest way to treat it any-where, save in the mildest climate, with the additional advantage that you could hang some ordinary netting, such as one uses to protect fruit buds later on, as a break against frost and wind. It is very stiff and stately, unlike its soft Corsican cousin, with a leathery texture in its dark green leaves, making a handsome plant even if it cannot be induced to flower as luxuriantly as beneath the Italian sun.

'Most of the rosemaries will flourish anywhere in the sun, pre-ferring a light soil, even a poor sandy stony soil, and will root very easily from cuttings taken off in September, stuck firmly into sand, and left to grow on until next spring when they can be planted out.'

If you want tons of flower, she adds, 'nip the stem tips out and then again, pick regular sprigs for the house'.

When Pam and Sybille arrived at Sissinghurst in 1959, there was already a chance seedling in the Tower steps, one with a darker blue flower than the ordinary, and with more feathery leaves. It was particularly beautiful so they propagated from it, and found it to be less hardy than the ordinary form but more able to stand our winters than either of the softer southern forms. It was probably a chance seedling of either the Tuscan or Corsican rosemary crossed with the standard variety, and has been preserved and propagated ever since as rosemary 'Sissinghurst Blue'.

This rosemary has become one of the emblematic plants of Sissinghurst. You'll find it around the base of Vita's Tower, and in spring its ceanothus-blue flowers are matched by those of the *Clematis alpina* trained to climb up and over the arch and the large-flowered pansies planted in all four bronze Bagatelle urns. This trio of plants and their colour, in contrast to the pink-red terracotta of the brick, are to me one of the most memorable plant combinations at Sissinghurst.

Vita also loved viburnums, and particularly the fragrant ones such as *Viburnum carlcephalum*. 'Have you got *Viburnum Carlcephalum*? If not, please get it at once. It is a hybrid of *Viburnum Carlesii*, which we all know and grow, and it is a far better thing. Its head of flower is tighter and denser; its scent is stronger; and its habit is vigorous. My own plant is young and small; but I am told by people who have seen it growing fully developed that it makes a huge bush in course of time. It is one of the most exciting things I have grown for years past; not very exciting as to its colour, which is white flushed with pink in the bud, but most exciting as to its powerful scent. It is flowering now – April–May.'

On the cusp of spring into summer come the flowers of the lilac, which Vita also relished. Lilac has gone out of favour in recent years and now few nurseries stock more than a few varieties, but – in a way because of this – the forms available for Vita to write about in the 1950s are almost the same as now. As she says, lilac was 'one of the few old favourites which has been definitely improved in recent years'. But not much has happened since:

Vita loved lilac, a flowering shrub with excellent scent, which she picked for the house.

'Frankly, the pale mauve type was a washy thing. The newer sorts have gained in colour, size, and scent. I suppose that everyone is by now familiar with the earlier improvements: *Souvenir de Louis Spaeth*, and *Charles Joly*, both dark red; or *Charles X*, deep purple; or *Madame Lemoine*, double white; none of which is easy to beat. But not everyone, I find, is familiar with the more recent hybrids, carrying truly noble plumes of immense weight: *Réaumur*, dark red; *President Poincaré* and *Pasteur*, both claret; *Congo*, very dark reddish-purple; *Jeanne d'Arc*, double white; *Mme F. Morel*, mauvish pink; *Maréchal Foch*, red.

'It is most advantageous to cut off the faded flowers, *this is really important*; they are perfectly hardy; and very long-lived unless they suddenly die back, which sometimes happens.

'The lilac grows grandly. It grows into a great tall treelike shrub, if you allow it to grow without restraint, so tall that after a few years it over-tops our own heads by several yards, so high that we can neither pick the heavy panicle of flower, nor enjoy the scent as we wander round the garden. It is too high out of reach ... You should cut your lilacs hard back. Take them right back to a new leaf-bud, and encourage them to break out afresh. Cut out all dead and twiggy wood, opening the centre to receive as much air and light as possible. June/July is the time to perform these surgical operations, just after the flowering; take note to do it without delay. And if you have got any manure available, put it round your lilacs now; they need feeding; they will appreciate a rich mulch. If you haven't got organic manure, or compost, give them some handfuls of bonemeal or hoof-and-horn, pricking the top-spit lightly with a fork to give them the benefit of a loosened top-soil so that the rain can wash it in. And they like the sun.'

SUMMER SCENT

On a hot day, with the York stone baking, the rosemary plants around the entrance radiate their clean, sharp smell. Turn right from the Top Courtyard and you're into the Rose Garden. Turn left and you're soon under the *Rosa mulliganii* in the White Garden –

Lathyrus 'Painted Lady' on a hazel tepee.

both places memorable for their voluminous scent.

No writing on summer scent could exclude sweet peas, which are still grown at Sissinghurst on hazel teepees – in the Rose Garden and in the Cottage Garden in red and orange – as well as in the cutting patch to supply flowers for Vita's room. The varieties in the Rose Garden are usually the highly scented 'Painted Lady' and 'Matucana', which is closely related to the original sweet pea – Vita's favourite – found wild in the hedgerows in Sicily.

'The true Sweet Pea, *Lathyrus odoratus*, small, hooded, and not remarkable for any beauty of colour,' she notes, 'was originally sent from Italy in 1699 by a Father Cupani to Dr. Robert Uvedale, headmaster of the Grammar School at Enfield, Middlesex. Of Father Cupani I know nothing, but Dr. Uvedale, schoolmaster and horticulturist, seems to have been something of a character. He had a fine collection of foreign plants, which after his death in 1722 were sold to Sir Robert Walpole for his garden at Houghton in Norfolk. Of Dr. Uvedale it was said that "his flowers were choice, his stock numerous, and his culture of them very methodical and

curious". Amongst them was the Sweet Pea, native of southern
Italy and Sicily, and it is this which I should like to see restored to
favour in this country.

'Undoubtedly the [newer] Grandiflora and Spencer hybrids
offer a greater range of colour, a greater solidity and length of
stalk, and more flower-heads to a stalk, nor can it be said that
they lack the fragrance which gives them their popular name.
But compared with the fragrance of the humble little wildling
they have nothing to boast about in that respect. It must be realized that the wild pea is not showy, in fact its pink and purple are
very washy and the individual flowers are small, but they have
a certain wistful delicacy of appearance and the scent of even half
a dozen in a bunch is astonishing ...

'Of course it is no good attempting to grow them on the
elaborate system of training one stem up a bean-pole and sup-
pressing all side shoots; they must be left to scramble up twiggy
pea-sticks in a tangle and kept entirely for picking, in an
unwanted but sunny corner of the kitchen garden.

'At the end of their season they can be left to set their own
seed and a supply be thus ensured. I know for a fact that they do
set and ripen their seed in this island, for I have seen them doing
it in a private garden quite far north, and came away, I am glad
to say, with a generous handful which I hope to have growing in
my own garden next summer.'

So Vita wanted the wild sweet pea, but the next-best thing is
'Cupani' or the larger-flowered 'Matucana'. All the sweet peas
flowering in our gardens today descend – as she says – from
the wild plant brought into cultivation in Sicily in the late seventeenth century. Franciscus Cupani, the Sicilian monk Vita
mentions above who in 1699 sent seeds to various institutions

and plant collectors including Dr Uvedale, was writing a flora of Sicily.

From then until 1870 a few new forms appeared; by 1793 the seedsman John Mason of Fleet Street in London had described five varieties in all. There were at that stage only a 'black' (probably maroon), purple (probably the 'Cupani' wild type), scarlet, white and 'Painted Lady', which remains one of the best and most highly scented sweet peas you can grow today.

Then appeared Henry Eckford, the creator of so many sweet peas that we still grow. He worked as a gardener until the age of sixty-five, then in 1888 set up his own nursery at Wem in Shropshire and dedicated the rest of his life to improving and expanding the small range of sweet peas then available. Eckford achieved two things – greatly increasing the size of the flowers and expanding the colour range. The products of his work are the group of sweet peas called *grandiflora*, including 'Matucana' which is hard to surpass even today.

Another annual to sow for its perfume is the night-scented stock. 'May is the time to sow that small, dim-coloured thing, *Matthiola bicornis*,' says Vita. 'I have just sown half an ounce of it all along the pathway at the foot of a yew hedge, and now look forward to some warm evening when the pale barn-owl is ranging over the orchard and the strong scent of the little stock surprises me as I go. This is anticipating the summer, when only recently snow lay upon the ground, but this modest little annual is so easily forgotten that a prod of reminder should not come amiss. If you mix the seed with the seed of Virginian stock, you will get a little colour in the daytime as well as the scent after dusk.'

You could never have a summer garden where scent was central without including as many roses as possible. They played a major part in Vita's summer garden. She loved them for the structure and abundance that they quickly gave her, and had many favourite varieties playing that role in her design. She also singles out a few particular roses for the magnificence of their scent.

In the list of her select few she includes a 'hedge of hybrid musk roses, especially *Penelope*', 'some bushes of the rugosa rose, *Blanc double de Coubert*' and 'a hedge of sweetbriar' – all front runners, which we should all seriously think of adding to our gardens. She writes:

Rosa 'Penelope'.

'Someone has been pleading with me to put in a good word for sweet-briar. I do so most willingly, for a hedge of sweet-briar is one of the most desirable things in any garden.

'It is thorny enough to keep out intruders, should it be needed as a boundary protection; in early summer it is as pretty as the dog-rose, with its pale pink single flowers; in autumn it turns itself into a sheer wall of scarlet hips; and on moist muggy evenings after rain the scent is really and truly strong in the ambient air. You do not need to crush a leaf between your fingers to provoke the scent: it swells out towards you of its own accord, as you walk past, like a great sail filling suddenly with a breeze off those Spice Islands which Columbus hoped to find.

'These are many virtues to claim, but even so we may add to them. It is the Eglantine of the poets, if you like that touch of romance. True, Milton seems to have confused it with something else, probably the honeysuckle:

'... through the sweet-briar or the Vine,
Or the twisted Eglantine ...

'But what does that matter? it is pedantic to be so precise, and we should do better to take a hint from Milton and plant a *mixed* hedge of honeysuckle and sweet-briar, with perhaps an ornamental vine twining amongst them – the purple-leafed vine, *Vitis vinifera purpurea*, would look sumptuous among the red hips in October.

'I have never seen a hedge of this composition; but why not? Ideas come to one; and it remains only to put them into practice. The nearest that I have got is to grow the common *Clematis Jackmanii* into my sweet-briar, planting the clematis on the north side of the hedge, where the roots are cool and shaded and the great purple flowers come wriggling through southwards into the sun. It looks fine, and the briar gives the clematis just the twiggy kind of support it needs.

'Sweet-briar is a strong grower, but is often blamed for going thin and scraggy towards the roots. I find that you can correct this weakness by planting your hedge in the first instance against a system of post-and-wire, and subsequently tying-in the long shoots to the posts and wire instead of pruning them. Tie the shoots horizontally, or bend them downwards if need be, thus obtaining a thick, dense growth, which well compensates you for the initial trouble of setting up the posts and the wire. They will last for years, and so will the briar.

'The common sweet-briar [is cheap], and the single plant will spread, horizontally, twenty feet or more. The Penzance hybrid briars are more expensive ... *Amy Robsart*, with deep rose flowers, and *Lady Penzance*, with coppery-yellow flowers, are particularly to be recommended.'

Vita went ahead and planted a hedge of sweet briar which still divides the Orchard from the path to the South Cottage back door, and its scent – particularly on a muggy June evening – is extraordinary.

The *rugosa* rose 'Blanc double de Coubert' and the Hybrid Musk 'Penelope' come up again and again in Vita's writing. It was for the length of their flowering season and the power of their fragrance that she most cherished them. She was also fond of 'Souvenir du Docteur Jamain', which she saved from extinction:

'There are roses which are "fast of their scent", requiring to be held to the nose, and others which generously spread themselves upon the summer air. Of these, I would signal three in particular: *rosa rugosa alba* and *rugosa Blanc double de Coubert*, and the hybrid musk *Penelope*. These all make big bushes, and should be placed near a corner where you frequently pass. They all have the merit of continuous flowering, and *rugosa alba* produces bright red hips in autumn, like little round apples amongst the yellowing leaves, adding to its attraction, interest and charm.

'The rugosa hybrid, *Parfum de l'Hay*, has the reputation of being one of the most strongly scented of all roses. Unfortunately its constitution is not as strong as its scent. Perhaps light soils don't suit it. Its companion, *Roseraie de l'Hay*, might do better, and smells nearly as good. Neither of them makes a big bush, so would be suitable for a small garden.

'*Souvenir du Docteur Jamain* is an old hybrid perpetual which

I am rather proud of having rescued from extinction. I found him growing against the office wall of an old nursery. No one knew what he was; no one seemed to care; no one knew his name; no one had troubled to propagate him. Could I dig him up, I asked? Well, if you like to risk it, they said, shrugging their shoulders; it's a very old plant, with a woody stiff root. I risked it; *Docteur Jamain* survived his removal; and now has a flourishing progeny in my garden and also on the market of certain rosarians to whom I gave him. *Docteur Jamain* is a deep red, not very large flowers, but so sweetly and sentimentally scented. Some writers would call it nostalgically scented, meaning everything that burying one's nose into the heart of a rose meant in one's childhood, or in one's adolescence when one first discovered poetry, or the first time one fell in love.

'I think *Docteur Jamain* should not be planted in too sunny a place. He burns. A south-west aspect suits him better than full south.'

Vita was also partial to the Bourbon roses – and who can blame her? – with their romantic history and intense, delicious scent. In my experience 'Madame Isaac Pereire' does have a magnificent scent, but is also prone to blackspot and mildew, which can defoliate a plant if not kept under control. When Vita was writing, it's possible the higher content of sulphur and other pollutants in the air, even in Kent, meant that the fungus scourge was less of a problem. It's counterintuitive, though: you'd think unclean air – unhealthy roses. But the reverse is the case.

'If you were born with a romantic nature, all roses must be crammed with romance, and if a particular rose originated on an island the romance must be doubled, for an island is romantic in itself.

'The island I refer to lies off the south-east coast of Africa, near Mauritius. It used to be called the Île Bourbon, now called Réunion. The inhabitants of this small island had the pleasing habit of using roses for their hedges: only two kinds, the Damask rose and the China rose. These two married in secret; and one day, in 1817, the curator of the botanic garden on the Île Bourbon noticed a seedling he transplanted and grew on, a solitary little bastard which has fathered or mothered the whole race we now call the Bourbon roses.

'It is curious to find Mr. Edward Bunyard writing in 1936 in his book *Old Garden Roses* that the Bourbon roses "are now almost forgotten", and listing only four as being "still obtainable". (*Hermosa, Bourbon Queen, Louise Odier,* and *Mme Pierre Oger.*) He does not even mention *Zéphyrine Drouhin,* the rose which so far back as 1868 decided to discard armaments and has been known as the thornless rose ever since. This shows how taste has changed within the last twenty years, for it is now possible to obtain at least two dozen different varieties.

'Far from being forgotten, now that the shrub roses have returned to favour, *Rosa bourboniana* includes some of the most desirable. Their scent alone makes one realize the extent to which they have inherited that quality from their damask parent; one has only to think of *Mme Isaac Péreire* and *Mme Pierre Oger,* admittedly two of the most fragrant roses in cultivation. We all have our scented favourites; and someone is bound to say, "What about *Parfum de l'Hay?*", but I must still support the claims of these two ladies in the Bourbon group.

'The cross has resulted in an oddly varied lot. There is *Coupe d'Hébé,* 1840, which you might easily mistake for a centifolia or cabbage rose; and if you like the striped roses there are *Honorine de Brabant* and *Commandant Beau-paire*, 1874, pink and white like *Rosa mundi*, but not, I contend, as good as that ancient Rose of the World. Among the more recent crosses, *Zigeuner Knabe*, 1909, makes the most swagger boastful bush you could set at any corner: a reddish purple, it looks more like a Cardinal fully robed, about to set off in procession, than like the *Gypsy Boy* we call it in English.

'The Bourbon roses should not be heavily pruned, and indeed their full beauty can be displayed only when they are allowed to grow into the great tall bushes natural to them. Dead and twiggy wood should be cut out. How easy to say, and how scratchy to do.'

On the disease issue with the Bourbons, she gives us some good practical advice: 'There are several schools of thought on the control of [blackspot], which causes complete defoliation in bad cases and must end in destroying the constitution of the plant, thus deprived of its natural means of breathing through the leaves. The orthodox method is spraying with Bordeaux mixture in January and February. T.M.T., or Thiram, sometimes supplied under the name *Tulisan*, is also recommended for fortnightly use from the end of May onwards. Some rose-growers also advise a thick mulch of lawn clippings, peat-moss litter, or even sawdust. Others put their faith (such as it is) in rich feeding, on the principle that a healthy, well-nourished plant is more resistant to infection. I must say that I found this works well. It may sound unscientific, since black spot is a fungus, and you might imagine that a fungus would establish itself on weak or strong plants equally once it had made up its mind to do so; but I am not a scientific gardener and can judge only by results. The result of some barrow-loads of compost was: no black spot on some particularly vulnerable roses two summers running, including the damp summer we have recently disenjoyed.'

Continuing with shrubs, Vita loved the scent of philadelphus – exotic and spicy, and as its common name, mock orange, implies, deliciously reminiscent of orange blossom and abelia which, as Vita says, smells of jasmine.

Philadelphus coronarius.

Starting with philadelphus, its name 'seems to suit it nicely, meaning brotherly or sisterly love in Greek, suggesting a purity of love distinct from any sexual passion.

'Yet the thing is bridal. It makes huge bushes of the purest white. The love of siblings may be all very well, but it is a truly nuptial thing, an epithalamium of a poem for young lovers.

'I saw it foaming about in two famous gardens I recently went to in Gloucestershire. I saw it also in all the cottage gardens of that incomparable Cotswold country. It was everywhere; all over the place. I scolded myself for not having planted philadelphus in masses when I first started to make my garden. Had I done so years ago, I should have had huge bushes by now, but it is never too late.

'I have got the dear old *Philadelphus coronarius*, that sweet-scented bush that takes one straight back to one's childhood. Three hundred years ago, Gerard the herbalist wrote that he had cut some flowers of this old plant, and laid them in his chamber, but found them of so unacquainted a savour that he could not take rest until he had cast them out. This can mean only that he found the scent too strong. What I hadn't realized was that some of the later flowering sorts were almost equally generous of their scent. Now I know better. The little *micro-phyllus* may not be very showy but smells delicious in its small white flowers. *Lemoinei erectus* is also sweet-scented. *Belle Etoile* isn't; or at any rate I can't detect any scent in it. Perhaps that is the fault of my nose; anyhow it is so magnificent a shrub that we all ought to grow it. You have *P. virginal*, with big white double flowers, a lovely cool green-and-white sight in midsummer; and *Belle Etoile* and *P. purpureo-maculatus*, white with a purple blotch in the centre; the last two scentless, alas, unlike the spring-flowering *P. coronarius*. *Grandiflorus* is the one with big single white flowers, very decorative but entirely scentless, which may be a recommendation for people who do not like heavily-scented flowers in their rooms.

'By the way, if you strip all the leaves from cut branches, they will last far longer, besides gaining in beauty. Try. And smash the woody stems with a hammer. [Or sear the stem ends in boiling water for thirty seconds.]

'The philadelphus family is so complicated that it is difficult to distinguish between them. They hybridize so freely amongst themselves that scarcely anybody knows now which are species or which are hybrids. Do we have to worry about this? Should we not rather plant as many as we can secure, this autumn [she's writing in July 1956], in the anticipation of great white bushes a few years hence?'

Another favoured shrub was *Abelia triflora*. 'It flowers in June, grows to the size of what we used to call Syringa [*Philadelphus*, above], and is smothered in white, funnel-shaped flowers with the strongest scent of Jasmine … do plant *Cytisus Battandieri*. This is a broom; and when it has grown into a large tree it is hung with gold-yellow tassels in June, with a peculiar scent. I could not think what the scent was, till my kind host who had it growing in his garden fixed it for me: "It is the scent of pineapple mixed with fruit salad." He was right.

'*Cytisus Battandieri* is supposed to be hardy, but I suspect that in cold districts it would be safer to train it against a wall.'

Lilies were very much part of Vita's summer garden repertoire, *Lilium auratum* appearing in her invaluable fragrance list (see p. 178) 'as a luxury'. This bulb is indeed a luxury as they are so expensive, so if you're going to grow them, they're most sensibly cultivated in a pot (see pp. 291–2). There are now various hybrids with some *auratum* genes, almost as good and a fraction of the price of the species. I grew the very similar 'Gold Band' last year and fell in love with it. It has vast flowers, the size of sideplates, white with a central gold band – like *auratum* – and a triumphant scent.

Lilium regale.

Vita also loved *Lilium regale,* 'that sweet-scented trumpet which is perhaps the easiest of that tricky family to grow'. They were and are a central plant in the summer White Garden.

'The tall white lilies,' she writes, 'have been a tremendous stand-by in the June and July garden. Their cool splendour at twilight came like a draught of water after the hot day. I like to see them piercing up between low grey foliaged plants such as artemisia, southernwood, and santolina, and rising above some clouds of gypsophila, for there is something satisfying in the contrasting shapes of the domed bushes and the belfry-like tower of the lily; an architectural harmony.

'Many people think lilies difficult to grow, and write them off as an expensive disappointment. I have myself. I try. I fail. I despair. Then I try again. This misconception must be due to several causes: (1) the notorious inverted snobbishness of the Madonna lily, which apparently refuses to flourish except in cottage gardens, (2) the prevalence of the fungus disease known as *botrytis* and the virus disease known as *mosaic*, (3) the belief that all lilies enjoy the same conditions, (4) the attempts of inexperienced gardeners to succeed with certain varieties which really defy all but the most expert handling. If the amateur, however, should content himself with half a dozen reliable kinds, triumph and not disappointment should be his.

'Start with the kinds that offer a reasonable hope of success, a short list in which the regal lily, *L. regale*, the Tiger lily, *L. tigrinum*, the yellow Turk's cap, *L. pyrenaicum*, the purplish Turk's cap, *L. martagon*, the vari-coloured *L. umbellatum* (or *hollandicum*) and the giant orange *L. henryi*, may safely figure ...'

Then she says – get advice from people who truly know how to grow them:

'Only last week did it occur to me to go and ask for advice from a famous grower of lilies in my neighbourhood, which was the obvious and sensible thing to do. I might have thought of it before. Surely he will not mind my passing on the hints he gave me, especially if it leads to an encouragement to grow some varieties of this supremely beautiful family.

'There are four cardinal points, he said, like the compass. Point 1: good drainage is essential; no stagnant moisture, even if it means digging out a hole and putting a layer of crocks or coarse clinker at the bottom. Point 2: make up a suitable bed to receive your bulbs, a bed rich in humus, which means leaf-mould, peat, compost, chopped bracken, or whatever form of humus you can command. Point 3: never plant lily bulbs which have been out of the ground too long or have had their basal roots cut off. Reject these, even if you find them offered at cheap rates in the horticultural department of some chain stores. Lily bulbs should be lifted fresh and replanted quickly, with their basal roots intact; therefore it is advisable to obtain them from any reputable nurseryman, who will pack them in moist peat and will never allow them to dry out before despatch. Point 4: divide when they become overcrowded.

'To these hints I might add another. Most lilies dislike what professional gardeners call "movement of air", which in plain English means wind or a draught ... so give them an abode within the shelter of shrubs. I have also discovered by experience that the Regal lily, *L. regale*, likes growing amongst some covering shelter such as Southernwood (Old Man) or one of the artemisias, I suppose because the foliage gives protection to the young lily-growth against late frosts, but also because some plants take kindly to one another in association.

'Finally, he said, remember that nothing makes a finer mulch than bracken cut green, chopped up into short pieces, and allowed to rot. He deprecated the use of lawn-grass mowings; of artificial fertilizers; and of over-fresh organic manure. Manure, he said, should never be allowed to come into contact with the bulb itself: it should be placed well beneath it, or used as a top mulch. Bone meal, he said, was always safe and useful.

'Also remember to acquaint yourself with the likes and dislikes of the lilies he intends to grow. Some hate lime; others demand it.'

To this list we'd now have to add the scourge of the scarlet-red lily beetle. This eats holes in the leaves – and the flowers – and weakens the bulb. They are notoriously difficult to squash, too, having very tough exoskeletons. The only thing guaranteed to get rid of them is a prophylactic spray with a systemic insecticide but many of us are reluctant to do this.

Increase your stock by raising lilies from 'seed or scales, a most fascinating occupation', which Vita recommends particularly for *L. regale*.

'[Lilies are not cheap] ... so if you want them in any quantity it will pay you to raise them from seed ... so look out for seeding heads in your own or a friend's garden. You can also buy seed [quite cheaply] ... but it is more fun to crack open a seed-pod and shake out those marvellously packed, paper-thin seeds for yourself. Every one of them should germinate, and one pod alone should give you more lilies than you will ever have space for. Choose the seeds from the strongest plant; sow them in a seed box and plant out the little bulbs next year in rows in a nursery bed where you can keep an eye on them; by the end of the second year you ought to be picking a few single flowers; by the end of the third year they ought to be fully developed. If you repeat the process yearly, thus staggering your supply of bulbs, you should never be without *L. regale* in your garden, at no cost.

'You realize, of course, that you can do the same with those little black boot-buttons that appear on the stems of the old tiger-lily?

'I cannot resist adding a note at a later date (1950) to pass on an amusing hint for growing lilies from seed. You need a screw-top jar, such as housewives bottle fruit in; a mixture of leaf-mould, peat, and loam, enough to fill the jar; and half a handful of seed. You make the mixture wet, and then squeeze it in your hand till it stops dripping and becomes a damp sponge. You then introduce it into the jar, sowing the seed in layers as you go, until the mixture and the seed have both reached the rim. You then screw on the top; put the jar on the window-sill in a warm room, and watch for the seeds which have come to the edge, where you can see them, to develop into little tadpole-like bodies which, you hope, will eventually become bulbs ...

'This method of obtaining lilies for nothing requires a considerable amount of patience, three to four years before you get a bulb old enough to flower, but how rewarding is the result. It also ensures that your bulbs have not been left lying about to dry up, a fatal destiny for any lily. It means also that you are not getting a stock infected by any virus disease; the plants may develop it later on, since no one can guarantee against this, but at least you know that you have started clean.

'I have found that seeds sown in fairly deep pans will make little bulbs ready to plant out in their second season. The seeds can also be sown in a prepared seed-bed in drills in the open, but pans are more easily controlled, especially in the matter of weeding. Stand them on a floor of ashes to prevent the incursion of undesirable insects.'

Vita was passionate about the empress of all lilies – *Cardiocrinum giganteum*, the giant Himalayan lily. There is none more extraordinary than this, over ten foot tall and still growing in the magnolia corner in the Lower Courtyard. She wrote at length about it, including it in her book of favourite plants, *Some Flowers*. They're a hassle to grow but are magnificent.

'[If *Cardiocrinum*] is too splendid to be called vulgar, she is still very decidedly over life-size. Unconsciously, one sets oneself some kind of limit as to what size a flower ought to be, and here is one which exceeds them all. It looks almost as though she had adapted

alarmed and overwhelmed. It was altogether too much like being growled at by Lord Tennyson in his later years.

'Anyhow, he did introduce me to the virtues of the Cheddar Pink, and I immediately ordered a packet of seed and grew it down my own garden path in the same way, not so much from any desire to imitate the Laureate as from a desire to reproduce that same delicious smell on a warm summer evening. And in doing so I learnt from experience a lesson which he had omitted to give me. For two summer seasons my Cheddar Pinks were a great success, and I thought they were going on forever, but, after that, they died out. I investigated indignantly and discovered that our native pink does die out when planted in ordinary garden soil, i.e. grown down the edge of an herbaceous border as Dr. Bridges was growing it. Its only chance of perennial survival is to live in starvation in a crack of a wall, where it may flourish happily year after year. This does not mean that it cannot be grown down the border path also; it means only that you have to renew your supply by fresh seedlings every alternate year – not an excessive trouble to take, when you remember the grey-green clumps which so agreeably throw up the colours of other flowers, and then the pinks themselves while they are blooming and giving off that special, incomparable smell which for me will always be associated with a June day and the cloaked figure of a beautiful, aged poet.'

For scent, it's not just the Cheddar pink which is remarkable – the whole dianthus family, whether annual, biennial or perennial, have fantastic scents, with 'Mrs Sinkins' famously the most fragrant. This is a great perennial pink, though its flowering season is shorter than many of the modern hybrids and its flowers a bit dishevelled; but even so, in terms of that characteristic clovey fragrance, it still reigns supreme. Vita planted it – and it's still here – in the White Garden.

'At this great planting season of the year [Vita was writing in December] we should do well to consider the vast tribe of Pinks, or *Dianthus*, 'for there are few

plants more charming, traditional, or accommodating. In old kitchen gardens one used to see long strips of *Mrs. Sinkins* bordering the paths, and what could be more desirable than that ragged old lady heavily scenting the air? She is a very old lady indeed. Some people think she may be as much as 140 years old, though others would make her a mere 80 or so, and say that she had her origin in a workhouse garden at Slough. Whatever the truth about Mrs. Sinkins

Dianthus 'Mrs Sinkins', Vita's favourite English garden pink.

may be, she appears proudly on the armorial bearings of the borough of Slough, firmly held in the beak of a swan.

' . . . Our native Cheddar Pink, *Dianthus caesius*, is almost as heavily scented as *Mrs. Sinkins* herself, and is as easy to grow.

'This applies to nearly all the pinks. They make few demands. Sun-lovers, they like a well-drained and rather gritty soil; and if you can plant them with a generous supply of mortar rubble they will be as happy as the years are long. This means, of course, that they prefer growing in lime or chalk, an alkaline soil; but they don't insist on it; they exact so little that they will put up with almost anything except a waterlogged place. They hate that; and will revenge themselves on you by damping off.

'The only other fault they have, a most endearing fault, revealing an all too generous nature, is that they may flower themselves to death in your service. You must be on the look-out for this, and cut the wealth of flowers hard back to the grey-green clumps, to protect and save them from their own extravagant generosity . . .'

AUTUMN SCENT

On the cusp from summer into autumn, you have to grow humea, the incense plant, one of my favourite discoveries this year. I read about it in Vita's writing and then came across plants at Chatsworth in Derbyshire, where they've had it all over the house for years from late summer through the autumn. It's a tender plant from Australia, an exotic-looking thing which stands four foot tall, like a finer, more elegant, cascading seed-head of a dock, not remarkable for its looks. But whenever you brush past it or touch the leaves, it fills the room with an intense, myrrh-like scent reminiscent of a great Byzantine cathedral. At Chatsworth, they use it as a house plant. Vita used it outside in the garden. Take your pick, or do both, but it's well worth seeking out. We've all got to grow it! Vita writes:

'A plant which I find always arouses a good deal of interest in the summer here is *Humea elegans.* Visitors walk round sniffing and saying: "What is that curious smell of incense? One might imagine oneself in an Italian cathedral instead of an English garden." They are quite right, for its other name is the Incense Plant.

'Eventually they track it down to a six- to eight-foot-tall plant, with large, pointed dark green leaves and a branching spike of feathery cedarwood-coloured flowers. It is neither showy nor conspicuous, and nothing but the scent would lead you to it among its more garish companions, such as the delphiniums; yet it is graceful in its growth and well deserves its adjective *elegans*. It makes its influence felt in more subtle ways than by a great splash of colour. It steals across the air as potently and pervasively as the sweet-briar on a damp evening. I stick it into odd corners, where people pass, or sit on benches, and pause for a moment before going on their way.

'A native of Australia, it is not hardy here, and must be treated as a half-hardy biennial sown under glass in early summer, kept away from frost, and planted out in the late half of May or beginning of June. For this reason I cannot advise anyone to grow it who has not the advantage of a frost-proof greenhouse in which to raise it; but those fortunate gardeners who have even a tiny warmed greenhouse might well experiment with a few seeds in a pot: six seeds will give six plants, and six plants will be enough to scent the garden, especially if planted under the windows. It will tolerate half-shade, but the flower develops a richer colour in the sun; in the shade it dims off into exactly the same dingy tan as an old flower-pot. It likes a rich soil; it would love to be fed with liquid manure, and will grow all the better if you have time to give it this extra diet or a handful of Clay's fertiliser; but if you have not the time – and who has the time to attend to all these extra and special requirements? – it will do adequately well in ordinary garden soil, and will give you all the reward you can reasonably demand.

'An additional attraction is that the flowering spike will last for at least a year indoors if you cut it off in autumn before the rain has come to sodden it. I kept some sprays of it in a vase for so long that I began to loathe the sight of the thing; it turned dusty long before it started to fade and die; it reminded me of those Everlasting Flowers, the *Helichrysums*, which are only too everlasting indeed.

'You can save and ripen your own seed of it by cutting a spray or two and laying it out on sheets of paper in a sunny place . . .

'I think I should add a word of caution. Some people appear to be allergic to *Humea elegans*, which brings them out in a rash which is anything but elegant. (Some primulas have this effect on some people.) It is a chancy danger which I would not wish any reader to incur owing to any fault of mine.

'A visitor to my garden went off with a plant of it in a pot in his motor-car and not only did he arrive home scratching, but also his dog.'

A final plant that Vita adored for its scent, flowering in the spring, is sweet woodruff. This is delicious, not while flowering but when it's dried in the autumn – it conjures up the sweet grassiness of newly mown hay. You want to pack lavender-style bags with it and stuff pillows. It has a deeply comforting smell:

'Some proverbs are piercingly true; some are not true at all; some are half true. One of the half-true ones is the one that says familiarity breeds contempt.

'Contempt is the wrong word. What we really mean is that we take certain virtues for granted when we live with them day by day. Our appreciation becomes blunted, even as the beautifully sharp blade of the pruning-knife someone gave us as a Christmas present has become blunted by Easter. There are things we grow in our gardens and forget about, and then remember suddenly, as I have just remembered the Sweet Woodruff, that meek, lowly, bright green native of Britain, so easy to grow, so rapid in prop-agation – every little bit of root will grow and extend itself – keeping weeds down and making a bright green strip or patch wherever you want it.

'Sweet Woodruff is its pretty English name. *Asperula odorata* is its Latin name.

'You can use it in many ways. You can grow it where other plants would not grow, in shade and even under the drip of trees. You can grow it as a covering plant to keep weeds away. Then, in the autumn, you can cut the leaves and dry them and make them into sachets which smell like new-mown grass and have the faculty of retaining their scent for years.

'It is not showy. Its little white flowers make no display, but it is a useful carpeter for blank spaces, and it certainly makes "sweet bags" for hanging in the linen cupboard to discourage the moth or to put under your pillow at night. Take note that it has no scent until it is cut and dried, so do not be disappointed if you walk beside it in the garden and catch no puff of scent as you stroll.'

Part 3

THE SMALLER CANVAS

Vita and Martin, her much-loved Alsatian, in the soon-to-be Rose Garden, 1934.

9

PAINTERLY PLANTS

Vita planted swathes of bearded iris to line the
stone paths, which flower to fill the colour gap
between the bulbs in spring and the roses of early
summer.

Vita was clear on her overall approach to designing her flower borders, and as to which were her favourites among the larger plants, the shrubs and climbers. Now to the more delicate things, the smaller plants she wanted to cram into her garden rooms so as to fill them to overbrimming.

In the early months of the year, she focused on the miniature flowers which weren't yet squeezed out by the garden's overall abundance; and she returns to this smaller scale in her plant choices for late autumn and winter. She sought out things which were, as she put it, 'shy, unobtrusive, demure; this is the way I like my flowers to be; not puffed up as though by a pair of bellows; not shouting for praise from gaping admirers'. And as she wrote in *Passenger to Teheran*, published in 1926, about a trip she'd made to Iran to visit Harold who was at the embassy there, 'I like my flowers small and delicate – the taste of all gardeners, as their discrimination increases, dwindles towards the microscopic.' You can see that from the plants she wrote about with the most affection.

Vita was especially fond of painterly plants, ones less noticeable outside in the general garden brouhaha, but when they come inside you can revel in their intricate beauty, sitting right in front of you in a pot or vase: 'The flowers I like best are the flowers requiring a close inspection before they consent to reveal their innermost secret beauty.' She was on the lookout for plants with a Fabergé delicacy, markings as if by the brush of a Chinese calligrapher. Vita would always have a good selection around her, including one or two things miraculous and exquisite, detailed and refined. She had lots of bearded irises, their texture and scent often as good as their colour; and delicates such as species crocus, *Iris reticulata*, meadow fritillaries and *Ixia viridiflora*.

This was why she loved to grow things in containers as well as in the garden itself. Then you could see the intricate flowers more clearly. She made a series of miniature gardens in troughs and old sinks and kept a clutch of pots at the entrance to the garden and at the top of the Tower steps. She also had indoor pots in a cold greenhouse. In there, whatever the weather, she could grow a few precious items: lily-of-the-valley and sweet violets forced into flower early, and elegant show auriculas, salpiglossis and tender nerines, all out of the worst of the weather and so still pristine.

She picked flowers all the time – some sprigs from her great range of flowering shrubs like hamamelis, mahonias, hoheria and *Magnolia grandiflora*, or a little bunch of spring bulbs, miniature iris, anemones, grape hyacinths, fragrant *tazetta* narcissus, mixed in with violets and primroses. Her relationship with the plant did not, then, stop at a fleeting whisk past in the garden, but could continue inside as a long hard stare.

Best known as Vita is for her all-enveloping, voluptuous gardening style and for her single-colour garden rooms, when you looked more closely there would always have been a good proportion of plants possessing a precise and exquisite beauty – something for which she had a great eye. It's these ideas – intricate plants for the garden and for pots both inside and out, plus lots of things for picking – that we can easily copy, whatever the size of our garden. We can fill our lives with the brilliance of Vita's ideas, on the small scale if we can't match the grand.

WINTER

Vita liked to have crocuses to pick – just a few – to arrange in an eggcup, scent bottle or sherry glass inside. They're one of the first

Crocus 'Spring Beauty'.

markers that the dreary winter is nearly over and that spring is, thank goodness, on its way. My favourite variety is newly bred, so Vita wouldn't have known it, but 'Spring Beauty' has all the delicacy and fineness of the ones she loved. 'Advance' and 'Snow Bunting' – which she mentions – are both splendid, forced in a pot or left to flower a little later in the garden, then admired or picked from there.

Crocuses are easy to grow and get better and better every year. Each of the *chrysanthus* varieties will cross-breed and self-sow, gradually studding your grass till it looks like Boticelli's *Primavera*. The best place to see this is in the late Christopher Lloyd's lawns and meadows at Great Dixter, magnificent for early bulbs at the end of winter. It's like walking into an Alpine meadow, but even better, distilled and heightened with all the best spring bulbs scattered through the grass. The *chrysanthus* varieties were Christopher's favourites. As Fergus Garrett, the head gardener at Dixter, says, there isn't an ugly one amongst them. There are many patches of 'Snow Bunting', deliciously scented, which clumps rather than spreads, with its pure white flowers and free-range-egg-yolk-yellow centres. If you follow Vita's recommendations, you'll have a succession flowering from January until the end of March. Here are some comments from *In Your Garden Again*, for February 1953:

'I now find myself regretting that I did not plant more of the species crocuses which are busy coming out in quick succession. They are so very charming, and so very small. If you can go and see them in a nursery garden or at a flower show, do take the opportunity to make a choice. Grown in bowls or Alpine pans they are enchanting for the house; they recall those miniature works of art created by the great Russian artificer Fabergé in the luxurious days when the very rich could afford such extravagances. Grown in stone troughs out of doors, they look exquisitely in scale with their surroundings, since in open beds or even in pockets of a rockery they are apt to get lost in the vast areas of landscape beyond.

'One wants to see them close to the eye, fully to appreciate the pencilling on the outside of the petals; it seems to have been drawn with a fine brush, perhaps wielded by some sure-handed Chinese calligrapher, feathering them in bronze or in lilac. Not the least charm of these little crocuses is their habit of throwing up several blooms to a stem (it is claimed for *Ancyrensis* that a score will grow from a single bulb). Just when you think they are going off, a fresh crop appears.

'*Ancyrensis*, from Ankara and Asia Minor, yellow, is usually the first to flower in January or early February, closely followed by *chrysanthus* and its seedlings *E. A. Bowles*, yellow and brown; *E. P. Bowles*, a deeper yellow feathered with purple; *Moonlight*, sulphur yellow and cream; *Snow Bunting*, cream and lilac; *Warley White*, feathered with purple. That fine species, *Imperati*, from Naples and Calabria, is slightly larger, violet-blue and straw-coloured; it flowers in February. *Susianus*, February and March, is well known as the Cloth of Gold crocus; *Sieberi*, a Greek, lilac-blue, is also well known; but *Suterianus* and its seedling *Jamie* are less often seen. *Jamie* must be the tiniest of all: a pale violet with deeper markings on the outside, he is no more than the size of a shilling across when fully expanded, and two inches high. I measured.

'I have mentioned only a few of this delightful family, which should, by the way, be planted in August.'

For the start of the year, Vita liked to have plenty of *Iris reticulata* in as many of its different forms as she could find. She planted enough so as to be able to admire their stalwartness out in the brutal February conditions, in the open borders or in one of her precious troughs (see p. 298), as well as some in pots to bring inside. They are marvellous inside, but the flowers are transient in the heat.

Very persistent bulbs, their numbers grew more and more each year and you'll still find lots at Sissinghurst, in the troughs in the Top Courtyard and popping up in patches in Delos and the Lime Walk. There are many forms, but I particularly love the luscious ruby-purple 'Pauline' (similar to 'Hercules' in Vita's list below), the bluer-purple 'Harmony', as well as the bright mauve 'Cantab', which she also mentions. And add to these the red-purple silk velvet, *Iris histrioides*, 'George'.

Iris reticulata 'Rhapsody'.

Vita's enthusiasm, as ever, is infectious:

'It seems extraordinary that anything so gay, delicate, and brilliant should really prefer the rigours of winter to the amenities of spring. It is true that we can grow Iris reticulata in pots under glass if we wish to do so, and that the result will be extremely satisfying and pretty, but the far more pleasing virtue of Iris reticulata is that it will come into bloom out of doors as early as February, with no coddling or forcing at all. Purple flecked with gold, it will open its buds even above the snow. The ideal place to grow it is in a pocket of rather rich though well-drained soil amongst stones; a private place which it can have all to itself for the short but grateful days of its consummation.

'Reticulata – the netted iris. Not the flower is netted, but the bulb. The bulb wears a little fibrous coat, like a miniature fishing-net. It is a native of the Caucasus, and there is a curious fact about it: the Caucasian native is reddish, whereas our European garden form is a true Imperial purple ...

'I do suggest that every flower-lover should grow a patch of the little reticulata somewhere in his garden. The variety *Cantab*, a pale turquoise blue, flowers about a fortnight earlier as a rule; *Hercules*, a subfusc ruby-red, comes at the same time as the species.'

Aconites would add to this delicate mix, putting in an appearance at a bleak and freezing moment early in the year. The great thing about aconites, as Vita says, is that without any pampering they will gradually spread all through any shady spot in the garden. Dig up a clump just after flowering – 'in the green' – and scatter it to several other places that would be cheered by a January–February carpet of gold. You'll forget about it for a couple of years, but then, settled in, it will start to put on a show

A bowl of winter aconites – *Eranthis hyemalis.*

and will do so for decades. Pick a few to arrange in a tiny vase or float some in a shallow bowl supported on crisp beech leaves.

'The courage of some small and apparently fragile flowers never ceases to amaze me,' Vita says. 'Here are we humans, red-nosed and blue-cheeked in the frost and the snow, looking dreadfully plain; but there are the little flowers coming up, as brave and gay as can be, unaffected by snow or frost. The winter aconite is a cheerful resister, coming through the white ground with puffs of snow all over his bright burnished face, none the worse in his January–February beauty, and increasing from self-sown seedlings year after year.

'We cannot be reminded too often of so dear and early a thing. It started flowering here, in Kent, on January 20th; I made a note in my diary. Then frost came, turning it into tiny crystallized apricots, like the preserved fruits one used once to get given for Christmas. They shone; they sparkled in the frost. Then the frost went, and with the thaw, they emerged from their rimy sugar coating into their full, smooth, buttercup yellow on a February day with its suggestion of spring, when the first faint warmth of the sun falls as a surprise upon our naked hands.

'I am being strictly correct in comparing the varnished yellow of the Winter Aconite to our common buttercup, for they both belong to the same botanical order of the *Ranunculaceae*.

'The proper name of the Winter Aconite is *Eranthis*. *Eranthis hyemalis* is the one usually grown, and should be good enough for anybody. These are cheap, but if you want a superior variety you can order *E. Tubergenii*. I daresay this would be worth trying. Personally I am very well satisfied with the smudge of gold given me by *hyemalis* (meaning, of winter). It has the great advantage of flourishing almost anywhere, in shade or sun, under trees or in the open, and also of producing a generous mustard-and-cress-like crop of self-sown seedlings which you can lift and transplant. It is better to do this than to lift the older plants, for it is one of those home-lovers that likes to stay put, and, indeed, will give of its best only when it has had a couple of years to become estab-lished. So do not get impatient with it at first. Give it time.

'There are many small early things one could happily associ-ate with it; in fact, I can imagine, and intend to plant, a winter corner, stuffed with little companions all giving their nursery party at the same time: *Narcissus minimus* [now known as *Narcissus asturiensis*] and *Narcissus nanus*; the bright blue thimbles of the earliest grape hyacinth, *Muscari azureus*; the delicate spring crocus *Tomasinianus*, who sows himself everywhere, scores of little Thomases all over the place ... but I must desist.'

Cyclamen give a similar delicacy and scale at almost any time of year, their leaves often as appealing as the flowers themselves. For January and February, you want *Cyclamen coum*, one of the first to appear in any garden. These come in a range of colours, but none better than that deep saturated pink. You can plant this right in amongst the roots of deciduous trees such as beech and oak, and they will poke their heads up through the coppery carpet of fallen leaves. They cope perfectly happily in the desert of dry shade, and Vita's selection (below) will give you a succession of flowers to cover most of the year. Like the species crocuses and aconites, these will gradually self-sow and naturalise.

One of the most beautiful winter containers I've ever seen was planted with *Cyclamen coum* as a carpet below the magnificent

snowdrop, 'Samuel Arnott'. This was created by Julian and Isabel Bannerman at Hanham Court, outside Bristol, and is just the sort of thing Vita might have done in one of her stone troughs, a simple sweep of something small-scale, jewelled and glorious.

Cyclamen coum and *Galanthalus* 'Samuel Arnott'.

Vita goes into detail: 'There are two kinds of cyclamen: the Persian, which is the one your friends give you, and which is not hardy [see more on this in the greenhouse section on pp. 282–3], and the small, out-door one, a tiny edition of the big Persian, as hardy as a snowdrop. These little cyclamen are among the longest-lived of garden plants. A cyclamen corm will keep itself going for more years than its owner is likely to live. They have other advantages: (1) they will grow under trees, for they tolerate, and indeed enjoy, shade; (2) they do not object to a limy soil; (3) they will seed themselves and (4) they will take you round the calendar by a judicious planting of different sorts. *C. neapolitanum*, for instance, will precede its ivy-like leaves by its little pink flower in late autumn, white flowers if you get the variety *album*; *C. coum*, pink, white, or lilac, will flower from December to March; *C. ibericum* from February to the end of March; *C. balearicum* will then carry on, followed by *C. repandum*, which takes you into the summer; and, finally, *C. europaeum* for the late summer and early autumn ...

'Anyone who grows the little cyclamen will have observed that they employ an unusual method of twiddling a kind of corkscrew, or coil, to project the seeds from the capsule when ready. One would imagine that the coil would go off with a ping, rather like the mainspring of a clock when one overwinds it, thus flinging the seeds far and wide, and this indeed was the theory put forward by many botanists.

'It would appear, however, that nothing of the kind happens, and that the seeds are gently deposited on the parent corm. Why, then, this elaborate apparatus of the coil, if it serves only to drop the seed on to a hard corm and not on to the soft receptive soil? It has been suggested ... that this concentration of the seeds may be Nature's idea of providing a convenient little heap for some distributing agent to carry away, and [a correspondent] points out that ants may be seen, in later summer, hurrying off with the seeds until not one is left. I confess that I have never sat up with a cyclamen long enough to watch this curious phenomenon of the exploding capsule; and I still wonder how and why seedlings so obligingly appear in odd corners of the garden – never, I must add, very far away from the parent patch.

'So accommodating are they that you can plant them at almost any time, though ideally they should be planted when dormant, i.e. in June or July.'

Winter has always been an important season in Vita's garden, and she came up with the idea of a special corner, jam-packed with all the plants just described: 'January to the end of March. I wish we had a name for that intermediate season which includes St. Valentine's Day, February 14th, and All Fools' Day, April 1st. It is neither one thing nor the other, neither winter nor spring. Could we call it wint-pring, which has a good Anglo-Saxon sound about it, and accept it, like marriage, for better or worse?

'My wint-pring corner shall be stuffed with every sort of bulb or corm that will flower during those few scanty weeks. The main point is that it shall be really stuffed; crammed full; packed tight ...'

In addition, 'there will be some early tulips, such as *Tulipa biflora* and *turkestanica* and *Kaufmaniana*, the water-lily tulip, flowering in March. There will be *Scilla biflora* and *Scilla Tubergeniana*, both flowering in February; and as a ground work, to follow after the winter aconites, I shall cram the ground with the Greek *Anemone blanda*, opening her starry blue flower in the rare sun of February, and with the Italian *Anemone Apennina*, who comes a fortnight later and carries on into March and is at her best in April. Terrible spreaders, these anemones; but so blue a carpet may gladly be allowed to spread.

' ... The winter corner should be cheap to plant; and needs, humbly, only a little patch of ground where you can find one. Let it be in a place which you pass frequently, and can observe from day to day.'

SPRING

Vita loved the meadow fritillary perhaps more than any spring bulb, partly for its subtlety, for, 'less showy than the buttercup, less spectacular than the foxglove in the wood, it seems to put a damask shadow over the grass, as though dusk were falling

Meadow fritillary – *Fritillaria meleagris.*

under a thunder-cloud that veiled the setting sun ...' She also
loved it for its hidden drama. It is, as she says in *Some Flowers*, 'a
flower to put in a glass on your table. It is a flower to peer into.
In order to appreciate its true beauty, you will have to learn to
know it intimately. You must look closely at all its little squares,
and also turn its bell up towards you so that you can look right
down into its depths, and see the queer semi-transparency of the
strangely foreign, wine-coloured chalice. It is a sinister little
flower, sinister in its mournful colours of decay.'

Vita planted lots of snakeshead fritillaries in the Orchard
underneath the fruit trees: 'In its native state the bulb grows
very deep down,' she explains, 'so taking a hint from Nature we

ought to plant it in our own gardens at a depth of at least six to eight inches. There is another good reason for doing this: pheasants are fond of it, and are liable to scratch it up if planted too shallow. Apart from its troubles with pheasants, it is an extremely obliging bulb and will flourish almost anywhere in good ordinary soil, either in grass or in beds. It looks best in grass, of course, where it is naturally meant to be, but I do not think it much matters where you put it, since you are unlikely to plant the million bulbs which would be necessary in order to reproduce anything like the natural effect, and are much more likely to plant just the few dozen which will give you enough flowers for picking.'

The heavy soil and poor drainage of the Sissinghurst Orchard make this ideal fritillary ground. They have been successful, and have self-sown for decades into robust patches flowering in April and May. That's where you see them in the wild – in damp, low-lying meadows, particularly in the Thames Valley, where they have self-sown now for millennia. As we've seen with other plants, that's just the look Vita wanted in her garden – damask shadows across her Orchard grass and enough for her to pick whenever she wanted. They only last three or four days in water, but there's nothing better.

Show auriculas might be extraordinary, but it is also worth growing the garden forms (see the section on her cold greenhouse for the show varieties, p. 269). As she said, 'we may have modestly to content ourselves with the outdoor or Alpine Auricula, but we have nothing to complain of, for it is not only the painter's but also the cottager's flower. It is indeed one of those flowers which look more like the invention of a miniaturist or of a designer of embroidery, than like a thing which will grow easily and contentedly in one's own garden. In practical truth it will flourish gratefully given the few conditions it requires: a deep, cool root-run, a light soil with plenty of leaf-mould ... a certain amount of shade during the hotter hours of the day, and enough moisture to keep it going. In other words, a west or even a north aspect will suit it well, so long as you do not forget the deep root-run, which has the particular reason that the auricula roots itself deeper and deeper into the earth as it grows older. If you plant it in shallow soil, you will find that the plant hoists itself upwards, away from the ground, eventually raising itself on to a bare, unhappy-looking stem, whereas it really ought to be flattening its leaves against the brown earth, and making rosette after rosette of healthy green. If your auriculas are doing this, you may be sure they are doing well, and you may without hesitation dig them up and divide them as soon as they have ceased flowering, that is to say in May or June, and re-plant the bits you have broken off, to increase your group next year.

'It is well worth trying to raise seedlings from your own seed, for you never know what variation you may get. The seed germinates easily in about ten days or a fortnight; sow it in a sandy compost, barely covering the seed; keep the seedlings in a shady place, in pots if you like, or pricked out on a suitable border till they are big enough to move to their permanent home.'

Vita was a great one for tulips, the showy 'parrots' for picking and the early-flowering, persistent and easy species for the Spring Garden (the Lime Walk) and Cottage Garden, and to include in her wint-pring corner – but it was *Tulipa clusiana*, the 'Lady Tulip', with its painterly quality, that stood out. Look for the white and red 'Peppermint Stick' cultivar that Vita writes about, as well as the creamy yellow and red hybrid, *T. clusiana* 'Cynthia'. They're both beautiful.

'[*Tulipa clusiana*] is familiarly called the Lady Tulip, but always reminds me more of a regiment of little red and white

soldiers. Seen growing wild on Mediterranean or Italian slopes, you can imagine a Lilliputian army deployed at its spring manoeuvres. I suppose her alleged femineity is due to her elegance and neatness, with her little white shirt so simply tucked inside her striped jacket, but she is really more like a slender boy, a slim little officer, dressed in a parti-coloured uniform of the Renaissance.

The Lady tulip – *Tulipa clusiana.*

'Clusiana is said to have travelled from the Mediterranean to England in 1656 ... Her native home will suggest the conditions under which she likes to be grown: a sunny exposure and a light rich soil. If it is a bit gritty, so much the better.'

On a different scale, but still a plant which rewards close examination, Vita loved the imperial fritillary (*Fritillaria imperialis*) and grew it in the Cottage Garden, as well as encouraging Harold to have good clumps of it to provide a rhythm down the borders of the Lime Walk. It's an unusual bulb and, like its relation the lily, is happy with some shade, plus a rich soil with lots of humus and leaf mould. In the right place this fritillary is

Crown Imperial – *Fritillaria imperialis.*

exceptionally long-lived, its bulbs surviving in the same place for decades. My mother has now had it in the same shady corner of their garden for over fifty years. Recently it has suffered the scourge of the lily beetle, which feeds and breeds on this too.

'It was once my good fortune to come unexpectedly across the Crown Imperial in its native home,' Vita notes. 'In a dark, damp ravine in one of the wildest parts of Persia, a river rushed among boulders at the bottom, the overhanging trees turned the greenery almost black, ferns sprouted from every crevice of the mossy rocks, water dripped everywhere, and in the midst of this moist luxuriance I suddenly discerned a group of the noble flower. Its coronet of orange bells glowed like lanterns in the shadows in the mysterious place. The track led me downwards towards the river, so that presently the banks were towering above me, and now the Crown Imperials stood up like torches between the wet rocks, as they had stood April after April in wasteful solitude beside that unfrequented path. The merest chance that I had lost my way had brought me into their retreat; otherwise I should never have surprised them thus. How noble they looked! How well-deserving of their name! Crown Imperial – they did indeed suggest an orange diadem fit to set on the brows of the ruler of an empire. That was a strange experience ... Since then, I have grown Crown Imperials at home. They are very handsome, very sturdy, very Gothic ...

'Like the other members of its family, the stateliest of them all has the habit of hanging its head, so that you have to turn it up towards you before you can see into it at all. Then and then only will you be able to observe the delicate veining on the pointed petals. It is worth looking into these yellow depths for the sake of the veining alone, especially if you hold it up against the light, when it is revealed in a complete system of veins and capillaries. You will, however, have to pull the petals right back, turning the secretive bell into something like a starry dahlia, before you can see the six little cups, so neatly filled to the brim, not overflow-ing, with rather watery honey at the base of each petal, against their background of dull purple and bright green. Luckily it does not seem to resent this treatment at all and allows itself to be closed up again into the bell-like shape which is natural to it, with the creamy pollened clapper of its stamens hanging down the middle.

'It always reminds me of the stiff, Gothic-looking flowers one sometimes sees growing along the bottom of a mediaeval tap-estry, together with irises and lilies in a fine disregard for season. Grown in a long narrow border, especially at the foot of an old wall of brick or stone, they curiously reproduce this effect. It is worth noting also how well the orange of the flower marries with rosy brick, far better than any of the pink shades which one might more naturally incline to put against it. It is worth noting also that you had better handle the bulbs in gloves for they smell stronger than garlic.

'Note: The disadvantage of this fritillary is that it is apt to

come up "blind", i.e. with leaves and no flower. I noted with interest that this occurred also in its native habitat.'

SUMMER

At the end of spring and through the summer, painterly plants
tend to get lost in the abundance and colour of the garden in
general, but there are still a few that Vita wrote about as cosier
garden, desk and greenhouse companions.

It was the intricate markings of the bearded iris – landing
lights for pollinators – as well as their unusual flower shape,
petal texture and their intense, spicy exotic scents which for Vita
put these in an early-summer class of their own. They are definitely flowers best peered into, nose and all. As she writes, 'No
adjective, however lyrical, can exaggerate the soft magnificence
of the moderns [the bearded irises], rivalled only by the texture
of Genoese velvet. We have to go back to the Italian Renaissance
to produce a flower as soft, as rich, as some of those velvets one
used to buy for next to nothing in Venice and Rome, years ago,
when one was young and scraps of velvet went cheap. Only the
pansy, amongst other flowers, shares this particular quality.

'Stately in their bearing, the irises look their best on either side
of a flagged path. The grey of the flat stone sets off both their
colour and their contrasting height … A straight path gives an
effect of regimental parade, which suits the irises, whose leaves
suggest uplifted swords.' (see photograph on p. 146.)

There were lots planted in the Cottage Garden in red, gold
and bronze, as well as drifts encouraged to establish themselves
in the Rose Garden. Here Vita grew the highly scented mauve

'Jane Phillips' as well as some dark velvet purples. The Purple Border and White Garden accommodated them too, with their huge ghostly flowers, pulsing out their scent most strongly at night, when this garden comes into its own.

The varieties available now are almost all different from the ones Vita could choose from when she was ordering in the 1930s, 40s and 50s, but the colour range available is much the same. The petals were less ruffled then, with a straighter edge, more elegant, more refined. Look out for these if you can find them, less fussy than our modern forms. '[Irises] are the easiest plants to grow,' she says. 'All they ask is a well-drained, sunny place so that their rhizomes may get the best possible baking; a scatter of lime in autumn or in spring; and division every third year.

'It may sound tiresome and laborious to divide plants every third year, but in the case of the iris it is a positive pleasure. It means that they increase so rapidly. Relatively expensive to buy in the first instance, by the end of the second or third year you have so large a clump from a single rhizome that you can break them up, spread them out, and even give them away.

'Dig up the clump, which looks like a cluster of fat brown crayfish, and you will find a number of white roots just beginning to grow. Cut out the centre of the clump, which is the part that has flowered, and retain only the younger side-bits. Replant these, singly, one by one, without burying them under the soil. This sounds easier than it is in practice, for you have to set them firmly in order to prevent them from getting loosened and wobbling about. It is one of those things that expert gardeners cheerfully advise one to do, and then go off leaving one wondering how to do it.

'An old argument concerns the shortening of the leaves. Some people say you shouldn't; other people say you should. The people who say you should, contend that the newly-planted rhizome runs less risk of being loosened by wind when it has not got a tall fan of leaves to be blown over. I am on the side of the shorteners. I would not cut the leaf down to the base, of course I would not, but I cannot see that it does any harm to cut the leaves half way down, because the top-tips will die off anyhow and turn brown, so there can be no loss of green vegetable nutriment to the root at the bottom, that secret store whence astonishing flowers astonishingly arise.

'The best time to do this is immediately after they have finished flowering – in other words, at the end of June or beginning of July.'

An abundance of bearded irises as a theme remains at Sissinghurst seventy years on: the May and June Rose Garden in particular is packed with many different varieties, both tall and dwarf. They thrive in its greensand, freely drained soil, of which most of the garden is made. As Vita said herself about the soils in this former vegetable plot, 'The soil had been cultivated for at least four hundred years and it was not bad soil to start with, being in the main what is geologically called Tunbridge Wells sand: a somewhat misleading name, since it is not sandy, but consisted of a top spit of decently friable loam with a clay bottom, if you were so unwise as to turn up the sub-soil two spits deep.' The bearded irises plug a gap, filling the garden with lushness after the spring abundance of bulbs, but before the roses have really got going.

On a different scale, but with their own particular delicacy, you can't fail to fall for the alliums and eremurus, or foxtail lily. Alliums are much more widely grown now than they were

Allium *christophii* and *Rosa* 'Mayflower' in the Rose Garden at Sissinghurst.

when Vita was gardening; there are so many excellent and non-invasive forms such as 'Purple Sensation', *christophii* and *hollandicum* now available.

Vita writes: 'Mr. William Robinson, in his classic work *The English Flower Garden*, was very scornful of the Alliums or ornamental garlics. He said that they were "not of much value in the garden"; that they produced so many little bulblets as to make themselves too numerous; and that they smelt when crushed.

'For once, I must disagree with that eminent authority. I think, on the contrary, that some of the Alliums have a high value in the June garden; far from objecting to a desirable plant making a spreading nuisance of itself, I am only too thankful that it should do so; and as for smelling nasty when crushed – well, who in his senses would wish wantonly to crush his own flowers?

'*Allium Rosenbachianum* is extremely handsome, four feet tall, with big, rounded lilac heads delicately touched with green. Its leaves, however, are far from handsome, so it should be planted behind something which will conceal them. If you are by nature a hoarder, you can cut down the long stems after the flowers have faded and keep them with their seed-pods for what is known to florists as "interior decoration" throughout the winter [see ideas for Christmas decorations, p. 341].

'Like most of the garlics, they demand a sunny, well-drained situation. Not expensive . . . for the effect they produce, they get better and better after the first year of planting.

'*Allium albo-pilosum*, a Persian, my favourite, is lilac in colour, two feet high or so. It's June-flowering, a native of Turkestan, it comes up in a large mop-sized head of numerous perfectly star-shaped flowers of sheeny lilac, each with a little green button at the centre, on long thin stalks, so that the general effect is of a vast mauve-and-green cobweb, quivering with its own lightness and buoyancy. [They are quite expensive,] . . . but even a group of six makes a fine show. Quite easy to grow, they prefer a light soil and a sunny place, and may be increased to any extent by the little bulbils which form round the parent bulb, a most economical way of multiplying your stock. They would mix very happily with the blue *Allium azureum*, sometimes called *A. caeruleum*, in front of them. These [are cheap] . . . not quite so tall, and overlap in their flowering season, thus prolonging the display.'

Eremuri give you a vertical firework display par excellence, and although they're expensive, they're worth every penny. On a heavy soil they're safest lifted after the leaves have begun to die back, but if your soil is freely drained leave them, as Vita says, just where they are. She was fond of them, and had groups planted in the Rose and Cottage Gardens. They have gone from here now as they don't seem to do well.

'Visitors to June and July flower-shows,' she notes, 'may have been surprised, pleased, and puzzled by enormous spikes, six to eight feet in height, which looked something like a giant lupin, but which, on closer inspection, proved to be very different. They were to be seen in various colours: pale yellow, buttercup-yellow,

Foxtail lilies – *Eremurus.*

greenish-yellow, white and greenish-white, pink, and a curious fawn-pink which is as hard to describe, because as subtle, as the colour of a chaffinch's breast.

'These were *Eremuri*, sometimes called the fox-tail lily and sometimes the giant asphodel. They belong, in fact, to the botanical family of the lilies, but, unlike most lilies, they do not grow from a bulb. They grow from a starfish-like root, which is brittle and needs very careful handling when you transplant it. I think this is probably the reason why some people fail to establish the eremurus satisfactorily. It should be moved in the last weeks of September or the first weeks of October, and it should be moved with the least possible delay. The roots should never be allowed to wait, shrivelling, out of the ground. Plant them instantly, as soon as they arrive from the nursery. Spread out the roots, flat, in a rather rich loamy soil, and cover them over with some bracken to protect them from frost during their first winter. Plant them under the shelter of a hedge, if you can; they dislike a strong wind, and the magnificence of their spires will show up better for the backing of a dark hedge. They like lime and sunshine.

'Thus established, the fox-tail lily should give increasing delight as the years go by. They get better and better as they grow older and older, throwing up more and more spires of flower from each crown of their star-fish root. I must admit that [they are expensive], but it is a good investment. There are several sorts obtainable: the giant *Eremurus robustus*, which flowers in June, and then the smaller ones, the Shelford hybrids and the Warei hybrids in their strange colours. Splendid things; torches of pale colour, towering, dwarfing the ordinary little annuals. Aristocrats of the garden, they are well worth [their price].'

For later in the summer, zinnias have the same sort of quality, with intricate flowers, which one wants to look at close to. Vita adored them, encouraging us to grow a good range of colours, in bold splashes rather than anything too discreet; but interestingly, she always recommended rogueing out the magentas. This was a coarse colour, she felt, which lowered the high zinnia tone.

Zinnias thrive in hot climates – the best ones I've ever seen were sown as a hedge in Sri Lanka – but they do fine here, particularly if sown direct (as she says), so they suffer no root disturbance. Don't sow too early. Wait even in the south of England until late May, early June.

Zinnias are no longer to be seen at Sissinghurst, apart from perhaps as a line left in a patch reserved for flowers for cutting,

Zinnia 'Giant Dahlia'.

hidden away in the nursery. They may be planted in drifts, the colours mixed together 'higgledy-piggledy', when they look like those pats of paints squeezed out upon the palette'. This is how they are grown so spectacularly at Great Dixter – and at Sissinghurst they could help with Vita's overbrimming theme.

'The original zinnia, or *Zinnia elegans*, was introduced into European countries in 1796, and since then has been "improved" into the garden varieties we now know and grow. Many flowers lose by this so-called improvement; the zinnia has gained. Some people call it artificial-looking, and so in a way it is. It looks as though it had been cut out of bits of cardboard ingeniously glued together into the semblance of a flower. It is prim and stiff and arranged and precise, almost geometrically precise, so that many people who prefer the more romantically disorderly flowers reject it just on account of its stiffness and regularity.

'"Besides," they say, "it gives us a lot of trouble to grow." It is only half-hardy in this country, and thus has to be sown in a seed box under glass in February or March; pricked out; and then planted out in May where we want it to flower. We have to be very careful not to water the seedlings too much, or they will damp off and die. On the other hand, we must never let the grown plant suffer from drought. Then, when we have planted it out, we have to be on the look-out for slugs, which have for zinnias an affection greatly exceeding our own. Why should we take all this trouble about growing a flower which we know is going to be cut down by the first autumn frost?

'Such arguments crash like truncheons, and it takes an effort to renew our determination by recalling the vivid bed which gave us weeks of pleasure last year. For there are few flowers more brilliant without being crude, and since they are sun-lovers the maximum of light will pour on the formal heads and array of colours. The disadvantage of growing them in seed boxes as a half-hardy annual may be overcome by sowing them where they are to remain, towards the end of May. I do believe that you get sturdier plants in the long run, when the seedlings have suffered no disturbance. Sow the seeds in little parties of three or four, and thin them remorselessly out when they are about two inches high, till only one lonely seedling remains. It will do all the better for being lonely, twelve inches away from its nearest neighbour. It will branch and bulge sideways if you give it plenty of room to develop, and by August or September will have developed a spread more desirable in plants than in human beings.

'In zinnias, you get a mixture of colours seldom seen in any other flower: straw-colour, greenish-white, a particular saffron-yellow, a dusky rose-pink, a coral-pink. The only nasty colour produced by the zinnia is a magenta, and this, alas, is produced only too often. When magenta threatens, I pull it up and throw it on the compost heap, and allow the better colours to have their way.

'Whether we grow them in a mixture or separate the pink from the orange, the red from the magenta, is a matter of taste. [And] personally I like them ... all by themselves, not associated with anything else.

'As cut flowers they are invaluable: they never flop, and they last I was going to say for weeks.'

AUTUMN

With abundance and growth curves tailing off by the autumn, the more delicate plants again come into their own. Vita was

sprays in flower six weeks before Christmas, and it will go on intermittently, provided you do not allow the buds to be caught by too
severe a frost, until March ... It was in full flower here in the open
during the first fortnight of November; I picked bucketfuls of the
long, white sprays; then came two nights of frost on November
15th and 16th; the remaining blossom was very literally browned-
off; I despaired of getting any more for weeks to come. But ten days
later, when the weather had more or less recovered itself, a whole
new batch of buds was ready to come out, and I got another buck-
etful as fresh and white and virgin as anything in May.

'There is a variety of this cherry called *rosea*, slightly tinged
with pink; I prefer the pure white myself, but that is a matter of
taste ... It is perhaps too ordinary to appeal to the real con-
noisseur – a form of snobbishness I always find hard to
understand in gardeners – but its wands of white are of so delicate and graceful a growth, whether on the tree or in a vase, that
it surely should not be condemned on that account. It is of the
easiest cultivation, content with any reasonable soil, and it may
be grown either as a standard or a bush; I think the bush is
preferable, because then you get the flowers at eye-level instead
of several feet above your head – though it can also look very
frail and youthful, high up against the pale blue of a winter sky.

'There is also another winter-flowering cherry, *Prunus serru-
lata Fudanzakura*, which I confess I neither grow nor know, and
I don't like recommending plants of which I have no personal
experience, but the advice of Captain Collingwood Ingram, the
"Cherry" Ingram of Japanese cherry fame, is good enough for me
and should be good enough for anybody. This, again, is a white
single-flowered blossom with a pink bud, and may be admired
out of doors or picked for indoors any time between November

and April. So obliging a visitor from the Far East is surely to be welcomed to our gardens.

'By the way, I suppose all those who like to have some flowers in their rooms even during the bleakest months are familiar with the hint of putting the cut branches, such as the winter-flowering cherry, into almost boiling hot water? It makes them, in the common phrase, "jump to it" [see pp. 345–6 for more flower-conditioning advice].'

INDOOR AND CONTAINER GARDENING

Nigel standing by one of Vita's troughs at Long Barn in the 1920s.

As an extension of her devotion to delicate, painterly plants, Vita was keen on containers. There you could see the intricacy of these things eye to eye, so to speak. She erected a series of shallow sinks and deeper stone troughs in the Top Courtyard to enable her to make some outdoor miniature gardens to house some of her favourites; and in 1936 she built a greenhouse attached to some stable buildings between the garden and the Victorian farmhouse. Victoria Sackville, Vita's mother, had died that year, and left Vita some money. Putting up the greenhouse was one of the first things she did, and there she immediately started to build up a collection of bulb pans and terracotta pots full of interesting things. Under cover of glass she could force plants a bit early, bringing forward the spring, and grow a few delicacies that would have been damaged by the weather if left outside all year. It would be lovely to see the greenhouse and collection re-established to increase the garden's richness in spring.

INDOOR GARDENING

Vita created a long, wide bed contained within the glass where she could grow a few plants which were not reliably frost-hardy – gerberas, *Euphorbia marginata* and borderline-hardy species of lilies such as *Lilium auratum* and *L. nepalense*. She describes her greenhouse as a 'long lean-to, sloped against the brick wall of an old stable, and all along the foot of the wall runs a bed about six feet wide.

'There are some flowers about which there is nothing interesting to say, except that they happen to have caught one's fancy. Such a flower, so far as I am concerned, is *Gerbera jamesonii*. It has

no historical interest that I know of; no long record of danger
and difficulty attending its discovery; no background of savage
mountains and Asiatic climates. It carries, in fact, no romantic
appeal at all. It has taken no man's life. It has to stand or fall on
its own merits.

'I first observed it in the window of a florist's shop, neatly
rising out of a gilt basket tied with pink ribbons. No more repel-
lent presentation could be imagined, or anything more likely to
put one against the flower for ever, yet somehow this poor ill-
treated object struck me instantly as a lovely thing, so lovely that
I suffered on its behalf to see it so misunderstood. I went in to
inquire its name, but the young lady assistant merely gaped at
me, as they nearly always do if one makes any inquiry about their
wares unconnected with their price. "It's a dysy of sorts," she
said' – Vita revealing herself as the social snob she was.

She went on: 'It was only later, at a flower-show, that I discovered it to be *Gerbera jamesonii*, also called the Transvaal daisy.
Neither name pleased me very much, but the flower itself pleased
me very much indeed. It seemed to include every colour one
could most desire, especially a coral pink and a rich yellow, and
every petal as shiny and polished as a buttercup. Long, slender
stalks and a clean, erect habit. It was altogether a very clean-
looking flower; in fact it might have been freshly varnished.

'The exhibitor was better informed than the florist's young
lady. It was only hardy in this country, he said, if it could be
grown in very dry conditions at the foot of a warm wall, in
which case it might be regarded as a reasonably hardy perennial.
I know, however, that nurserymen are frequently more optimistic
in their recommendations than they should be, so privately
resolved to grow it in an un-heated greenhouse.'

In fact, gerberas are surprisingly easy to grow, and long-flowering. They're almost evergreen perennials in a greenhouse and produce flowering stems from May until October. You'll readily find them in dwarf as well as tall-stemmed forms. Once cut, they last well in water for at least a couple of weeks. They've become a well-known florist's flower, available in all sorts of colours including a delicious rich burgundy called 'Chateau'.

Gerbera jamesonii.

If you have a cold greenhouse you could grow your own, as Vita explains. 'I wonder indeed why those who are fortunate enough to possess such a lean-to, do not more frequently put it to this use. It is true that it entails sacrificing all the staging down one side of the house, but the gain is great. Staging means pots, and pots mean watering, and "potting on" if you are to avoid root-starvation, whereas plants set straight into the ground can root down to Australia if they like. You can, moreover, make up the soil to suit every separate kind; you can work under cover in bad weather; you can snap your fingers at hailstorms, late frosts, young rabbits, and even, to a certain extent, slugs. There is certainly a great deal to be said for this method of gardening.

'I once saw a lean-to house which had been adapted in this way, with a special view to growing lilies. The wall had been distempered a light blue, of that peculiar shade produced by spraying vines with copper sulphate against the walls of farm-houses in Italy: in the centre was a sunk rectangular pool, with blue nymphaeae [waterlilies] growing in it and clumps of agapanthus at each of the four corners. Tall lilies rose straight and pure and pale against the curious blue of the wall. I liked best going into this house after dark, when the single electric reflector in the roof cast down a flood-lighting effect more unreal and unearthly than anything I had ever seen.'

It's a good image, and one I have followed. I now grow many of my lilies in my cold greenhouse, where they flower pristine, away from the lily beetle, and make the whole place smell intoxicatingly good. Once they've died down, remember to label where they are carefully so you don't slice them when you're putting other stuff in.

POTS FOR THE COLD GREENHOUSE

WINTER

Vita loved visiting her cold greenhouse in the winter, somewhere she could enjoy a blast of spring a few weeks earlier than in the garden.

For this she had staging down one side where she could grow pans of her treasured small-scale plants – things to move in and out of the house, as well as to admire clustered together on the greenhouse bench. 'There is no more amusing toy for the amateur gardener than a small greenhouse,' she notes. 'It need not necessarily be heated, if he can be satisfied with plants that do not dread the frosts of winter but whose fragile petals suffer from the onslaught of heavy rain or hail. Such plants are better grown under the covering of glass, that transparent canopy which admits the light and excludes the unkindly deluge descending from overhead.

'Surely many owners of such small greenhouses have turned them into a sort of Alpine house by now, filled with pans of winter-flowering bulbs such as the little crocuses, and early irises.'

Vita did just this, filling the benches with her favourite painterly plants: '[T]he squat pans stuffed with such treasures should be filled in the early autumn,' she continued. 'Do not make the mistake I made last year of putting in the crocuses too sparsely. I thought they would look nicer if they had more room to develop, but I was wrong. They need to be crammed tight, as tight as can be, bulb touching bulb, like people squeezed together in a crowd. (I am referring, of course, to the species crocus and their hybrids, not to the ordinary garden variety.)

'The little irises, on the other hand, the *reticulata* irises for instance, gain by being given enough space to expand their lovely heads in liberty. Their bulbs should not be set nearer than a couple of inches apart.'

These trays of bulbs gave her the optimistic flavour of spring, somewhere to visit to reconnect with the outside, whatever the weather: 'Looking back over the nastiest weeks of our late unlamented winter, I try to remember with gratitude the things that gave me pleasure when all was grey and colourless and cold outside. I managed then to keep a few square yards on a shelf or staging in an unheated greenhouse, and those few square yards were crowded with tiny bright things from New Year's Day to Easter. Their brilliance contrasted with the snow and the leaden skies; it was like coming into an aviary of tropical birds or

butterflies, yet they were all easy to grow, nothing odd or rec-
ondite, just a few pans of the early species crocus; a pot of
Cyclamen coum which flowered so madly I thought it might kill
itself by its generosity; a pan-full of grape hyacinths dug up out
of the garden; some snowdrops lifted just before they intended
to flower; some saxifrages sprouting into miniature nail-head
size of flower, hugging close to the tight grey-green rosettes
they pinkly star; some early flowering narcissi and jonquils; a
pot-plant of the lovely pink camellia *Donation*; some early primu-
lus, *frondosa* and *marginata* var. *Linda Pope*; a pot of the scented
daphnes *collina* and *tangutica*; and, bravest and earliest of all, the
miniature sky-blue iris *histrioides major*, which I recommend to
everybody, either for indoors or out. It is ideal in an Alpine pan
and ideal in a sink or trough.

'A sprinkling of grey granite or limestone chippings goes a long
way towards enhancing the colour and delicacy of the flowers.'

Vita was all for digging up the odd clump of aconites, as we saw
earlier. Here she uses them for a different purpose: 'Another early
treasure on a staging under glass is the winter aconite. I somewhat
nervously lifted a few clumps from the garden just as they were
beginning to hump themselves in their round-shouldered way
through the ground before the snow came, and transferred them
with a fat ball of soil into a couple of low pans. They do not seem
to have minded in the least, and are flowering like little suns, a gay
sight on a winter morning. It is remarkable how frost-resistant
their soft petals are. There is no heating in that greenhouse, and
the pans are frozen solid, yet the golden petals remain untouched
and I know that when the snow has cleared away, their garden
companions will flaunt regardless of how many degrees may
follow after the disappearance of the warm white blanket.'

She also recommends copying a neighbour who 'digs up clumps of violets from her outdoor garden and has them blooming exuberantly in pots, the small pink violet and the little almost-blue one; and as she takes the trouble to whitewash her pots, instead of leaving them to their normal hideous terra-cotta colour, you may imagine how the flowers gain in beauty as they pour over those blanched containers, white and clean as blancoed tennis-shoes. She digs up clumps of snowdrops and crocuses, and packs them into an ordinary pudding basin.'

Bouvardia ternifolia.

A less well known plant which made it into Vita's select indoor spring crew was bouvardia. 'Bridal Wreath' is a white scented variety, a hybrid of *Bouvardia jasmini-flora*, and she also grew a non-scented pink, both of them slightly easier to grow than their relation stephanotis. Bouvardia flowers – with minimal background heat – under cover in the winter. Vita comments:

'I was surprised and pleased to come upon an old friend in a florist's shop. Frankly, it was so long since I had seen it that I had forgotten all about it, and then discovered that it is much less widely grown than it used to be. There seems to be no particular reason for this, since it demands only a temperate greenhouse, is by no means difficult, and is certainly most desirable as a pot-plant. (It does not pick well.) The thing I mean is called *Bouvardia*.

'At first sight, you might take it for a tightly compressed bunch of a white jasmine which had been subjected to that iniquitous fashion of dyeing flowers an unnatural colour by standing them in water diluted with the requisite tint of ink. It shares the tubular shape of a jasmine, growing in a corymb or cluster, each individual flower flattening out at the tip to the circular size of a farthing. More fleshy than a jasmine, it looks as though it ought to be as strongly scented as a gardenia or a stephanotis; one's first impulse is to bury one's nose, only to meet with disappointment; the waxy appearance is most misleading; the thing has no scent at all.

'Colour it has, and that is the point of it. How to describe colour in words? If I say cyclamen-pink, or cherry-pink, or Rose du Barry, or Persian red, I may be conveying quite the wrong impression to another person. All I can say is that those bunches of *Bouvardia* were warming to the heart and eye in contrast with the snow outside. They looked as genial as gleed or embers on a hearth-fire.

'As a matter of fact, there are three *Bouvardias* said to be scented: *B. humboldtii, B. jasminiflora*, and *B. longiflora*. These are all white. Must we be driven to the conclusion that we cannot exact both scent and colour? Would that be asking too much? For my own part, I think I would forgo the scent in favour of the crammed bunches so softly pink, so deeply roseate, of *B. angustifolia* or *B. triphylla*.'

Jasmines, both the unscented, hardy, winter-flowering *Jasminum nudiflorum* and the tender, highly scented form, *Jasminum polyanthum*, were high up on Vita's list of favourites. They would be moved into rooms in the house from the cold greenhouse when they were looking and smelling their best. She liked to have them trained onto a frame to maximise their impact, which also helped prevent their long stems getting into a tangled mess. She writes:

'I hesitate to insult readers of *The Observer* by recommending the merits of so well known a plant as the winter-flowering jasmine, *Jasminum nudiflorum*, introduced from China in 1844. We all grow it now. I picked long sprays of it on December 4th and all the buds opened indoors in water, lasting for several weeks. The flowers and buds are not very frost-resistant out of doors; so here is a hint: grow a plant of it in a large pot; leave the pot standing out of doors all summer and autumn; bring the pot indoors in November; train the shoots round some bamboo canes; stand the pot on the floor in a corner of your room; don't forget to water it; put a large plate or bowl under the pot or your carpet will suffer; and having done all this you may confidently expect a golden fountain for two or three months unaffected by the weather outside.

'As a rule I try to be practical in these articles, recommending only such plants as can be grown with some hope of success by the amateur gardener having no advantage of glass or any similar luxury. For once, however, I would like to introduce a climber which does demand shelter from frost, although it may stand out of doors in its pot happily throughout the summer, and, failing a greenhouse, could be safely preserved in a warm room in winter. To do this, you would have to keep it within reasonable bounds by training it round some hoops of sticks, when it makes the most charming pot-plant imaginable. It is so pretty, it flowers so continuously, and smells so deliciously sweet, that it justifies all this extra trouble.

'Its name is *Jasminum polyanthum* ... As it strikes very readily from cuttings a home-grown stock may be raised within a very short time if wanted. To look at, it resembles the familiar white summer-flowering jasmine, *officinale*, but the flowers are larger, the scent twenty times as powerful, and the rosy, pointed buds are so pretty among the dark green leaves as to be like little jewels in themselves. I have a sprig six inches long on my table, today in January, carrying twenty-two buds, so its name *polyanthum*, meaning many-flowered, is manifestly well deserved. On the parent plant, now standing in an unheated glass lean-to, a few flowers are already open, a real boon in January. I hope I have said enough to stir temptation.

'In the milder counties it could, of course, be grown out of doors, and I have in fact seen a magnificent specimen reaching as high as the eaves of the house in Highdown, near Goring-on-Sea, in Sussex. Here it has the wall to protect it from the north wind, and the sea-air which always means less frost. In Devon or Cornwall, or in some sheltered parts of Somerset, Dorset, and Wales, I imagine that it would grow exuberantly and to a great height. Like all such twining things, it tends to get into a tangle, which, as all gardeners know to their cost, leads to a lot of dead wood in the centre and is plaguy to control. The best way of thwarting this airless, lightless jungle is to train some strong shoots sideways, away from the main stem; otherwise we shall find ourselves with a task like unravelling several milesworth of mad hanks of string.

'For those whose interest I may have caught by this mention of the Chinese jasmine, I might end by a reference to the Cape jasmine, *J. angulare*, which is said to be even more fragrant.'

SPRING

Vita was devoted to auriculas, which reveal their beauty best close to. She had a good collection. When they were in flower, they would come inside to take pride of place, to be admired for their velvet texture and their extraordinary range of colours. She comments:

'There is no denying that the kind known as the Show Auricula [as distinct from alpine, garden types], which demands

Auricula 'Argus'.

to be grown under glass, is the more varied and exquisite in its colourings and markings and general strangeness. Above the mealy stems and leaves, looking as though they had been dusted with powdered chalk, rise the flat heads, curiously scalloped with a margin of contrary colour, it may be of white or gold or green, or of purple or a reddish bronze, all as velvet as a pansy.

'The show auricula is perfectly hardy but demanding protection from the rain which would make a porridgy mess of its floury-white powder. The pure whiteness of the mealy *farina* is an essential character of the show auricula; and if it runs all the beauty is lost.

'The plants, however, should never be coddled; an unheated greenhouse suits them, with plenty of ventilation, and when they have finished flowering they can spend their time out of doors, their pots sunk to the rim in a bed of sand or sifted ashes, away from a hot sun ...

'In the eighteenth and nineteenth centuries, when the passion for auriculas equalled the earlier passion for tulips, especially and I think rather touchingly among the miners and cotton-spinners of Lancashire, growers had their theories about the best kind of ingredients to use in potting.

'Goose guano and the soil thrown up by moles both had their advocates. Today, the John Innes compost is recommended: two parts sterilized and sifted loam, three parts peat, two parts sand, to which you may add an ounce of hoof and horn per bushel, and some crushed charcoal.'

Mary Keen, the garden designer, has a great collection of show auriculas. She recommends an easier potting-medium recipe: 4 parts loam-based John Innes no. 2; 2 parts leaf mould; and 1 part grit. The pots should be topped off with grit after planting.

Vita writes: 'Repotting should be done in June; don't use too large a pot and keep the pots shaded until re-rooting has taken place ... Bearing in mind what I said about rain spoiling the mealy *farina*,' she goes on, 'it should be superfluous to add that watering from a can must be done carefully, from a spout not a rose. Watering will be necessary, because the plants must never be allowed to dry out while they are in their glassy palace. This presents a difficulty in prolonged frosty weather, when the soil in the pots might freeze up during the night if left damp after a drink during the day. The only solution, if you are really compelled to water a flagging misery at so unpropitious a time, is to carry it into a temporary shelter where frost cannot harden and clutch with cruel claws.

'So greatly did the old florists esteem the Show auricula, that they used to stage it in miniature theatres, something like Punch and Judy, painting pictures in the interior of the theatre in order to give interest to their gardens when the plants were not in flower.'

Mary Keen displays her collection in an 'auricula theatre' of great glamour and beauty, and she has a smaller metal stand with hoops for the pots, shaped like a pyramid. This shows them off brilliantly, sitting in the middle of a table, and is a perfect system for those of us who have fewer to show.

Vita also liked the odd grand, stately indoor plant, a shrub or climber brought in from the greenhouse, which she could stand in the Priest's House dining room or Harold's workroom in the South Cottage. The natural place for these impressive potted plants would have been the Big Room (now called the Library), which was intended for entertaining, but after 1930 and the beginning of their new life at Sissinghurst, Vita became much less social. She wanted to see fewer people – and those, often alone – so this room was hardly used. Socialising apart, she still took pleasure in having these few exotic items around her.

Billbergia was much favoured, easy to grow and ideal for moving from the greenhouse to a prominent window or table when it was looking its best in March or April. Few people would know or recognise it – introducing others to something unusual always gave Vita a frisson of pleasure.

'It is a most amusing pot-plant for a cool greenhouse,' she enthuses, 'or even for a room indoors, since it is so nearly hardy that it asks only to be kept free from frost. I have even seen it described as "a common cottage window plant", though I must admit that I have never seen it on any cottage window sill. This should be enough to recommend it in these days when so many people go in for indoor gardening.

'What is it like? It is difficult to describe. If I were describing it in botanical terms I should have to say its flowers were zygomorphic, stamens inserted into the base of the perianth, and what sort of a picture would that convey? No, I would rather say that it is more like a crazy jeweller's dream than a flower, an immensely long earring in the most fantastic mixture of colours: bright pink stem and bracts, with a 4-in-long dingle-dangle of green, blue, pink, and yellow, a thing to swing from the head-dress of a Balinese dancer or from the ear-lobes of a beauty in a Persian miniature. Yet even that amateurish pictorial effort cannot make you see it. Does it help if I add that it belongs to the spiky pineapple family?

'*Billbergia nutans* [also called the 'friendship plant' and 'queen's tears'] is the easiest to grow. There are other varieties, some of which sound even more alluring, such as *Billbergia zebrina*, stripy as a zebra, but *nutans* is the most reliable so far as flowering goes; in fact, it has never disappointed me, flowering with the utmost liberality every March into April. If you want to increase it, you break it up after flowering into rosettes which can then be repotted, and the old ones thrown away; or else you can repot the whole plant into a larger pot with some fresh soil, rather on the light side and well drained. Kept in this way, a single plant may produce over a score of its strange, hanging flowers. The native home of the Billbergias extends from Brazil to Mexico.'

For the end of spring, Vita had another unusual recommendation, which looks more exotic and difficult to grow than it is, a plant you rarely see now apart from at Royal Horticultural Society or Alpine Garden Society shows:

'[M]ight I recommend something which will give pleasure under glass in May? We have such a foison [an abundance] of flowers out of doors in May that perhaps we do not want to be bothered with a pot plant just then. Still, I hope you will try it. It is an orchid, called *Pleione Pricei*.

'Orchids sound difficult and expensive and far beyond our reach, but this one is easy and very pleasing to those who have eyes to see. It can be grown in the open, in a pocket of the rock-garden, for it is perfectly hardy, but then it suffers injury from the weather beating down on it, spoiling the flower just as it comes towards its consummation, so on the whole it is wiser to grow it in a pot or pan. It comes from Formosa; it likes a mixture of leaf-mould, sand, loam, and peat; and it must never be allowed to get dry.'

When I was a child I spent a lot of time botanising with my father, and part of that experience involved going to Alpine Garden Society shows. These were the moments when everyone brought plants from their alpine houses and set them out to compete on the show bench. They would select the best-looking species with the most flowers at that moment, wash their terracotta bulb trays and top them off with granite chipping to show the flowers to maximum effect. In May, 'best in show' was always won by the same plant belonging to the same man – a vicar from three villages away – an amazing *Pleione pricei* (now *Pleione formosana*, commonly called the Taiwan pleione), a carpet of flowers on one huge plant, its fringed trumpet – as if cut with crimping shears – and its bright pink wings. Whenever he turned up, all the rest of us would inwardly groan, 'Oh no, not him again.' We all longed for the vicar to be ill on the day so that someone else stood a chance. We loved to hate his orchid, but I can picture it now nearly forty years later. It was quite a thing.

SUMMER

For summer, potted plants for the greenhouse are less necessary, and perhaps too much hassle with so much going on in the garden, but Vita recommends one or two. She loved salpiglossis, whose velvet flowers can look like Venetian paper at its best – particularly the purple marked with gold, and the brown, 'Royale Chocolate'. This is most beautiful when there are some flowers in bud and some fully open. Then you get a mint-chocolate colour duo – from the buds, a greeny-white, to the full-out flowers, a rich dark chocolate.

Salpiglossis is a plant that struggles in a wet summer, the petals splotching readily in the rain, and its delicate stems do not cope well in the wind, but it's so velvety and exotic it's worth a

Salpiglossis was one of Vita's favourite summer-flowering annuals for growing under cover, out of the rain. That's when it looks at its best – velvety and pristine.

go. It will flower happily in a conservatory or cold green-house, or even – as Vita tells us – grown as a pot plant for a sunny window ledge in summer, or even winter:

'The salpiglossis arrived in this country from Chile as long ago as 1820 and is one of those flowers which has benefited incredibly from the attentions of horticulturists to the original form ...

'It is entirely lovely. To my mind it far exceeds its relation the petunia in every way. The range and richness of its colour is amazing. Like the Assyrian, it can come up in cohorts of purple and gold, or in ruby and gold, or in white and gold, when it has the milky purity, gold-embroidered, traditionally associated with the robes of saints and angels. Then you can also grow it in brown and gold, a very rare colour in flowers, for it is a true brown – the brown of corduroy, with all the depth of the velvet pile. The veining is drawn as though by the stroke of a fine brush; and, moreover, suggests what is in fact the truth: that the salpiglossis shows to great advantage as a cut flower.

'Out in the garden it is apt to look bedraggled rather too easily, for unless it has been carefully staked its brittle stems suffer badly from wind or heavy rain, but in a vase its intense livery glows unsullied. Place it for choice in a window or on a table where the sun will strike it, and then ask yourself whether it has not proved itself worthy of all the care it entailed.

'For the same reason, try growing it as pot-plant for the winter months. It adapts itself very graciously to this treatment. Of course you must keep it warm; forty to fifty degrees should be a safe temperature. In fact, you might try rescuing half a dozen plants from the garden in the autumn before the frosts come, potting them, and seeing whether they would not carry on, getting even sturdier as they grew older. Experiments are always interesting, but if you prefer the safer course, sow a few seeds in pots in March and grow them on in what gardeners descriptively call a gentle heat.'

Salpiglossis has made the odd appearance in the Sissinghurst borders in the last few years, and it would make an excellent reintroduction if Vita's cold greenhouse were restored. It could join a good collection of plants she loved, better suited for inside than out.

She liked to grow a few 'joke' plants, things she could wheel out when she wanted to amuse. Her favourite was the 'humble plant', *Mimosa pudica*. Adam remembers having a pot of this in the middle of the dining-room table when he was a child. Harold would encourage him to touch it, then instantly that part of the plant (just that branch) would collapse, as if you'd killed it. It would then perk up so you could do it again and again, to great hilarity all round.

'Amongst other seeds for spring sowing,' Vita tells us, 'I ordered a sixpenny packet of *Mimosa pudica*, the Humble Plant. Most people, including some nurserymen, call it the Sensitive Plant, a name that should be reserved for *Mimosa sensitiva*, which contradictorily, is less sensitive than *M. pudica*. So humble is the Humble Plant, so bashful, that a mere touch of the finger or a puff of breath blown across it will cause it to collapse instantly into a woebegone heap ... One grows it purely for the purpose of amusing the children. The normal child, if not an insufferable prig, thoroughly enjoys being unkind to something; so here is a harmless outlet for this instinct in the human young. Shrieks of delight are evoked, enhanced by the sadistic pleasure of doing it over and over again. "Let's go back and see if it has sat up yet." It probably has, for it seems to be endowed with endless patience under such mischievous persecution.

'I must admit that I would like to see it in its native home in tropical America, where, I have been told, acres of pigmy forest swoon under the touch of a ruffling breeze. Nominally a perennial there, it is best treated as a half-hardy annual here. This means that we must sow our sixpenny packet in a pot or a pan under glass or on the window-sill of a warm room. By late summer it will have grown up into quite a tall plant about a foot high; and then you may observe that, like most sensitive people, it is not only sensitive but prickly. It develops large spiky thorns, but still retains its shivering fright. It then becomes not only an amusement for children but a symbol for many of our friends.'

I have found it slow to grow sown in April, so this is a half-hardy for early sowing in January or February, or even October or November with a bit of heat – and it must be kept frost-free as it grows on through spring.

Vita goes on: 'If these joke plants interest you I have several more in mind. For instance, the Burning Bush, *Dictamnus fraxinella* or Dittany, which you can set alight into a blue flame, especially on a warm summer day, without any harm to the plant. The explanation of this apparent miracle is the presence of a volatile oil; but why seek for explanations when you can so easily entertain your young guests?'

AUTUMN

As autumn continues, garden abundance peters out again and it's good to revert to some spectacular pot-grown things. Vita built

up a good number, including the Scarborough lily, crinums and belladonna lilies, growing them in pots which could be moved around and used in key places when they came into flower. Feeling the lack of colour, she could stroll out to her greenhouse at almost

Scarborough lily – *Cyrtanthus elatus*   any moment and pick up a pot of something interesting to bring inside to have with her for the next few weeks.

'One of the most beautiful of early-autumn flowering bulbs is surely the Scarborough lily,' she says. 'That is its everyday name, but botanically it is known as *Vallota purpurea* or *Vallota speciosa* [now called *Cyrtanthus elatus*]. Like the Belladonna lily, it belongs to the family of the Amaryllidaceae, and comes from South Africa, not from Scarborough. Usually regarded as a pot plant for the cool greenhouse, there has long been some dispute as to its hardiness ... If you want to grow it out of doors you should give it the warmest possible place, say at the foot of a south wall, and plant it fairly deep, say 6 in., with a generous allowance of sand, and a covering of bracken or pine branches in winter. Like the Belladonna lily, it appreciates water when the leaves begin to appear but should be kept on the dry side during its resting period, from November to March or April, advice which is more easily followed when the bulbs are grown in pots under glass. Grown out of doors, a cloche or handlight might be the solution.

'Kept in pots it gives little trouble, as it does not need constant repotting, but seems rather to enjoy becoming cramped in a pot that you might imagine too small for so large a bulb.

'The colour is variously described as scarlet or bright scarlet, a description I find most misleading, almost as misleading as the botanical adjective *purpurea*. Scarlet may be the official term on the R.H.S. colour chart, but to my mind it suggests a Guardsman's tunic or the zonal pelargonium so aptly named Grenadier. The Scarborough lily has far more orange in it. Allowing for the difference in texture between a hard substance and the soft translucent petal of a flower, it exactly resembles coral. I have held them side by side to compare, and if only a stray bloom of the *chaenomeles* Knaphill Scarlet would make its appearance at this time of year, as sometimes happens, I fancy that I should find very little difference in colour. But there again, this variety of *chaenomeles* is dubbed scarlet, so evidently I am at variance with the authorities, and, unrepentant, shall remain so.'

The other thing Vita recommends using a cold greenhouse for – if you can remember – is sowing some hardy annuals in early autumn to flower inside for Christmas or early in the New Year. I sow schizanthus, the butterfly plant, in early August for flowering in the greenhouse the next spring, but it's worth experimenting with the following annuals, which might flower even earlier. As Vita says:

'People with the advantage of even a tiny greenhouse may have a great deal of fun with a few pots of half-hardy annuals sown in August. They bring a summer look into winter. What could be more summer-like than a pot crammed with nemesia, either in separate colours or in that gay mixture we so often see bordering a cottage-garden path? Nemesia will give this reward by Christmas or New Year's Day. Ten-week stocks are well known as a winter pot-plant. People who are successful with mignonette in the open can grow this delightful, old-fashioned, sentimental, sweet-scented friend, which always looks to me like a miniature forest of spires of dust-devils. It needs a firm soil, and some lime, and sometimes will elude the skill of the most experienced gardener, though it will often flourish in the little plot of the most inexperienced child. It seems to be one of those inexplicably tricky things with minds and prejudices of their own.

'I am assured on good authority that the beautiful Morning Glory, Heavenly Blue, if sown now, will produce its wealth of blue trumpets indoors in mid-winter. Trained up some tall bamboo sticks, twiddling in and out, with its delicate tendrils and its pale, heart-shaped leaves and its amazing azure flowers, it would indeed offer a wonderful summer-sky reminder on a January day.'

CHRISTMAS

As well as the usual 'Paper White' narcissus and Roman hyacinths, Vita offers us the excellent idea of forcing garden lilies-of-the-valley for Christmas, in a pot, to bring inside. This calls for a bit of heat but is easy to do. If you have a good spread of this plant – as you often do in the shady part of an old garden – it's worth the sacrifice of a small clump, whose hole will be filled rapidly with the romping roots of this tuberous perennial.

'A temptation and a suggestion reach me, hand in hand, in the shape of a leaflet about retarded crowns of lily of the valley. If this leaflet did not come from one of the most reliable and reputable of our nurserymen I should mistrust it, for it sounds too good to be true. As it is, I accept their word that I can have lilies of the valley in flower within three to four weeks of planting, at any time of the year, including just now when they would come in appropriately for Christmas. It is a real extravagance, because the crowns will just have to be thrown away; it would be no good planting them out as one plants out the bulbs of narcissus and hyacinths, which have been forced.

'All that you do is to order [or dig up] and plant them ... They do not like to be left lying about, waiting. You can plant them either in a frame, provided that you can keep the night temperature up to the day, which is not easy unless you have bottom heat; or else in pots or in boxes not less than 4 in. in depth, which

means that an ordinary seedbox won't do; or else in bowls filled
with peat fibre, put into a warm cupboard of about 60 degrees,
if you have such a thing – I suppose that a hot-air linen cupboard
would meet this requirement, and would keep them in the dark
until 5 or 6 in. of growth had risen from the crowns. They must
not be exposed to strong light until then, and in any case never
to the rays of the sun. For the same reasons, of warmth and
shade, I imagine that they could be successfully started in their
boxes, pots, or bowls under the staging of a greenhouse. They
must always be kept moist, and the tips of the crowns should not
be covered with soil.

'The ordinary old English lily of the valley has the sweetest
scent of all, but the large-flowered variety called *Fortin's Giant*
has its value, because it flowers rather later and thus prolongs
the season by about a fortnight.'

Christmas rose – *Helleborus niger.*

Hellebores also make ex-
cellent winter house plants,
potted up and brought inside.
Helleborus niger in particular,
with its architectural seed-
pods, is very long-flowering,
from Christmas until April
or even May, and can be
replanted in the garden. You
can also force it into flower a
little early. It'll take a year or
two to recover, but if you
have plenty, it's worth it.

'Let me pass on a hint,'
Vita says. 'It concerns the

Christmas rose, *Helleborus niger.* If you happen to have an old clump in your garden, dig bits of it up and pot them into deep pots; put an inverted pot over each; keep them in the dark for a couple of weeks, and see what happens. You will find that the stalks are taller, and above all you will find that the flowers are of a purity and a whiteness they never achieved outside, not even under the protection of a cloche.

'I know I shall be told that the Christmas rose does not like being disturbed. It is one of those plants with that reputation, but I am not at all sure that the reputation is wholly deserved. If you lift your clump with a large ball of soil, I guarantee that you will find it settling down again quite happily. It may not give of its best the first year, and for that reason it is advisable to stagger the potted clumps, some this year and some the next, planting them out into the open turn by turn.'

Cyclamen *persica* on a Sissinghurst window ledge.

With just the minimal addition of a little background heat, you could bring inside slightly tender things such as Persian cyclamen, *C. persica.* Cyclamen were then, as now, an excellent winter and a particularly good Christmas mainstay. This is what Vita has to say about *persica*:

'I went to a Christmas party given by a neighbour of mine, a member of a great hereditary firm of seedsmen, almost feudal in their family tradition. His baptismal name, most appropriate to the season, was Noel. All the things appertaining to a cocktail party were standing about, on tables; but the thing that instantly caught my eye was a pot-plant of cyclamen I had not seen for years.

'Delicate in its quality, subtle in its scent, which resembles the scent of wood-violets, it stood there in a corner by itself, looking so modest and Jane-Austen-like among its far grander companions. It had a freshness and an innocence about it, a sort of adolescent look, rather frightened at finding itself in company of orchids and choice azaleas and glasses filled with champagne cocktails.

'It was the little Persian cyclamen, in its original size before it had got "improved" by nurserymen and swollen into its present inflated form. May I here make a protest against the fashion for exaggerating the size of flowers? Bigger, but not thereby better. Those vast begonias; those tree-trunk delphiniums; those mops of chrysanthemums, all those things called *giganteum* – does anyone really like them, except the growers who get the gold medals?

'Ah, no, I thought, looking at the little Persian cyclamen, white, pink-tipped, shy, unobtrusive, demure . . .

'I have never seen it growing wild in Persia. Apparently it grows wild also in Cyprus and in Rhodes.

'I wish it were easier to obtain. You can buy or be given the big cyclamen at any florist's shop, and I am not saying anything against them. They are a wonderful stand-by at this time of the year, and with due care their corms should last year after year, reviving again in July or August to start on their job of flowering once more before next Christmas. But handsome though they are, these big Christmas-present cyclamen, they do not possess the Tom-tit, Jenny-wren, leveret-eared character of the little Persian.'

Vita also gives us practical advice about how to look after any indoor cyclamen after Christmas:

'This is the time of year [February and March] when people begin to get worried about their pots of cyclamen and how to treat them in the ensuing months. Don't throw it away. It will repeat its beauty for you year after year if you treat it right. Treating it right means (1) keeping it moist so long as it continues to flower and to carry leaves; (2) letting it dry off by degrees after the last buds have opened and faded away; (3) keeping it, still in its pot, *unwatered*, in a frost-proof place during the remaining cold weeks, and then standing it out of doors, still unwatered, still in its pot, throughout the spring and early summer in a shady place; (4) starting it into life again in July or August. Starting it into life again merely means giving it water again – very simple. It will then begin, quite quickly, to show new buds all over the corm; but to get the best out of it you ought then to re-pot it. It likes a rather loose soil, made up of fibrous loam, some gritty sand, and a handful of bonemeal, all mixed well together. *Do not bury the corm*; it should sit on top, three-quarters visible. Do not water too much at first, water more generously when autumn comes and you bring your pots into the shelter of a warm greenhouse if you have one; or on to a warm window-sill if you have not.

'Do not ever, at any time, give too much water. If you do, your plant will very quickly notify you by turning its leaves yellow and by developing a soft rot in the stems of the flowers.

'[Once they've finished flowering,] sink the pots out of doors in a shady place into a bed of peat or ashes, up to the rim. This . . .

retains just the right amount of moisture without any need for watering throughout the months when the corm needs to rest. Do not keep the same corm for more than two or three years. At the end of that time the quality of the flowers begins to deteriorate, although a second-year corm should produce a larger quantity of flower than a first-year corm. I should not mind the diminished size, myself, since whopping ogreish flowers hold no special charm for me, but that is a matter of taste ... Never, pull a yellowing leaf away. In so doing you may strip off a bit of the skin of the corm, and thus do damage. Cut it off with a knife. Don't tug. On the other hand, always pull the flower stalk away vertically should you want to detach it from the corm. I did know that much, though the bit about the leaf was new to me.'

For something more exotic, orchids such as those of the genus *Phalaenopsis* have become very fashionable as easy-to-look-after house plants for us all – they can be stored not necessarily in a greenhouse but on a deep, cool window ledge. But the pansy orchid *Paphiopedilum* is much more beautiful and extraordinary:

'Anyone with a slightly heated greenhouse, say 45 degrees to 50 degrees can count on a succession of flowers from a few pots of *Cypripedium insigne* [now called *Paphiopedilum insigne*], the most easily grown of all orchids, the Lady's Slipper type, with the big pouch and the wing-like petals. I cannot imagine a better Christmas present than a well-filled pot, for the flower has an astonishing faculty for lasting several weeks either on the plant or picked for a vase, and the plant itself will survive for many years. I don't believe that a greenhouse would be necessary: a window-sill in a room where the temperature never dropped below 45 degrees should suffice. They do not like very strong sunlight, and they do like plenty of water.

'They need re-potting every three years or so, and it is best to get a ready-made mixture from a nurseryman. Re-plant as firmly as you possibly can, ramming the sphagnum compost down with strong fingers and a blunt stick like an enormously fat, unsharpened pencil, and use plenty of small crocks for drainage.'

I was sent a couple of varieties of these – the so-called pansy-flowered orchid – a white and purple and a rich green and white form, for Christmas last year and they flowered on a regime of almost total neglect until the middle of spring. They're one of the longest-flowering indoor plants I've grown.

POTS FOR OUTSIDE

Vita liked pot gardening. It was at the base of her Tower, on the brick steps, as well as by the main arch entrance that she collected together many of her favourite things, grown in terracotta groups. These plants were raised under cover in the hot or the cold greenhouse and just came out for their summer season. She says:

'I like the habit of pot gardening. It reminds me of the South – Italy, Spain, Provence, where pots of carnations and zinnias are stood carelessly about, in a sunny courtyard or rising in tiers on the treads of an outside stair, dusty but oh how gay! I know it entails constant watering, but consider the convenience of being able to set down a smear of colour just where you need it, in some corner where an earlier flower has gone off. We should take this hint from other lands. We do not make nearly enough use of pots in our country, partly, I suspect, because we have no tradition of pot-making here, nothing to compare with the camellia-pot, a

A huge copper that Vita filled every year with tulips. It was
found when all the rubbish was cleared out of the piggery.

common thing in Italy, swagged with garlands looped from a
lion's mouth. Several times have I tried to persuade brick-makers
to reproduce this standardized Italian model. They look at it with
suspicion and alarm. "Oh, no, we couldn't do that. We have never
done anything like that. Sorry, we can't oblige."'

Before so many tender perennials became available through
the 1970s and 80s – things like arctotis, gazanias, argyranthemums and a wide range of salvias, which we all take for granted
for our outdoor summer containers – there was a much more
limited range of summer bedding. Vita had a favoured one or
two, which she propagated from one year to the next in her
greenhouse, some for pots and some for planting in her beds in
prominent corners:

'People who have a frost-proof greenhouse in which to winter

some tender plants, might well consider keeping a stock of the Blue Daisy, *Felicia amelloides*. It is a little shrub, or sub-shrub, about 18 in. high, from South Africa, easily raised from seed or cuttings as a pot-plant, to set out in the open border towards the end of May, when it will flower continuously until the time comes to dig it up and re-pot it and carry it back into shelter for the winter. Its constant supply of starry, bright blue flowers makes it a very desirable asset in the summer border, even if it cannot claim to share the rich sapphire of the gentians. The forget-me-not comes closer within its range of colour; or some blue Northern eyes.

'It is botanically related to the asters. *Aster amellus* is a familiar term in gardening language, but perhaps only a very small percentage of gardeners who talk glibly about *Aster amellus* realize that they are going right back to the poet Virgil, who in the first century B.C. gave the name *Amellus* to a blue-flowered plant found wild on the banks of the River Mella in Italy. Thus do classical times connect with our present-day gardening. Rather romantically, I think, as well as classically.

'There is another form of this pretty blue daisy which can be grown from seed as a half-hardy annual. This is *Felicia Bergeriana*, the Kingfisher daisy, well named since it really does suggest a flight of kingfishers stopped on the wing and held stationary for our enjoyment. No one could arrest a kingfisher in flight, that flash of blue; but the Kingfisher daisy is the next best thing.'

Felicia amelloides still puts in an appearance at Sissinghurst in pots, as does *Tweedia caerulea*, which is planted in a beautiful verdigris copper, found in the garden in its ruined state and placed by Vita to the right of the Tower steps. Pam and Sybille

The marble bowl resting on three lions in the Herb Garden –
brought back by Vita and Harold from their time in
Constantinople.

Black-eyed Susan – *Thunbergia alata*.

One of four Bagatelle urns, which Vita was given from the Wallace Collection by her mother, containing *Verbena* 'Sissinghurst'.

Sparaxis tricolor, a favourite of Vita's for instant colour.

established a tradition with this container, which has remained ever since. There are several tweedia plants in the copper and another clutch around the base, to one side, as if the colour is spilling on to the ground beneath. It's a beautiful bit of planting.

More of us should grow tweedia – it's easy, and you can keep it going from one year to the next:

'The happy few who still maintain a greenhouse, however small, sufficiently warmed in winter to keep the frost out, will find themselves repaid if they can make room for a few pots of the unfamiliar, pretty, blue-flowered *Oxypetalum caeruleum* ... [Vita added later: '*Oxypetalum caeruleum* is now known as *Tweedia caerulea*, or *Amblyopetalum caeruleum.*'] It is a native of Brazil.

'This, admittedly, is subtle rather than showy, but I notice that it always attracts attention when we stand the pots out of doors for the summer in the garden. It has downy-green leaves and flowers of a curious greyish-blue, with a bright blue button no bigger than a flattened seed-pearl in the middle. I like to associate it with some pots of *Plumbago capensis*, whose stronger blue marries into a mist of blues reinforcing one another. Both, of course, are cool greenhouse plants, but they will live very happily in the open from the end of May until October.'

It's on the Tower steps that the extraordinary verdigris flower *Puya alpestris* (see p. 83) was placed, and often still is, a truly magnificent flower which takes many years to get to a sufficient size to bloom, but is hugely worth it if you have the patience. It looks like something straight out of the Malaysian rain forest.

Pride of place should also be reserved for Vita's 'luxury', the incredible *Lilium auratum*, which she describes in *Some Flowers*:

'Less wayward than [the famously tricky Madonna lily], *L. candidum*, in fact not wayward at all, [for] there is no reason why the golden-rayed lily of Japan should not grow satisfactorily for all of us. It is said that the Japanese complacently ate the bulbs as a vegetable, much as we eat the potato or the artichoke, until, fortunately for us, they realized the commercial value to European gardens, when the slopes of Fujiyama started yielding a profitable harvest of bulbs timed to reach this country shortly after New Year's Day.

'There are two ways in which we can grow this superb lily: in the open, preferably with the protection of shrubs, or in pots. I do not, myself, very much like the association of lilies with shrubs. It always looks to me too much like the-thing-one-has-been-told-is-the-right-thing-to-do. It savours too much of the shrubbery border effect, and suggests all too clearly that the lilies have been added in order to give "an interest after the flowering shrubs are over". This is not quite fair an accusation, since shrubs do certainly provide an ideal shelter for lilies, but still I retain a personal distaste for the arrangement. I cannot agree, for instance, that *Lilium auratum* looks more "handsome" against a background of rhododendron or azalea; I think they look infinitely more handsome standing independently in pots set, let us say, on a flight of garden steps. Of course this method involves a little more trouble. It means carrying the pots to the desired position, and watering them throughout the growing season. Still it is worthwhile, and if they can be placed somewhere near a garden bench their scent alone is sufficient justification.

'Luckily, they are very amenable to life in pots, provided the pots are large enough and are filled with a rich enough compost of peat and leaf-mould. It is as well to stake them when planting the bulbs, remembering that they may grow to a height of seven feet, especially the variety platyphyllum which is the finest of all.

White and gold and curly, it unfolds to expose its leopard-like throat in truly superb and towering arrogance.'

Tigridias, Mexican tiger flowers, are ideal for pots too, ten or fifteen bulbs planted in a shallow tray. You can plant these in a very sheltered position, at the base – as Vita says – of a sun-drenched wall with big eaves to protect them from the rain, but they're ideal, and safer, grown in a pot.

'This is a wildly beautiful exotic-looking thing,' she writes. 'It throws only one flower at a time, and that flower lasts only one day, but it is of such superlative beauty and is succeeded by so many other blooms, day after day, that it is well worth the money you will have to pay for a dozen of mixed varieties. They are low-growing, not a foot in height, and they are of an amazing brilliance and diversity of colour: coral, orange, buttercup-yellow, red, and the purest white. If you have grown them before they will need no recommendation from me. If you have never grown them I beg you to give them a trial; I think you will be surprised. A sunny place is essential.'

You can either keep them in their pot or take them out in the autumn, storing them in a frost-proof shed, and replanting them again the following spring.

Sparaxis was another Vita choice of bulb for early-summer flowering, just thrown willy-nilly into a pot for weeks of blooms. I've had a large pot containing thirty bulbs planted five years ago which I store on the floor in a cold greenhouse. When it's about to flower, I bring it into pride of place for the six weeks or so it goes on looking good. Every day, new flowers emerge, saucers in cream, yellow and red, each one precisely eyeliner-pencilled around its golden heart.

'I also like the true sparaxis ... which you should grow ... in a warm south-facing bed under a wall, or in a pan under glass for early flowering, or in the rock-garden, where it should live happily for years, given the sharp drainage all these South Africans need.

'I have kept a pan of sparaxis for years, cruelly neglected, but coming up and flowering gallantly every spring. There is a particularly showy one amongst them, which I think must be *Excelsior*, a very brilliant dark red with a yellow eye and black splotches.'

Vita also liked to have pots of the more delicate gladiolus, such as 'The Bride', and she loved the fragrant *Acidanthera*. Her advice for crocuses in pots (see p. 262) is true for gladioli too. You want to cram them in almost touching:

'That frail and lovely little gladiolus *colvillei The Bride* should have been potted up before Christmas, but it is not too late to do so until the end of February. If I had a stony, sun-baked terrace on the Riviera I should grow it by the hundred; as it is, I content myself with a dozen in two pots under glass [which can be moved outside]. I know very well that people do grow it out of doors in England, lifting the corms each autumn as you would do with other gladioli, but its white delicacy is really seen to better advantage as a picked [or potted] flower than lost in the competition of the garden.

'Some gardeners have a theory that the corms are not worth keeping after the first year and that it is better to renew annually. I believe this to be an unnecessarily extravagant idea. The little offsets always to be found clustering round the parent corm may be grown on until they come to flowering size in their second year. Naturally, this means a preliminary gap of one season, but once the rhythm is established the succession is assured.

'I have found that the same system works with *Acidanthera*

bicolor Murieliae, itself a form of gladiolus, and with those tiny starry narcissi *Watereri*, which are difficult to keep otherwise and rather expensive to buy. These, by the way, are a real treasure for a pan in an Alpine house, or in a raised trough out of doors where they can be examined at leisure and more or less at eye-level.'

When frost threatened, it was 'time to bring the tender pot-plants under cover for the winter. What a lot of pleasure they have given, throughout the summer months, those pots of the scented ivy-leaf pelargonium, those pots of the lemon-scented verbena, standing about in a casual way round our front doors or in odd corners of the garden, where you can tweak a leaf off and put it in your pocket or your buttonhole each morning. I wonder why people don't use pot-plants more frequently in this country, especially those people who have not a large garden and want to make use of every yard of space, easy to set a pot down on, taking up little room and giving little trouble apart from watering when the pots threaten to get dry.

'Cottage people and people living in rural villages always seem so clever and so green-fingered about this sort of thing. They keep plants on their window-sills, flourishing for years, without any light or any attention at all, or so it seems. We might all usefully take a tip from the cottagers, and grow more pot-plants to set out of doors during the summer months and to bring indoors as soon as frost threatens, and then just to set them down on a window-sill in a room warmed by an ordinary fire, enough to keep the frost out.

'This is also a suitable time to take cuttings of any favourite shrub to keep up the supply. There is something immensely satisfactory about a nursery of little rooted plants, growing along, waiting to be planted out or given away. They strike most easily in small pots or in a propagating frame, which need be nothing more elaborate than a shallow wooden box with some sheets of glass or a handlight placed over it until the roots have had time to form. You can save yourselves trouble by getting the prepared John Innes Compost for cuttings, supplied by any nurseryman or seedsman, or you can make it for yourselves out of one part loam, two parts peat, and one part sand. This is especially useful for cuttings to be raised under glass, but you will find that many cuttings will root out of doors, if you set them *very firmly* (this is important) in a shallow trench made by one slice of the spade and filled in with coarse sharp sand. You must not expect every single one of them to respond to this rougher method, but even if you get only twenty-five out of a hundred it is still very much worth while.

'And by the way, a bottle of hormone preparation, such as Seradix A, will go a long way towards helping your cuttings to strike the desirable roots.'

OUTDOOR SINKS AND TROUGHS

Miniature gardens and landscapes in troughs and sinks were also very much Vita's thing. She'd started growing stuff in troughs at Long Barn and carried on doing this increasingly at Sissinghurst. When the buildings and rubbish were cleared soon after their arrival at Sissinghurst in 1930, she had found in the centuries of chaos more things to add to her collection of pots and troughs, which she stored away for later use. For those of us who can't find such things in our back gardens, you can buy them or make your own copies.

As Vita says, 'by sink or trough, we mean either those old-fashioned stone sinks now rejected in favour of glazed porcelain or aluminium; or the stone drinking-troughs with which pigs and cattle were once content before they had heard of concrete. Repudiated now by man and beast, they can be picked up in a house-breaker's yard for a few shillings.' That's sadly not true today, but my parents had a good system of buying a cheap sink and then encasing it with a coating of concrete. Twenty-five years on, one block of concrete has fallen off, but in the main these still look remarkably good. You can paint them with 'cow tea' (liquid manure made from a cowpat) or live yoghurt diluted 50:50 with water, and quite quickly they look almost like stone, colonised gradually by mosses and lichens.

Vita was passionate about this miniature form of rock gardening, and inspired others to do the same:

'Trough gardening is one of the handiest and most intimate forms of gardening, adapted to the large garden or the small, the town garden or the country; and especially to the rheumatic or the sufferers from lumbago, or the merely rather stiff-jointed elderly. The point is that the sink or trough can be raised to waist-level on four little supports of brick or stone, one at each corner, thus obviating all need to stoop and also permitting a close-up view of the small subjects it may have been found desirable to grow. These little things, these precious alpines, these tiny delicate bulbs, demand to be seen very close, almost through a magnifying glass, if their especial quality is not to be missed. One has to peer right into them. I think the mistake that people often make is to set their sink or trough gardens low on the ground, when half the enjoyment and half the convenience are lost.'

On the practicalities: 'you need a big hole for drainage, covered over by a large crock or a broken tile; then a layer of crocks all over the bottom; then some rough stuff, such as fibrous leaf-mould; then the all-important soil. This will have to depend on what you intend to grow. You may, for instance, wish to grow nothing but scree-loving plants, in which case you will obviously fill up your trough with a gritty mixture; or you may wish to grow the peat-lovers, the lime-haters; and here is one of the great advantages of trough-gardening: you can make up the bed to suit any type of plant of your choosing.

'As a general rule,' she went on, 'unless you have anything special in mind, it is safe to say that a good rich mixture of loam, leaf-mould, and sharp sand will satisfy most demands. I would implore you, however, to heap the soil-bed as high and deep as you can. Sinks, and even troughs, are apt to be shallow, too shallow, so this fault must be corrected by piling up the soil mixture above the edge-level and keeping it in place with little rocks or stone, otherwise it tends to wash away under heavy rain. These little rocks need not look artificial or pretty-pretty; they are there for the functional purpose of holding the soil up, though at the same time they may contribute to the landscape lay-out of so tiny a garden.'

All you then need do is choose what plants to grow. It's miniature gardening, quick and cheap, and good for getting children enthused – and one step up from the miniature tray gardens of the local horticultural show. 'Fidget is perhaps the right word [for this sort of gardening], for ... the sink-gardener is like a jeweller working in precious stones. He makes his designs, trying experiments which he can alter when they fail to satisfy him, if he had the wisdom to keep a few pots in reserve. Out comes the offending colour, and in goes the befitting colour, neatly dropped in without any root disturbance.'

One of Vita's troughs in the Top Courtyard.

My parents, who used to travel abroad collecting plants in Greece and Italy, grew some of their most treasured things in troughs, raising them up so that you could see them clearly and enabling them to create just the right growing conditions needed for each precious plant. They grew species crocus, Italian anemones and the widow iris (*Hermodactylus tuberosa*), as well as auriculas, special snowdrops, sempervivum and autumn-flowering gentians. In a garden where the soil is limy – as theirs is outside Cambridge – growing gentians in a sink is good as they can be put in a lime-free mix.

Vita has many suggestions, starting with planting a mass of one thing, selecting species that look good for most of the year. 'You may wish to stick to one family such as the saxifrages which will eventually join up to form a close silvery mat, very pretty at all times of the year, but delicately lovely when starred all over by their tiny flowers, rosy, yellow, white, or red. It is impossible to give a complete list here, and all I can do is to urge you to make your choice in a nursery, where they are mostly grown in small pots and can be carried off when in full flower and planted out for an immediate effect. The wise thing to remember is that nearly all the saxifrages need limestone chips in the soil bed.

'The sempervivums, or house-leeks, are perhaps the easiest subjects for a sink garden. Practically indestructible, they would be a good thing to arouse the interest of the very youthful gardener who might be allowed a sink of his or her very own. The cob-web house-leek is one of the most curious and attractive.'

She also suggested planting a mix of different plants, a combination to flower in succession. 'If you would prefer a miscellaneous collection which will carry you all through the spring and summer, with something coming out the whole time, something always new and fresh to look at ... there are dozens of small hardy treasures.

'Try carpeters such as *Gypsophila fratensis* or *Raoulia australis*; tufts such as the little thrift, *Armeria caespitosa,* or some of the smaller dianthus and violas; the choice is endless, and don't forget that the whole thing can be inter-planted with small bulbs coming up through, thus doubling the available area with no detriment to any of its occupants. Some of the species, crocuses and tulips and narcissi and irises, are especially suitable.

'You could also try: *Thymus serpyllum* for carpeting; *saxifrages* of the Kabschia or the encrusted kind; the tiny Alpine forget-me-not, *Myosotis rupicola*; the tiny Alpine poppy; *Bellis Dresden China,* a very bright pink little daisy; *Erinus alpinus,* pink; *Veronica Allionii,* violet spikes; *Allium cyaneum,* a five-inch high blue garlic; and even the midget roses, *Roulettii* and *Oakington Ruby*; and the innumerable bulbs such as the early species crocuses (*Sieberi, Tomasianus*), and the early species tulips such as *linifolia,* bright red, or *dasystemon,* green and grey; or *orphanidea,* bronze; and scillas and chionodoxas and grape hyacinths ... There is plenty of scope.'

Vita used her sinks to show off things like her garden auriculas to best effect, planting them out for their flowering months and then swapping them for something like tweedia when the auricula season was over.

'Practical note: leave a space between the house-wall and the back of the container, or the house-wall will get damp.'

1 1

Cut Flowers

Small pots of simple flowers were always to be found on Vita's desk.

Vita always had a few simple vases of flowers on the desk and table in her writing room in the Tower, as well as scattered around the rooms they used at Sissinghurst. It was important to her to have at least a sprig to pick every week of the year. As she says in *In Your Garden*, 'A flowerless room is a soul-less room, to my thinking; but even one solitary little vase of a living flower may redeem it.'

Typical of women of her class and time, she had Mrs Staples to look after her in the kitchen, so she never had to cook, as well as employing increasing numbers of gardeners; but flowers she always picked for herself. She was not one for the great Dutch still-life style, those complicated mixed arrangements, preferring casually chosen stems of one thing or another, or perhaps a big vase of blossom such as philadelphus, or a bunch of zinnias or dahlias to put on the central table in her writing room, or on the lapis lazuli table in the Big Room on the rare event they used it.

She often sent Harold back to London with flowers for his flat. Once he reported in a letter to her during the war, 'the stylosas [*Iris unguicularis*] have unfurled themselves quite beautifully back in London. It is as if all the Ladies at Longchamps had suddenly unfurled pale blue sunshades.' Even when Harold was posted to Berlin in 1929, Vita sent flowers from the garden at Long Barn – daphne, iris, hyacinths and tulips – in the diplomatic bag.

WINTER

Winter flowers were particularly precious – the harbingers of greater abundance just around the corner. Vita loved to have plenty of things to pick for that time of the year – once the garden is chock-a-block, cut flowers are not so crucial. By late spring, you only need take a walk in the garden and you will feel replenished, but in winter, cut flowers inside are key.

'Flowers come so thick in summer that one hesitates which to pick among so many, one is apt to forget the bare cold days when the earth is a miser offering only one or two, take it or leave it. Wrapped in mufflers and overcoats we go and peer about for a stray sprig of winter-sweet, a splashed and muddy hellebore, a premature violet – anything, anything to fill one solitary glass with some pretence of spring long before spring has really arrived. There are the bulbs, of course, which one has carefully plunged in ashes or placed in a dark cupboard, according to the instructions in the garden books and catalogues: but somehow there is always something a little artificial about any flower which has been compelled to bloom before its time. Even though we may not number ourselves among the rich who languidly fill their rooms on an order to the florist with lilac at Christmas and tulips on New Year's Day, there is still, I think, a great difference between the flowers which we force and those which we have the patience to wait for at their proper season. For one thing, the forced flower always slightly spoils our delight in its outdoor successor when it normally arrives; and for another, the forced flower itself, however welcome, is always something of a fake. To the true lover of flowers, these arguments are disturbingly potent.

'The moral of all this is, that we especially welcome any flower which lightens the gloom of winter of its own accord. The more fragile and improbable-looking, the better.'

I was brought up with *Iris unguicularis* on my parents' doorstep. They had a large clump they could pick from whenever they wanted, right through the winter until the middle of spring. I loved the purple cigars, chalky mauve on the outside, with a glimpse of rich plush purple within. My mother usually had a small glass vase of four or five stems by her telephone.

Iris unguicularis 'Walter Butts'.

'The Algerian iris are most obliging plants,' Vita tells us, 'even if maltreated, but a little extra kindliness and understanding will bring forth an even better response. As is true of most of us, whether plants or humans.

'Kindliness, so far as the Algerian iris is concerned, consists in starving it. Rich cultivation makes it run to leaf rather than to flower. What it really enjoys is being grown in a miserably poor soil, mostly composed of old lime and mortar rubble and even gravel: a gritty mixture at the foot of a sunny wall, the grittier and the sunnier the better. Sun and poverty are the two things it likes. To give it the maximum of sun to ripen itself off during the summer, you should chop down its leaves in May or early June and let the sun get at it for so long as our climate allows. There is no more that you can do for it except to guard it against snails and slugs. It is vital to do this if the flower is not to be nibbled and tattered by these creatures, which hibernate so happily within the leaves and in the cracks of the wall. Any proprietary slug-bait will do the job for you ... It may be unkind to the snails, but one has to make one's choice.

'If you have not yet got this iris in your garden and want to acquire it, you can plant it in March or April; but September is the best time for transplanting. It does not much like being split up and moved, so, whenever you acquire it, do make sure that it does not get too dry until it has had time to establish itself. After that, it will give you no trouble.'

You can pick the odd aconite and float it in a shallow bowl, but snowdrops are even better for January and February vases. Arrange a few stems mixed with a sprig of ivy, or show off a bit and use a mini-noughts-and-crosses grid. Make this from straight stems of hazel or brightly coloured dogwood, cut just long enough to rest on the top of a small bowl, and tie them at every cross-over with a reef knot, all the knots arranged in the same direction so the grid can fold away. Then slide the mini-posies in, one to each square. The grid holds the flowers up out of the water, while still giving them plenty to drink, and transforms the delicate stems into something with impact. Slot the odd sprig of ivy in between.

'We all love snowdrops, with a sentimental love going back to our childhood,' Vita comments. 'They bravely appeared through the snow, justifying their French name of *Perce-neige*, but perhaps we never knew very much about them beyond the fact that we could pick a bunch in January when there was very little else to pick.

'There are many varieties, and it may come as a surprise to learn that at least three are autumn-flowering, even so early as September. Personally I prefer my snowdrops at the accustomed time, in the depth of winter.

'Cultivation is easy, though it must be remembered that the commonest form, *nivalis*, will do better in some localities than in others, notably in Scotland and the northern counties. I suppose everybody knows that the time to dig up and replant the bulbs, dividing the clumps if necessary, is when the flowers are just beginning to fade. Move them quickly, and do not let them come into contact with any animal manure: they hate it.'

For a shady spot, we'd be mad not to grow hellebores, both for the garden and – in the case of *H. niger* – picking for inside:

'There are several kinds of Hellebore, but the two varieties usually seen in English gardens are more familiar under their prettier names of Christmas rose and Lenten rose, *Helleborus niger* and *Helleborus orientalis* respectively. They are true to their association with the calendar, which means that from December to April the clumps of one or the other are in flower.

'Why the Christmas rose, which is white, should be called black in Latin I could not imagine until I discovered that the adjective referred to the root; but I still cannot imagine why people do not grow both these varieties more freely. They will fill up many an odd corner; their demands are few; and they will give flowers at a time of year when flowers are scarce. They like a rather shady place; moist, but well drained. A western aspect suits them. The one thing they will not stand is a poor sandy soil which gets dried out in the summer. Once planted, leave them alone. They will grow in strength from year to year especially if you give them an occasional mulch of compost, leaf-mould, or rotted manure. I have a plant in my garden which to my certain knowledge has been there for fifty years. It was bequeathed to me by an old countrywoman of the old type, who wanted me to have the enjoyment of it after she had gone.

'It is, of course, cheaper to grow them from seed than to buy plants, and the seed germinates very readily if it is freshly harvested, say from the garden of a friend, in May or June.'

Both *H. niger* and the Corsican hellebore (now called *H. argutifolius*), with its large, leathery, dark green leaves, make good cut flowers, the Corsican lasting up to a month in water if you've seared its stem ends, which I find makes them last longer than the splitting Vita advises.

'The Christmas rose is ideal for picking, lasting for weeks indoors if you split the stems. Cover the clump with a hand-light [a glass cloche] to avoid splashing with mud from heavy rain. I have been told that the way to get long stems is to heap sand over the centre of the plant, when the flower-stalks, under the obligation of reaching for the light, will force their way upwards.

'Those who share my taste for greenish flowers may like to grow the Corsican hellebore (*H. corsicus*), a tough and handsome plant whose tightly packed head of strangely livid blossoms will last either out of doors or in a bowl of water from early March to May. Before the flower buds open they look not unlike a bunch of

Lenten Rose – *Helleborus orientalis.*

Muscat grapes, but presently they open out flat, when they look like a miniature pale green water-lily, if you can imagine a water-lily about the size of a penny.'

The Lenten hellebore (or Lenten rose), *Helleborus orientalis* – and the modern Garden Hybrids bred from them – are more temperamental as cut flowers, often not lasting on a long stem even if you sear the ends (see pp. 345–6). These are best cut short, the flowers held out of the water on a grid – using the same system as for snowdrops (see p. 305). Or wait until one flower on each stem is just starting to form a seedpod. They usually have enough lignin (the substance which many plants possess that gives them their woodiness) in the cell walls by that stage to remain upstanding.

Spring

Vita relished what she called a tussie-mussie, a small mixed bunch of winter and early spring bulbs for arranging in a sherry glass to sit on her desk as she wrote. These were her favourite mini-flower arrangements, best before the garden had properly got going. That's when you can really appreciate the delicate small-scale perfection of these tiny mixes of flowers and leaves. It's in late February when they really come into their own – you can have one or two sitting near you by your bed or on your desk every week for a month or two.

When I was young my father had to have an operation for a duodenal ulcer. He was in bed for weeks in early spring and every Saturday I'd pick him a little posy which would just about keep going until the following weekend. As a result I've always loved them, two or three flowers of seven or eight different things – coloured polyanthus, *Cyclamen coum*, scillas, snowdrops, miniature highly scented *Narcissus canaliculatus*, the more delicate species crocus and a grape hyacinth or two – adding up to a bunch no bigger than the palm of my hand. That's what Vita would call a tussie-mussie.

'A dear near neighbour brought me a tussie-mussie this week,' she writes in February 1950. 'The dictionary defines tuzzy-muzzy, or tussie-mussie, as *a bunch or posy of flowers, a nosegay* ... It is composed of at least five different flowers, all perfectly chosen. She goes always for the best, which I am sure is the secret of good gardening: choose always the best of any variety you want to grow. Thus, in the bunch she brought me, the violets were *pink* violets, the sort called *Coeur d'Alsace*, and the one *Iris Reticulata* she put in was the sort called *Hercules*, which is redder than the familiar purple and gold. The grape-hyacinths were the small sky-blue *azureus*, which flowers earlier and is prettier than the dark blue later sort. The crocus in her bunch was not the common yellow, but had brown markings on its outside; I think it may be *C. susianus* or it may be Moonlight, but I forgot to ask her. The anemone that she put in must be a freakishly early bloom of *Anemone St. Bavo*, amethyst petals with an electric-blue centre. How wise she is to grow *Anemone St. Bavo* instead of the coarser *Anemone St. Brigid.*'

One of Vita's favoured spring cut flowers was the widow iris, *Hermodactylus tuberosa*. She loved iris, particularly this one with its delicious sweet scent and extraordinary green and black velvet flowers. I have grown these very successfully in a well-drained spot with soil on top of builders' rubble – it's the iris referred to earlier that my parents had a good clump of in one of their Vita-inspired sinks. The key thing is not to move them, as they'll get better and better, the clumps eventually huge and covered with flowers for several weeks at a stretch. They don't last long in water but their exotic colour, texture and scent make them hugely worthwhile. Arrange them simply on their own or with the beautiful white, green-outlined bells of the spring snowflake (*Leucojum*) which flowers at the same time.

'Several correspondents have asked me to say something about that strangely coloured black and green flower commonly called *Iris tuberosa*, or the Snakeshead iris, which is to be found in florists' shops during March and April, sold in bunches, rather cheap,' Vita wrote, in one of her *Observer* articles that would later be published in *In your Garden*. 'I like being asked these questions, because they come as a challenge to my own many failures in gardening and make me examine my conscience to see where I have gone wrong. I have certainly gone wrong over my *Iris tuberosa*. I planted it in rather too shady a place, under an apple tree, in a rich old soil, and I now see that it ought to be given the maximum of sun, in a gritty, well-drained soil, exposed to as much baking as our English summer will afford.

'It should not be difficult to grow. The tuber is not expensive and it should increase itself if you put it in the right sort of place, dry, hot, and sunny. An Italian by origin, it grows wild in other parts of southern Europe, all indicating that it would enjoy conditions as near as we can get to the Mediterranean coast.

'A wise precaution: mark its position in the garden by a stick or a ring of stones, because it disappears altogether during the summer, and thus is liable to get dug up by mistake.'

Gardeners and plantsmen and women can be terrible snobs – asserting that this zinnia or that dahlia is vulgar and should never be planted in your garden, however long it flowers and however easy it is to grow. One of the good things about Vita was that was not the case. She was confident enough in her own eye that she could rise above this kind of thing and make her own decisions, even if it pushed her outside conventional good taste: the familiar anemones were 'a trifle coarse, perhaps ... but how useful and flaunting!' she enthused. 'One should not be too much

Vita habitually put flowers on Harold's desk in South Cottage.

of a snob about one's flowers. One should always preserve the nice balance between the elect and the ordinary. There is room in even the smallest garden for something to suit all tastes. I would never despise any flower just because you see it everywhere, provided it has its own beauty in its own right and is grown in the place that suits it. The common foxglove can give as much pleasure as the rarest lily – no, perhaps that isn't quite true, but I hope you see what I mean.'

For planting in March but picking from late spring onwards, these *Anemone coronarias* take ten to twelve weeks from planting to flower. Vita loved the luscious-coloured and -textured so-called poppy anemones, with their velvety, open saucer flowers. You can buy these with the colours mixed – purple-blue, pink, red and white – but that tends to give you quite a few where the saturated purity of colour is mixed with a little white and becomes wishy-washy. Better are the single-coloured cultivars, the current ones being 'Mr Fokker' for the deep purple-blue, 'Cristina' for purple-crimson, 'The Bride' for white, 'Hollandia' for a luscious scarlet; and one of my favourites, 'Sylphide', for a brilliant pink, no white in its tone at all.

These should be planted in March and April, Vita tells us, 'at intervals for succession; in fact, the more you stagger the planting of anemone corms the longer succession you will get. Cheap to buy ... I would advise you to get them from a reputable nurseryman rather than from a chain-store where the corms may have been hanging about for weeks, getting dried up and losing their vitality. They need no description; we all know those tight little eightpenny bunches which start arriving from Cornwall on to the street-barrows in January, and open in the most surprising way once they are released from the constriction of their elastic band and are put into water and last so long that we begin to think them immortal. They are the sorts known as *Anemone St. Brigid* and *Anemone de Caen*. There are more beautiful kinds of anemone, but these are the familiar ones.'

Extending out from the coronarias, Vita wrote about the whole anemone group. She gives valuable advice as to how to make them grow well in your garden:

'In the seventeenth century anemones were called by the charming name of Parsley Roses, because of their fringed and curly leaves.

'Many people complain that they cannot get anemones to do well. I think this may be due to two or three causes. Planting the corms too deep is a very common reason for failure. One and a half to two inches is quite deep enough. Another mistake frequently made is to buy the large-size corms in preference to the smaller, in the very natural belief that top-sizes, known as Jumbos in the trade, will give finer flowers. The reverse is true. Avoid Jumbo.

'It should also be remembered that most anemones like an alkaline soil, which should be good news for the lime dwellers. An exception, of course, is the woodland *nemerosa* and its varieties *robinsoniana* and *alleni*; but you have only to think of our other native, *Anemone pulsatilla*, to realize that it occurs in its natural state on the chalky Downs. I am not saying that anemones will thrive only in soil where lime is present; in my own garden, for instance, where the soil, thank God, is neutral, many of them sow themselves all over the place, even in the grass of an orchard; but I do suggest that if your anemones disappoint you might well consider giving them a top dressing of lime.

'Another thing that amateur growers do not always realize is that anemones of the *St. Brigid* and *de Caen* strain will not persist for ever. One has to renew after two or three years, but as non-Jumbo corms cost [very little per thousand], they should be well within the purse of anybody who would like to share the thousand out among friends.

'*Anemone fulgens*, on the other hand, the brilliant red windflower of Mediterranean coasts, may be left for years in the same place and indeed dislikes being dug up. I think the same would apply to its descendant, the *St. Bavo* anemone, which sows itself in cracks of pavement and comes up year after year in ever more varying colours. I often wonder why people don't grow the *St. Bavo*. They don't seem to know about it, and are surprised when they see it, with its subtle colour of petals with an electric-blue blotch at the base.'

Although Vita didn't do lots of forcing of leaves and flowers for inside, usually preferring them when they came naturally, she did pick and force the odd bucket of flowering currant for a large vase to cheer up the early spring:

'The old flowering currant, *Ribes sanguineum,* is a familiar sight in cottage gardens, where it may sometimes be seen clipped into shape as a hedge, and a very dense, pretty hedge it makes, clothed at this time of year with a mass of pink flowers. A most reliable shrub, never taking a year off, and demanding the minimum of care or cultivation, it cannot lay claim to great distinction, and indeed some people despise the somewhat dingy pink of the individual flower; these people, with whom I find myself in agreement, should not be satisfied with the original type, introduced from the west of the United States in 1826, but should obtain its varieties *splendens* and *King Edward VII,* both far brighter in colour and just as accommodating in temperament.

'I suppose that most people know the tip of cutting generous sheaves of the common flowering currant in January and putting them in a pail of water indoors [in a dark cupboard. When they are brought] out into the light in March, they will find not a pink but a snow-white sheaf, a bride's sheaf, to reward them.'

SUMMER

For late spring and early summer, Vita – like most of us – loved peonies, her 'gross Edwardian swagger ladies'. Along with delphiniums, peonies were one of the few herbaceous perennials she mixed in her borders and from which she picked the odd vase. Unlike delphiniums, though, peonies did well at Sissinghurst, not succumbing so readily to the scourge of the slug. Sybille Kreutzberger told me that Vita used to joke about the failure with delphiniums – 'Hayter [one of the two gardeners who started working at Sissinghurst in 1930] treads on them,' she would whisper. But their scanty growth was almost certainly due to the lack of slug control.

Paeonia mlokosiewiczi, called by many 'Molly-the-witch' (as its proper name is so unpronounceable), is a magnificent pale primrose-yellow single, and many people's favourite. Vita mentions a couple of others – 'Sarah Bernhardt' and 'Duchesse de Nemours', which remain hugely popular and rightly so. Each individual flower lasts at least a week in water, and even the green bullet buds will unfurl into fully blown flowers, one stem giving you up to three weeks of bloom at a stretch. These two varieties in particular give off a good scent, the white 'Duchesse' a delicious mix of roses crossed with lily-of-the-valley. I would add *Monsieur Jules Elie* as another highly scented top performer.

Peony lactiflora hybrid.

'There are few more repaying plants,' Vita asserts. 'Rabbits dislike them; their flowering season extends through May and June; they last for a week or more as picked flowers for the house ...

Larger than any rose, [each flower] has something of the cabbage rose's voluminous quality; and when it finally drops from the vase, it sheds its vast petticoats with a bump on the table, all in an intact heap, much as a rose will suddenly fall, making us look up from our book or conversation, to notice for one moment the death of what had still appeared to be a living beauty ...

'[T]hey will flourish in sun or semi-shade; they will tolerate almost any kind of soil, lime-free or otherwise; they will even put up with clay ... Slugs don't care for [them] ...; and the only disease [they] may seriously suffer from is *wilt*, a fungus, *Botrytis*. If this appears, you must cut out the diseased bits and burn them; but in the many years I have grown peonies in my garden I have, touch wood, never found any trace of disease amongst my gross Edwardian swagger ladies ... They never need dividing or transplanting; in fact, they hate it; and they are so long-lived that once you have established a clump (which is not difficult) they will probably outlive you. Add to all this, that they will endure neglect. Mine struggled through the weeds of war and seem none the worse for it ... They will go ahead, and probably outlive the person who planted them, so that his or her grandchild will be picking finer flowers fifty years hence ...

'Of course, if you want to do them well, they will respond as any plant will respond to good treatment. If you have a little bonemeal to spare, fork it in during the autumn. But it is not really necessary. The only thing which is really necessary is careful planting in the first instance, and by this I mean that you should dig the hole eighteen inches deep; put in some rotted manure or compost at the bottom; fill it in with ordinary soil and *plant shallow*, i.e. don't bury the crown more than a couple of inches underground. This is important.

A vase of lilies on Vita's desk at Long Barn with a humea, the incense plant, in a pot to the left.

'There are, roughly speaking, two different kinds of peony: the herbaceous, in which we may include the species, and the Tree peony (*Paeonia suffruticosa*, or *Moutan*). The Tree peony is not very easy to get nowadays [and is expensive]. Still, it is worth the investment, especially as it will start to flower young and will flower more and more copiously as it advances in age. *Never cut it down.* Mine were destroyed for ever by a jobbing gardener . . . when he cut them to the ground one autumn.

'The herbaceous peony is the one we are accustomed to see in some not very attractive shades of red or pink in cottage gardens. Do not condemn it on that account. There are now many varieties, either single or double, ranging from pure white through white-and-yellow to shell-pink, deep pink, and the sunset colour you find in *P. peregrina*. This really flames; and its companion, *P. lobata Sunbeam*, is as good, if not better. As a yellow I would recommend *P. Mlokosiewiczi*, did it not cost 30s. a plant; I grew it from a sixpenny packet of seed myself, but you have to be very patient to do that. Apart from this, *P. Laura Dessert* is probably the best yellow and at a more reasonable price of 7s. 6d. *Sarah Bernhardt*, at 6s., has enormous pale pink flowers, double; *Kelway's Glorious*, at 12s. 6d. is a fine white; *Duchesse de Nemours*, at 5s., is white with a slightly yellowish tinge and smaller flowers; *Martin Cahuzac* at 6s., a dark red, has leaves which colour well in autumn.'

In contrast to the showiness of a peony, Vita also appreciated the delicacy of ixias to pick for a vase on her desk in June. You rarely see these now, but more of us should grow them – elegant and long-lasting once cut. Like freesias but without the scent, these are finer-looking, the flowers held on thread-like stems.

'Brave gardeners who have a sunny corner to spare, at the foot of a south wall for choice, and a poor sandy soil, should plant some bulbs of Ixia, the South African Corn-lily, in just such a place as you would set Iris *stylosa* [*unguiculari*], starved and baked to flower at its best … Ixias are not entirely hardy, though hardier than the freesias which they somewhat resemble. Deep planting of about six inches, and a little cover throughout our damp winter, should, however, ensure their survival. On the whole I have found the ixias reasonably reliable, even in an ordinary flat bed. It is true that they diminish instead of increasing with the years, but they are so cheap, even for named varieties, that a dozen or so can be added each year to replenish the stock …

' … graceful … about eighteen inches high, [they have] rush-like leaves and a flower-spike in various colours: white, yellow, coral-pink, and sometimes striped like the boiled sweets of our childhood. These, in a mixture, [are cheap to buy]. There is also a particularly lovely and rather strange variety, green with a black centre, *Ixia viridiflora,* more expensive [and difficult to find but worth it.] ...

'Of course, the more you can plant, the better. They flower in June and take up very little room. They are ideal for picking, as they last a long time in water and arrange themselves with thin and slender elegance in a tall glass.

'They do also very well as pot-plants in a cold greenhouse or a conservatory, not requiring any heat but only protection from frost. If you grow them this way, you must disregard the advice to plant them six inches deep, and cover them with only an inch or so of soil – sandy loam and a handful of leaf-mould mixed to each pot, and crocks for drainage at the bottom.'

Vita liked the small-flowered, delicate butterfly gladiolus. She recommends planting in March, or any time at intervals between March and May, to get a succession for picking from midsummer. Many people have reservations about gladioli, associating them with the huge-flowered hybrid varieties made famous by Barry Humphries' Dame Edna. Vita was not keen on these, but the butterfly types with fine structured flowers in pretty colours make excellent cut flowers, and she liked them. They are, as she says, surprisingly perennial if mulched six inches deep for the frosty winter months:

'I am never quite sure what I feel about the [large-flowered hybrid] gladioli. Handsome, yes; wonderful in colour, yes; helpful for picking, yes; invaluable in the August–September garden, providing colour at a time of year when flowers are becoming scarce, yes; supreme in the late summer flower shows, yes, in those great peacock-tail displays like swords dipped in all the hues of sunrise, sunset and storm. Here I come to a full stop and start saying No. I don't like their habit of fading at the bottom before they have come out at the top. I don't like the top-heaviness which entails staking if you are to avoid a mud-stained flower flattened to the ground. Finally, I don't like the florist-shop look of them. No, take it all round, I cannot love the big gladiolus. It touches not my heart.

'The little *Gladiolus primulinus* is a far less massive thing. Not so showy, perhaps, but more delicate to the fastidious taste. They can be had in an astonishing range of colour. If you want named varieties you will have to pay for them, but you can also get a mixture quite cheaply.

'They are as showy as the dahlia and far less of a nuisance, for I have proved to my satisfaction over a number of years that they can be left in the ground through the winter – yes, even the winter of 1956 – and will reappear at the appropriate moment. There was a colony I did not much like, and could not be bothered to dig up and store, so left them to take their chance, almost hoping that they would miss it; but there they were again, and have been ever since. I suppose the corms had originally been planted fairly deep, at least 6 to 8 inches, and thus escaped the hardest freezing of the ground.

'I know that what I am saying goes against all orthodox advice, but can only record my own experience. Don't blame me if it goes wrong for you.

'I like calling the gladiolus the Sword-flower. The name goes right back to the elder Pliny, who gave it that name as a diminutive of *gladius*, a sword; Pliny, a gardener and a naturalist, who got overwhelmed by the eruption of Vesuvius over Pompeii, 1,878 years ago.

'Pliny would certainly have been amazed by our twentieth-century garden hybrids. He might, and probably would, have preferred them to the species indigenous to the Mediterranean, which is all he can have known. I should disagree with Pliny: I like the little gladioli far better than the huge things so heavy that they need staking. I like the *primulinus* and the so-called *butterfly* gladioli, in their soft colouring and their hooded habit of turning back a petal, rather after the fashion of a cyclamen. I remember – could I ever forget? – picking a bunch of little wild gladioli at sunset off a mountain in Persia and putting them in a jam-jar on the wooden crate that served as our supper-table in our camping place.

'They made all the garden hybrids look more vulgar than Hollywood.'

Moving on from bulbs for summer and autumn flowering, Vita writes enthusiastically about the currently out-of-fashion alstroemerias. And rightly so – they flower for months and have an exceptional vase life of up to three weeks. The Ligtu Hybrids, the commonest ones available in the 1930s, 40s and 50s, are great doers, but almost too much so. My mother planted some beneath standard roses in her formal front garden and they filled the bed in no time and were then tricky to contain.

This is not true of lots of new florists' varieties, which have been bred to be better-behaved. 'Friendship' and 'Elvira' are my modern favourites, both with stupendously long flowering seasons from May until almost Christmas in a mild year. If you keep pulling them or cutting them right to the ground if they go over, they're quick to re-emerge and flower. They make a good simple vase, their tall, arching stems at least three foot high. The key with picking alstroemerias is to pull them, like rhubarb, rather than cut their stems.

'There are some moments when I feel pleased with my garden, and other moments when I despair,' Vita admits. 'The pleased moments usually happen in spring, and last up to the middle of June. By that time all the freshness has gone off; everything has become heavy; everything has lost that adolescent look, that look of astonishment at its own youth. The middle-aged spread has begun.' Goodness, don't we all know that feeling, when the garden suddenly seems out of control, not enough staking done early on, and the really strong weeds, the nettles and thistles, romping away, the whole place already feeling tired – and with only half the year gone.

'It is then,' says Vita, 'that the *Alstroemerias* come into their own. Lumps of colour just when you need them ... *Alstroemerias* or Peruvian lilies are rather oddly named since they all come from Chile or Brazil. They are just coming into flower, (now in late June) and should be at their best during the next two or three weeks, so this is the time to see them and judge for yourself. The common old rather dingy form, *A. aurantiaca*, is no longer worth growing, when you can have such superb varieties as *A. haemantha*, like the inside of a blood orange, or the *Ligtu hybrids*, which burst into every shade of colour from a strawy-buff to a coral rose, and apart from their garden value are among the loveliest of flowers for picking, since they not only arrange themselves in graceful curves in water but last for an unusually long time.

'A bed of *Alstroemeria Ligtu hybrids* in full sun is a glowing sight. *A. haemantha* glows even more richly, though you may object that a flaming red-orange is an awkward colour to manage in a small garden. Personally I should like to grow half an acre of them, somewhere in the distance, if only in order to hear people gasp.

'May I insist on two or three points for growing them, dictated to me by practical experience? First, grow them from seed, sown on the spot where you wish them to continue their existence. This is because the roots are extremely brittle, and they loathe being transplanted. So suspicious are they of transplantation that even seedlings carefully tipped out of pots seem to sense that something precarious and unsettling is happening to them, and resent it in the unanswerable way of plants by the simple protest of death. Second, sow them either when the seed is freshly harvested, or, better still, in early spring. Third, sow them in a sunny, well-drained place. Fourth, cover them over with some protective litter such as bracken for the first winter. After observing all these instructions you will not have to worry about them any more, beyond staking them with twiggy sticks as soon as they reappear every year 6 in. above the ground, for the stems are fragile and easily broken down by wind or heavy rain. You will find that the clumps increase in size and beauty, with self-sown seedlings coming up all over the near neighbourhood.'

There were a few other cut flowers Vita grew from seed, mostly in lines in the Kitchen Garden. She particularly cherished the annual 'Chabaud' carnation and tried to persuade everyone to grow them. She loved the fleck and stipple of their petals – which, as she said, were straight out of a Dutch still-life:

'There are two sorts of carnations, the annual and the perennial. The annuals are divided into the *Giant Chabaud*, the *Enfant de Nice*, and the *Compact Dwarf.* They should be sown in February or March in boxes of well-mixed leaf-mould, soil and sharp sand. They require no heat; but in frosty weather the seedlings should be protected. Do not over-water. Keep them on the dry side. Plant them out when they are large enough, in a sunny place with good drainage. (I think myself that they look best in a bed by themselves, not mixed in with other plants.) Their colour range is wide: yellow, white, red, purple, pink, and striped. They are extremely prolific, and if sown in February should be in flower from July onwards. If you care to take the trouble, they can be lifted in October and potted, to continue flowering under glass or indoors on a window-sill, i.e. safely away from frost, well into the winter.

'"Carnation" is perhaps a misleading term, since to most people, myself included, carnation suggests a greenhouse plant of the Malmaison type; an expensive buttonhole for a dandy at Ascot or Lord's. The *Chabaud* carnations are more like what we think of as our grandmothers' pinks, as pretty and scented as anyone could desire. They can be had in self-colours, or flaked and striped like the pinks in old flower-paintings; with their old-fashioned look they associate perfectly with the Damask and Gallica and Cabbage roses.'

Vita knew how important it is to grow plenty of good summer foliage plants as well as flowers if you want to pick bunches for the house. Dill is one of the best and easiest-to-grow of these, and Vita encouraged lots of it to self-sow.

'May I put in a good word for Dill?' she asks. 'It is, I think, extremely pretty, both in the garden and picked for indoors, per-haps especially picked for indoors, where it looks like a very fine golden lace, feathery amongst the heavy flat heads of yarrow, *Achillea eupatorium*, one of the most usual herbaceous plants to be found in any garden.

'Dill, of course, is not an herbaceous plant; it is an annual, but it sows itself so prolifically that one need never bother about its

Dill – *Anethum graveolens.*

renewal. It sees to that for itself, and comes up year after year where you want it and in many places where you don't. It has many virtues, even if you do not rely upon it "to stay the hiccough, being boiled in wine", or to "hinder witches of their will". Amongst its virtues, apart from its light yellow grace in a mixed bunch of flowers, is the fact that you can use its seeds to flavour vinegar, and for pickling cucumbers. You can also, if you wish, use the young leaves to flavour soups, sauces, and fish. All mothers know about Dill-water, but few will want to go to the trouble of preparing that concoction for themselves, so on the whole the most practical use the cook or the housewife will find for this pretty herb lies in the harvest of its seeds, which are indistinguishable from caraway seeds in seed-cake or rolled into scones or into the crust of bread. Once she has got it going in her garden, she need never fear to be short of supply for seed-cake, since one ounce is said to contain over twenty-five thousand seeds; and even if she has got a few seeds left over out of her thousands she can keep them waiting, for they will still be viable after three years.

'The correct place for Dill is the herb garden, but if you have not got a herb garden it will take a very decorative place in any border. I like muddling things up; and if a herb looks nice in a border, then why not grow it there? Why not grow anything anywhere so long as it looks right where it is? That is, surely, the art of gardening.

'By the way, the official botanical name of Dill is *Peucedanum graveolens* [now *Anethum*], for the information of anyone who does not prefer the short monosyllable, as I do.'

Along the same lines, she loved bells of Ireland (*Moluccella laevis*), one of the best and longest-lasting annual foliage plants you can grow. It can be tricky to germinate. Try putting the seed in the freezer for a week before you sow – that usually jolts it into life. Then it lasts for many weeks in a vase and will dry for arrangements through the winter. Here's what Vita says about it:

'Have you grown *Molucella laevis*? It was introduced into this country from Syria in 1570, nearly 400 years ago, and seems to have been somewhat neglected until a recent revival of its popularity. I tried it and was disappointed when it first came up; then, as it developed, I saw that it did deserve its other name, the Shell-flower, and from being disappointed I came round to an affection for it. One must be patient with it, for it takes some leisurely summer weeks before it shows what it intends to do.

'I was given to understand that it could be picked and kept in a vase indoors throughout the winter, but alas the ruthless hoe came along before I had time to arrest it, and my Shell-flower got carted off on to the rubbish heap.'

She also had a soft spot for the white and green variegated *Euphorbia marginata* – 'an old friend, a hardy annual spurge, more attractively known as Snow-on-the-mountain. It grows about 2 ft. high; its long pointed, pale-green leaves are edged with white, some of them coming white altogether, and in place of flowers it produces pure white bracts. Not only is it extremely effective, but it has the merit of lasting for months.' This makes an excellent garden and vase foliage plant, but can also be tricky to grow. I find it does best – particularly in a wet summer – under cover, growing in a greenhouse.

AUTUMN

One of the very best bulbs for picking and for containers, from late summer right through the autumn, is the scented cousin of the gladiolus, *Acidanthera murieliae*. One of Vita's favourite late-flowering bulbs, she describes it as a 'lovely, fragrant thing', 'an exquisite dandy'. *Acidanthera* has a delicacy and fineness – a painterliness – typical of the species wild gladiolus, which she much preferred to the larger, coarser hybrids:

'It is, perhaps, a thing for the choosy fastidious gardener, not for the gardener who wants a great splash. It will not give a showy display. Perhaps, above all, it is to be cherished for cutting, when you get the full benefit of the strong, sweet scent. Slender and graceful, on wiry stems two to three feet high, with starry white flowers blotched with a maroon centre, it comes from the aromatic hills of Abyssinia, so we may truly say of it that it hangs "like a rich jewel in an Ethiop's ear", and may say also that it likes the sunniest, driest place, and likes to be taken up for the winter and stored away from frost and damp.'

For flowers right through until November, plant a batch every couple of weeks in succession from March until May or June. It takes a hundred days from planting to flower.

Another autumn-flowering bulb, or strictly speaking a rhi-
zomatous perennial, useful for picking, is the Kaffir lily, or
schizostylis (now called *Hesperantha*), a valuable stalwart which
Vita planted in various patches in the garden such as on the edge
of the moat and around the Lion Pond. That's the sort of conditions it likes – a moist soil with good drainage, in a sunny,
sheltered spot.

'I would recommend the Kaffir Lily,' she says, 'officially called
Schizostylis coccinea, with its pretty pink variety called *Mrs.
Hegarty*. It resembles a miniature gladiolus, and it has the advan-

Kaffir lily – *Schizostylis coccinea.*

tage, from our point of view,
of flowering in October and
November, when it is difficult to find anything out of
doors for indoor picking.

'The Kaffir Lily [is not
an expensive plant]. One
dozen will give you a good
return, if you plant them in
the right sort of place and
look after them properly.
Planting them in the right
sort of place means giving
them a light, well-drained

soil in full sun. Looking after them properly means that you
must give them plenty of water during their growing period,
when their leaves are throwing up, rather as you would treat an
amaryllis, the Belladonna lily. You should realize that they are
not entirely hardy, especially in our colder counties; but they are
reasonably hardy in most parts of England; a thin quilt of

bracken or dry leaves next winter will keep them safe for years. It is remarkable what a little covering of bracken will do for bulbs. Speaking for myself, I cannot imagine anything less adequate than a draughty scatter of bracken on a frosty night, give me a thick eiderdown and blankets every time, and a hot-water bottle, too, but bulbs which are buried deep down in the earth will keep themselves warm and safe with the thinnest cover from frost above them.'

By the middle of autumn, finding plenty to pick for a vase inside becomes more of a challenge, but the question of which flowers to pick for October onwards was an important one for Vita. For that reason she became 'very fond of [the] modest rose, *Stanwell perpetual*, who truly merits the description *perpetual*. One is apt to overlook her during the great *foison* of early summer; but now in October, when every chosen flower is precious, I feel grateful to her for offering me her shell-pink, highly-scented, patiently-produced flowers, delicately doing her job again for my delectation in a glass on my table, and filling my room with such a good smell that it puffs at me as I open the door.

'*Stanwell perpetual* grows taller than the average Scots rose. It grows four to five feet high. It is ... a hybrid. It has another name, according to Miss Nancy Lindsay, who is an expert on these old roses, the *Victorian Valentine rose*. This evokes pictures of old Valentines – but, however that may be, I do urge you to plant *Stanwell perpetual* in your garden to give you a reward of picking in October.'

Another good rose for autumn and even winter picking is 'Comtesse du Cayla', mentioned earlier. At Sissinghurst this is in the toolshed bed where Vita had it, easy to pick just outside the South Cottage, and is still used – just the odd flower – for

putting in a single-stem vase on Vita's desk. She describes it
in 1952 in *In Your Garden Again*: ' ... a China rose, so red in the
stem on young wood as to appear transparent in a bright light;
very pointed in the coral-coloured bud; very early to flower,
continuing to flower throughout the summer until the frosts
come (I once picked a bunch on Christmas morning); somewhat
romantic in her associations, for the lady in whose honour she is
named was the mistress of Louis XVIII; altogether a desirable
rose, not liable to black spot or mildew; needing little pruning
apart from the removal of wood when it has become too old, say,
every two or three years.'

There is callicarpa too, the purple-bead shrub which looks
nothing for most of the year, but in autumn emerges with a dash
of glamour you'd almost forgotten it's capable of. It's good to
have a few plants like this, parts of the chorus who step forward
to bowl you over, if only for a short time. Vita says it 'gives some
colour in November and December, also looks pretty in a glass
under an electric lamp. The flowers, which come earlier in the
year, are inconspicuous; the point is the deep-mauve berry,
growing close to the stem in clusters, about the size of those
tiny sugar-coated sweets which children call Hundreds and
Thousands. I doubt if it would be hardy enough for very bleak
or northern districts, though it should do well in a sunny corner
in a line south of the Wash, as the weather reports say; it came
undamaged through 18 degrees of frost in my garden last
winter.

'There is one vital thing to remember about *Callicarpa*: it is
one of those sociable plants which like company of their own
kind, so you must put at least two or three in a clump together,
otherwise you won't get the berries. It is not a question of male

and female plants, as, for example, with the Sea Buckthorn, which will not give its orange fruits unless married; the explanation appears to be simply that it enjoys a party.

'This, of course, is true of many of the berrying shrubs, as well as of many human beings.

'I am told that it makes a pretty pot-plant, grown in a single stem, when the berries cluster even more densely, all the way up. Here, again, it would be necessary to have several pots, not only one.'

Hardy chrysanthemums come into their own for this moment in the year, but as Vita points out, you need to take care to grow the right ones. There are plenty of good-looking chrysanths, but there are plenty of ugly ones too. She liked the garden singles – the Korean varieties – rather than the great pom-pom greenhouse types. One of the reasons people love to hate chrysanths is that they have such a long vase life and have become too commonplace. But they are such good value, so don't throw the baby out with the bath water – find a few varieties you like, because there's nothing better for picking towards the end of the year.

Always keen to be one step ahead, Vita would lose no time: 'The day after Christmas Day . . . we may begin to look forward to the next great happy feast of the Church, Easter, knowing that the evenings are gradually lengthening and that the moment has come to examine the catalogues and to decide on what we are going to order.

'One must look forward, but one must also look back. Looking back, we shall probably remember that there was an ugly blank gap from the middle of November onwards. The ordinary Korean chrysanthemums lasted extremely well, and even put out a fresh crop of flowers after a touch of frost; they are truly invaluable plants, with none of the coarseness of the greenhouse monsters (I know I shall get into trouble for saying this), and they may now be had in a variety of ravishing colours: a dusty pink, a bracken brown, a brick red, a maize yellow, a port wine red, and many others which you will find enumerated in the nurserymen's lists. This is the time to order them for spring delivery, if you have not already got some which you wish to increase. If you have, you can take cuttings off them any time between now and March, from the shoots which come from the roots, and dibble them into sandy soil in pots or boxes. They root more readily if you can keep them in a greenhouse with a temperature of 40 deg. to 45 deg.

'It is probably quite unnecessary for me to tell anyone how to take chrysanthemum cuttings, since it is the common practice, and I set out with no such purpose. What I really wanted to mention was a late-flowering section of the Koreans, to carry us on over that awkward time in late November and December. These do best, i.e., go on flowering longer, if they can be lifted from the open ground and kept in pots or boxes in a cold greenhouse, for picking for indoors, which is what one wants at that time of year. You can get these in five different sorts: *Crimson Bride, Lilac Time, Primrose Day, Red Letter Day* and *Wedding Day.* As its name suggests, *Wedding Day* is white and claims to be the first white Korean to be put on the market.

'There is another section of the Koreans, called the dwarf or cushion Koreans. These grow only to 1 ft. or 18 in. high, and are thus ideal plants for the front edge of a border, or for a windy place. They flower profusely throughout August, September, October, and into November, according to the varieties you choose, and share the same lovely range of colour as their taller cousins.

'Order all your Korean plants now, for delivery next spring. They will look tiny and scrimpy when they arrive, but they will grow into big plants by the end of the summer.'

As with the first two months of the year, having flowers to pick during the last two, when the garden was dingy and the weather not beckoning you outside, was a Vita priority. As she says, 'I find, and do not doubt that most people will agree with me, that November and December are quite the bleakest months of the year for finding "something to pick for indoors" ... I propose to suggest some things that everybody can grow with a prophetic eye on next winter so that the usual blank period may not occur again. These will be things that flourish out of doors. I am not here concerned with greenhouses.' What she had in mind were a few flowering shrubs, some with good berries, as well as one or two roses that

Rosa 'Fru Dagmar Hastrup' hips in frost.

were invaluable for their hips at this late stage in the year, both in the garden and for the vase. And with less around, it was time for the return of the tussie-mussie (or 'tuzzy-muzzy'), the little mixed bunch – one or two sprigs of several different things tied together:

'Prowling round through the drizzle with knife and secateurs, I collected quite a presentable tuzzy-muzzy. Some bits were scented; some were merely pretty; and few of them had been grown with a special view to picking in November.

'Among the scented bits were *Viburnum Bodnantense* and *Viburnum fragrans*; some sprigs of *Daphne retusa*; a few stray roses, notably the Scots *Stanwell perpetual* and the hybrid musk *Penelope* who goes on and on, untiringly, and whose every bud opens in water. To these I added some lemon-scented verbena and some ivy-leaved geranium; they had been growing all summer in the open and had not yet suffered from frost.

'*Viburnum fragrans* will start producing its apple-blossom flowers in November, and unless interrupted by a particularly severe frost will carry on until March. It is a shrub growing eventually to a height of ten or twelve feet; it is extremely hardy; easy-going as to soil; and has the merit of producing a whole nursery of children in the shape of young self-rooted shoots. Picked and brought into a warm room, it is very sweet scented.

'Among the scentless but more brightly coloured bits, I still had some gentians and some cyclamen *neapolitanum*, both pink and white, coming up through their beautifully marbled leaves which, if you look carefully, are seen to be never quite the same from plant to plant. They surprise with their infinite variety, more innocently than Cleopatra surprised her Antony.

'Then I picked some sprays of *Abutilon megapotamicum* – it does not last well, once cut [for more on this see pp. 113–14] – which has been flowering since last June and shows no sign of stopping until a bad frost hits it. It grows against a south wall and is given some protection in winter, not very much protection, just a heap of coarse ashes over its roots and a curtain of hessian or sacking drawn across it when the weather becomes very severe.

'I found some fine heads of polyanthus, entirely out of season, the blue Californian variety and some of the butter-and-cream *Munstead*, raised by Miss Gertrude Jekyll, that grand gardener to whom we owe so much. That was not a bad little bunch from out-of-doors in November.'

Finally, as Vita says, some of the rose leaves and hips are good for vases before they shrivel or drop: 'The leaves of the rugosa rose, *Blanc de Coubert*, in either the single or the double form [I think there is only a double now available], also turn a very beautiful yellow at this time of year and are good for picking. This rose has every virtue; the flowers are intensely sweet-scented, they persist all through the summer, they are succeeded by bright red hips in autumn, as round as little apples, and the whole bush is a blaze of gold in November. The only disadvantage, for a small garden, might be the amount of room the bush takes up; it is a strong grower, like most of the rugosas, and will eventually spread to a width of four or five feet and to a height of a tall man. It is, however, very shapely, with its rounded head, and it never straggles.'

DECEMBER AND CHRISTMAS

'We are into December, *Mid-winter-monath* in old Saxon, and what a difficult time it is to produce flowers to fill even a few vases in the house!' Vita laments in 1954.

It's easy for us to get tempted to buy stuff – amaryllis, lilies, bowls of forced hyacinths and 'Paper White' narcissi – but there's something nicer about picking as much as possible to decorate your house from the garden, even if it's quite a challenge.

'The weeks between December 1st and January 1st are probably the most awkward from the point of view of the gardener who is asked to produce something to pick for the house. He, poor man, is expected to supply a succession of bunches and branches to enliven the rooms, especially over Christmas. His chrysanthemums are all over; and a good thing too, if they were those shaggy things the size of an Old English Sheepdog's face. The far lovelier Korean chrysanthemums were over long ago, unless he had facilities for keeping them under glass. He must fall back on the autumn-flowering cherry, on the winter jasmine, on *Viburnum fragrans*, on the berrying cotoneasters, on the waxy tassels and red fruits of *Arbutus unedo* if he had the foresight to plant one in his garden years ago. There is very little else that he can find except a few stray Algerian iris poking up through their untidy leaves.

Prunus subhirtella 'Autumnalis' – autumn-flowering cherry.

'I am in deep sympathy with this worried gardener, being a worried gardener myself, with a house clamouring for flowers when I haven't got any.'

It is to the autumn-flowering cherry (see p. 254), the winter jasmine (see p. 186), *Viburnum fragrans* (see pp. 334–5), the berrying cotoneasters and berberis, as well as *Arbutus unedo*, that Vita turns:

'One has to fall back upon the berried plants and amongst these I think *Cotoneaster rugosa Henryii* is one of the best. It is a graceful grower, throwing out long, red-berried sprays, with dark green, pointed, leathery leaves of especial beauty. It is not fussy as to soil and will flourish either in sun or shade, in fact, it can even be trained against a north wall, which is always one of the most difficult sites to find plants for in any garden. *Berberis Thunbergii*, either the dwarf form or the variety called *purpurea*, both so well known that perhaps they need no recommendation, will also thrive in sun or shade, and at this time of year flame into the sanguine colours of autumn. They should be planted in clumps in some neglected corner, and be left to take care of themselves until the time comes to cut them for what professional florists call "indoor decoration", but what you and I call, more simply, something to fill the flower vases with. They have the additional merit of lasting a very long time in water.'

One of the loveliest things for Christmas picking, and particularly brilliant for adding long-lasting colour to festive door wreaths, is the strawberry tree *Arbutus unedo*, with its strawberry-crossed-with-lychee fruits at their best exactly now, for Christmas. '[It is] not very often seen in these islands, except in south-west Eire, where it grows wild, but is an attractive evergreen of manageable size and accommodating disposition. True, most varieties object to lime, belonging as they do to the family of *ericaceae*, like the heaths and the rhododendrons, but the one called *Arbutus unedo* can safely be planted in any reasonable soil.

'To enumerate its virtues. It is, as I have said, evergreen. It will withstand sea-gales, being tough and woody. It has an amusing, shaggy, reddish bark. It can be grown in the open as a shrub, or trained against a wall, which perhaps shows off the bark to its fullest advantage, especially if you can place it where the setting sun will strike on it, as on the trunk of a Scots pine. Its waxy, pinkish-white flowers, hanging like clusters of tiny bells among the dark green foliage, are useful for picking until the first frost of November browns them; a drawback which can be obviated by a hurried picking when frost threatens. And, to my mind, its greatest charm is that it bears flower and fruit at the same time, so that you get the strawberry-like berries dangling red beneath the pale flowers. These berries are edible, but I do not recommend them. According to Pliny, who confused it with the real strawberry, the word *unedo*, from *unum edo*, means "I eat one", thus indicating that you don't come back for more.

'After its virtues, its only fault: it is not quite hardy enough for very cold districts, or for the North.'

There are a couple of other plants which Vita liked for December vases and which are particularly useful for Christmas wreaths – celastrus and our native stinking iris (*Iris foetidissima*), which both have brilliantly coloured orange berries and last well in or out of water.

'[In] November and December ... [o]ne has to fall back on the berrying plants; and amongst these I would like to recommend the seldom-grown *Celastrus orbiculatus*. This is a rampant climber, which will writhe itself up into any old valueless fruit tree, apple or pear, or over the roof of a shed, or over any space not wanted for anything more choice. It is rather a dull green plant during the summer months; you would not notice it then at all; but in the autumn months of October and November it produces its butter-yellow berries which presently break open to show the orange seeds, garish as heraldry, *gules* and *or*, startling to pick for indoors when set in trails against dark wood panelling, but equally lovely against a white-painted wall.

'It is a twisting thing. It wriggles itself into corkscrews, not to be disentangled, but this does not matter because it never needs pruning unless you want to keep it under control. My only need has been to haul it down from a tree into which it was growing too vigorously; a young prunus, which would soon have been smothered. Planted at the foot of an old dead or dying tree, it can be left to find its way upwards and hang down in beaded swags, rich for indoor picking, like thousands of tiny Hunter's moons coming up over the eastern horizon on a frosty night.'

The wild *Iris foetidissima*, with its orange seeds filling its shiny green pods in December, is another stalwart: 'A spike of the brightest orange caught my eye, half hidden by a clump of *Berberis Thunbergii* which had turned very much the same colour. They were both of an extraordinary brilliance in the low afternoon sunshine. I could not remember if I had planted them deliberately in juxtaposition, or if they had come together by a fortunate chance. Investigation revealed further spikes: three-sided seed-pods cracked wide open to expose the violent clusters of the berries within. This was our native *Iris foetidissima* in its autumn dress, our only other native iris being the yellow water-side flag, *I. pseudo-acorus* . . .

'No one would plant *I. foetidissima* for the sake of its name, which in English is rendered the Stinking iris and derives from the unpleasant smell of the leaves if you bruise them. There is, however, no need to bruise leaves, a wanton pastime, and you can call it the Gladdon or Gladwyn iris if you prefer, or even the Roast-beef Plant. Some etymologists think that Gladdon or Gladwyn are corruptions of Gladiolus, owing to a similarity between the sword-like leaves; but I wish someone would tell me how it got its roast-beef name.

'Its flowers, small, and of a dingy mauve, are of no value or charm, nor should we be wise to pick them, because it is for the seed pods that we cherish it. Not that it needs much cherishing, and is even one of those amiable plants that will tolerate shade. Strugglers with shady gardens, or with difficult shaded areas, will doubtless note this point. The seedpods are for late autumn and winter decoration indoors, for the seeds have the unusual property of not dropping out when the pod bursts open, and will last for a long time in a vase; they look fine, and warm, under a table-lamp on a bleak evening. Miss Gertrude Jekyll used to advise hanging the bunch upside down for a bit, to stiffen the stalks; I dare say she was right; she was usually right, and had an experimental mind.

'Let me not claim for the Gladdon iris that its crop of orange berries makes a subtle bunch or one which would appeal to flower-lovers of very delicate taste; it is frankly as coarse as it is showy, and has all the appearance of having been brought in by a pleased child after an afternoon's ramble through the copse. Nevertheless, its brightness is welcome, and its coarseness can be lightened by a few sprays of its companion the berberis.'

Vita liked to have a few skeletal seedpods for winter decoration – and none better than alliums, brilliant June and July garden plants and something we should all collect for winter vases and Christmas decorations. You want to harvest them in July and

Dried allium *christophii* heads for winter decoration.

August, before they get blown to pieces by the wind and rain of autumn, and then spray them silver for the Christmas tree. You can stand well away from the tree and just throw the alliums at it and they stick. The complex structure of their heads meeting the spines of the fir makes a firm union without any ribbon or string. That's how I decorate our tree at Sissinghurst – with mainly natural things including lots of different alliums such as *Allium rosenbachianum, A. hollandicum, A. christophii* and the vast sparkler heads of *A. schubertii,* one of these perfect for the top of the tree.

Finally for Christmas, Vita always had a bunch of mistletoe, 'pearled and dotted with tiny moons', and was keen to encourage the odd clump to establish itself in the trees in the orchard:

'Shakespeare called [mistletoe] baleful; but, as everybody knows, it is possessed of most serviceable properties if only you treat it right. It can avert lightning and thunderbolts, witchcraft and sorcery; it can extinguish fire; it can discover gold buried in the earth; it can cure ulcers and epilepsy; it can stimulate fertility in women and cattle. On the other hand, if you do not treat it right it can do dreadful things to you. It may even kill you as it killed Balder the Beautiful, whose mother neglected to exact an oath from it not to hurt her son "because it seemed too young to swear".

'The important thing, therefore, seems to be to learn as quickly and thoroughly as possible how to treat it right.

'You must never cut it with iron, but always with gold. You must never let it touch the ground, but must catch it in a white cloth as it falls. This seems easy compared with the first stipulation, since even in these days most people do still possess a white cloth of some sort, a sheet, or a large handkerchief, whereas few of us can command a golden bagging-hook or even a knife with a blade of pure gold. You must never put it into a vase but must always suspend it, and after every traditional kiss the man must pick off one fruit – which is not a berry, although it looks like one – and when all the fruits have gone the magic of the kiss has gone also.

'Folk-tales? He would be a bold man who attempted to explain or to explain away such ancient and widespread superstitions, ranging from furthest Asia into Europe and Africa. Mysterious and magical throughout all countries and all centuries, these tales may be read in Sir James Frazer's monumental work in which he honoured that queer parasite, the mistletoe, with the title *The Golden Bough*.'

Mistletoe is just as popular now as it was in Vita's day, grown in the old fruit orchards of Hereford and Shropshire, which are at the heart of its trade. There are still mistletoe auctions in Tenbury Wells in Worcestershire, where people travel from all corners to bid for great bundles to break up and sell in the build-up to Christmas.

Vita goes on to say: 'So here let me concentrate rather on some botanical facts which Sir James Frazer disregards, and try to correct some popular misconceptions about the nature of the mistletoe.

'We think of it as a parasite, but it is not a true parasite, only a semi-parasite, meaning that it does not entirely depend upon its host for nourishment, but gains some of its life from its own leaves. It belongs to an exceptional family, the *Loranthaceae*, comprising more than five hundred members, only one of which is a British-born subject – *Viscum album*, the Latin name for our English mistletoe.

'The mistletoe, as we know it, grows on some trees and not on others. The worst mistake that we make is to believe that it grows most freely on the oak. It seldom does; and that is the reason why the Druids particularly esteemed the oak-borne mistletoe, for this was a rarity and thus had a special value. The mistletoe prefers the soft-barked trees: the apple, the ash, the hawthorn, the birch, the poplar, the willow, the maple, the Scots pine, the sycamore, the lime, and the cedar. It is seldom found on the pear, the alder, or the beech; and is most rare on the oak.

'Another popular mistake concerning the propagation of this queer plant. It is commonly believed that birds carry the seeds. This is only half true. What really happens, by one of those extraordinarily complicated arrangements which Nature appears to favour, is that the bird (usually the missel-thrush) pecks off the white fruit for the sake of the seed inside it, and then gets worried by the sticky mess round the seed [which is indeed as sticky as chewing gum] and wipes his beak, much as we might wipe our muddy shoes on a doormat, and thereby deposits the seed in a crack of the bark, where it may, or may not, germinate.'

If you want to propagate it yourself and not leave it to the birds, 'save the Christmas decorations; or, better still, get some fresh berries in February or March', Vita urges. 'These will be less withered and stand a better chance of germination. Squeeze the berry until it bursts, and stick the seed to the underside of a healthy young twig by means of the natural glue. Stick as many seeds as possible, to ensure a good percentage of germination, and also to ensure getting more than one plant, necessary for purposes of fertilization; in other words, you won't get berries if you haven't more than one plant. The best host-trees are the apple and the poplar, and you can be very successful also in starting it on hawthorns. Some people advocate cutting or scraping the twig before sticking the seed on to it, but you'll get the best results from a healthy shoot with a smooth and clean bark.

'After all this, apparently, you have to be very patient. The infant plant, always assuming that germination has taken place, will do very little for the first two years of its life. In its first April, that is to say a couple of months after it has been sown, it ought to show a green disc or finger, and that is all it will do until the following spring, when the first two leaves ought to appear, and after that it ought to go on increasing "at a rate of a geometrical progression", until such time as you can cut your own berried bunch instead of buying it, to hang over the dinner-table.

'It sounds all right and feasible, and would in any case be an amusing experiment for the amateur with a bit of extra leisure and an orchard of old apple trees to practise on. Commercially, it might prove profitable. Our Christmas mistletoe is quite expensive, and is, I understand, imported in vast quantities from abroad. Travellers between Calais and Paris must surely have noticed the lumps and clumps darkening like magpies' nests the many neglected-looking strips of trees along the railway line in the North of France. Perhaps the neglect is deliberate; perhaps they pay a good dividend from all our markets, not only from Covent Garden.

'Such are a few, a very few, legends and facts about the strange and wanton bunch we shall hang somewhere in our house this Christmas.'

CONDITIONING CUT FLOWERS

As an avid picker of home-grown flowers, Vita was keen to know all she could about the ways to extend the vase life of the plants she harvested, and she passed on the advice.

'Perhaps I should entitle this article "In Your House", or "Your Garden in Your House", because I want to write something about cut flowers, inspired by an interesting letter from a gentleman describing himself as a botanist and horticulturist who has carried out researches on the subject [of making cut flowers last. In the spring] owners of gardens begin to pick more recklessly, with less dread of spoiling their outdoor show, but this pleasurable occupation does take a long time, and the busy woman wants to make her flowers last as long as possible.

'"The cause of difficulties with cut flowers," says my correspondent, "lies in the entry of air into the water-tubes of the flower stems during the period between cutting the flowers and placing them in water." To prevent such disappointment, he recommends that you should place your newly cut flowers in recently boiled water while it is still just above tepid, i.e. not hot enough to sting your hand but warm enough to give your fingers an agreeable sensation of warmth.' In my experiments with conditioning cut flowers I use just-off-boiling water, and know this to be very successful in extending the vase lives of most flowers. Particularly in the spring, when most stems are growing rapidly and so have little time to lay down any woodiness, or lignin, in their cell walls, I sear almost everything except bulbs (which do not need it – except for cut bluebells, which benefit from it hugely). By autumn, when stems have become more solid, it is much less important. Sear the bottom 10 per cent of the stem length.

'Cut your flowers, he says, during dull, sunless hours,' Vita continues. A particularly good time is when all the plant cells are in a positive water balance at the beginning or end of the day. 'My correspondent,' she goes on, 'condemns as an old wives' tale the placing of aspirin tablets or copper coins in the water.' In fact, a soluble aspirin (which contains salicylic acid) changes the pH, acidifying the flower water and so cutting down bacterial build-up. Bacteria are what create the slime at the end of the stem, and with that block water uptake. In my experience aspirin helps prolong vase life, and vinegar works just as well. Or you may find a drop of bleach easier.

Vita's correspondent 'gives a slight approval to lumps of charcoal, in so far as they absorb air from the water. I suppose that we all have our theories, but this idea of air entering the stems is worth consideration. I pass it on to you.'

1 2

THE RECENT PAST

Vita and Harold outside South Cottage in the late 1950s.

Having created their garden together, Harold and Vita spent as much time as they could planting, pruning, weeding and watering. Harold was in London during the week, but Vita rarely spent time away from her garden. Throughout the last thirty years of her life she went on the occasional cruise and the odd French or Italian holiday, but she did not travel or socialise much, preferring to concentrate on a few close friends, her writing and Sissinghurst. Vita wrote in 1957: 'May I assure the gentleman who writes to me (quite often) from a Priory in Sussex that I am not the armchair, library-fireside gardener he evidently suspects, "never having performed any single act of gardening" myself, and that for the last forty years of my life I have broken my back, my finger-nails, and sometimes my heart, in the practical pursuit of my favourite occupation?'

Vita's enthusiasm for gardening remained undiminished, as did Harold's, particularly in the Lime Walk. But they gradually took on more help, moving from two gardeners plus one part-time handyman-chauffeur at the start in 1930, to five including Jack Vass as head gardener through the 1940s (with a break for wartime service in the RAF) and most of the 50s.

Vita and Harold decided in 1938 to open the garden under the National Gardens Scheme, for just two days a year. A couple of years later they increased this to daily opening (in the main growing season) and charged a shilling entrance fee, with an honesty bowl left under the arch.

Vita liked the garden being open. Visitors – 'the Shillingses', as she called them – often, particularly towards the end of the day, reported seeing her weeding or planting, when she would be happy to have a chat and answer questions on plant names and

The entrance to Sissinghurst, with the stall from which plants were sold.

show them her favourites, flowering at that moment. She wrote
in the *New Statesman* in 1939 that she liked having the garden
visitors around because they were old-fashioned, well behaved
types who 'had a particular form of courtesy ... a gardener's
courtesy, in a world where courtesy is giving place to rougher
things'. Harold didn't always agree, and visitors reported him as
being sometimes rather gruff.

Jack Vass and Vita fell out in 1957, and she took on Ronald
Platt as head gardener, who stayed only two years. So in 1959 she
was again looking for someone new. With increased opening and
with garden visitor numbers already at six thousand (huge numbers for a private amateur garden. By comparison, fewer than
half come to Perch Hill on open days), she needed more staff. It

was then that she employed Pam Schwerdt and Sybille
Kreutzberger, who had written to her looking for a place to run
a nursery. They would be Sissinghurst's head gardeners for over
three decades. With their arrival, the next era of the place and its
garden was about to begin.

As Tony Lord's book *Gardening at Sissinghurst* tells us in some
detail, when Pam and Sybille arrived, Harold's and Vita's ages
and their health meant that the garden was not at its best. The
two new women had trained at the rigorous Waterperry School
of Horticulture in Oxfordshire and had stayed there ten years.
They could not have been more highly trained, and as soon as
they were taken on they set out to reinvigorate the Sissinghurt

Head gardeners, Pam and Sybille. They arrived in 1959 and
stayed at Sissinghurst for over thirty years.

garden. As Sybille said to me recently, from day one it was easy
to see how they could improve things.

They left the four other gardeners already there to get on with
their own work, while the two of them got stuck into the areas
they felt were crying out for care and attention. For a start, the
hedges had become too tall and too thick, so they cut them hard
back. They tackled the ever-encroaching perennial weeds; they
conditioned the soil; and they then started on the planting. Vita
was growing a lot of short-season plants – peonies, Ligtu Hybrid
alstroemerias and bearded iris, the varieties available in the
1930s, but the range of plants had grown hugely in the thirty or
so years since. For Vita and Harold and their private garden, it
was fine for each room to have its weeks of glory and then for the
next to set out its stall, but this sort of garden and this sort of
gardening did not work for somewhere open to the public from
mid-spring to autumn.

Pam and Sybille, with their up-to-date plant knowledge, knew
these varieties could be replaced by newer, longer-flowering
forms, as well as supplemented by other plants that would perform for not just weeks but many months. They both felt that
each garden room could easily be flowerier for longer, whatever
the season, and they achieved this by gradually introducing a
wide range of half-hardy perennials. These included new varieties of salvias, verbenas, arctotis and argyranthemums, as well
as dahlias, aiming to make sure that nowhere had a blank
moment during the main growing season. As Sybille says, 'I
cannot believe that if VSW had been exposed to these things, she
would not have chosen them too.'

They added *Arctotis* 'Mahogany' and 'Flame' to replace the
wallflowers on the south side of the South Cottage, still planted

out there today where they flower from June until November; they put in *Verbena merci*, a beautiful, rich compact burgundy verbena, as well as the purple *Verbena rigida*, which both flower for four or five months in the Rose Garden; then the brilliant pink *Verbena* 'Sissinghurst', still filling the four bronze urns in the entrance courtyard throughout the summer and autumn; as well as argyranthemums in the White Garden and *Salvia guaranitica* in the Purple Border, and many more.

They also refined Vita's system of generous planting, putting in large groups of things, with seven or nine of one variety in a drift, but – a deft touch – continuing those same plants across the path in a smaller group. As Lex, until recently the head gardener, has commented, the Sissinghurst way of planting things is very distinct. Gardeners usually aim to plant, not in a line, but with everything equally spaced – but not at Sissinghurst. The style is 'fake amateurishness', with things strewn in an apparently random way, 'twiddling the group through other plants in a typically informal Sissinghurst way'.

Pam and Sybille also added even more climbers, particularly clematis such as 'Perle d'Azur', flanked by ceanothus to extend its colour season, on the Powys curved wall in the Rose Garden; plus on the north wall behind the Purple Border some summer and early-autumn-flowering clematis in the red and purple range.

Gradually the garden got tidier, more cohesive, but it remained full, and almost all of it luscious with colour from early in the year till late. Harold's brilliant structure and Vita's inspired choice of place, plants and style made Sissinghurst a garden unparalleled in its beauty. Added to all this were the practical skills, the plant knowledge and the creative eye of Pam and Sybille, combining to make a garden that seemed to reach its peak of perfection in the mid-1960s.

You can see this so clearly in the photographs by Edwin Smith taken the year Vita died, and this high point continued for many years after that. Vita knew that she had created something of lasting value, and that there was every chance it might remain so in the hands of the dynamic duo she called 'the girls'. Harold survived her by six years, sad and lonely. Visitors would see him sitting on the Tower Lawn with tears running down his cheeks. Their son Nigel was 'awed by his desolation', but when Harold died in 1968 he too collapsed to a depth he had never known.

Vita in the garden at Sissinghurst in 1956 in her distinctive, impressively stylish gardening garb of silk shirt, cotton breeches and tight leather lace-up boots.

Pam and Sybille pre-dated the National Trust, which took over Sissinghurst in 1967. Vita was a founder member of the National Trust Gardens Committee from 1948, but did not want them involved with her own garden. Nigel, rather than the older Ben, was to inherit Sissinghurst and the garden on Vita's death. Ben, a renowned art historian based in London, preferred urban life.

Famously, when Vita was asked by Nigel in 1954 what he should do about the future of Sissinghurst after her death, and whether she would be happy for him to transfer ownership to the Trust, this was the response she gave in her diary: 'I said Never, never, never. Au grand jamais, jamais. Never, never, never! Not that hard little metal plate at my door! Nigel can do what he likes when I'm dead, but so long as I live, no Nat Trust or any other foreign body shall have my darling. No, no. Over my corpse or my ashes, not otherwise ... It's bad enough to have lost my Knole, but they shan't take S/hurst from me.'

By the end of her life her view had softened, and she left Nigel a letter saying she realised it would be difficult for him to keep Sissinghurst and she would understand if he wanted to choose the National Trust option.

With large death duties and little capital, Nigel faced the choice either to let the garden gradually go downhill, sell it, or the farm around it, or persuade the National Trust to take it. He and Harold both felt this was the best course to take, ensuring the garden and the buildings at Sissinghurst would be preserved. The National Trust, after much negotiating, took Sissinghurst over in April 1967, with Nigel's family having the right to live in the south range and South Cottage in perpetuity. The visitor numbers were already at twenty-eight thousand in 1966, but within a year they had almost doubled.

Once they had moved down from London in 1963, Nigel and his wife Philippa became more involved with the garden. Philippa got the famous American garden designer Lanning Roper to come and give advice, but it was Pam and Sybille who were very much at the helm. Their horticultural expertise showed, and the garden became even more popular. The two

Adam, Juliet and Harold a few days after Vita died in 1962.

of them, along with the other gardeners and the books that Nigel wrote about both the garden and his parents, helped to make Sissinghurst famous, and one of the most visited places in Britain.

Pam and Sybille stayed at Sissinghurst until 1991, when they retired to make their own garden in Gloucestershire, and Sarah Cook then took over. Sarah had been trained by 'the girls' at Sissinghurst for four years, from 1984 to 1988, and returned for a few months' handover early in the New Year of 1991. She added her own touches, but she was much influenced by the 'Pam

Adam and our dog, Frizzy.

and Sybille way'. That year the visitor numbers hit the all-time high of 197,000 and the famed timed tickets were started. This entry system was introduced to try to stop the increasing wear and tear on the garden; the aim was never to let numbers exceed two thousand people at one time.

After Sarah came Alexis Datta. She was trained by Sarah and had been her deputy at Sissinghurst for many years. Lex left in 2013 and was replaced by Troy Scott Smith in July that year. Troy, who had worked at Sissinghurst in the 1990s, was previously head gardener for seven years at Bodnant Garden near Colwyn Bay.

This succession of gardeners, along with the National Trust, have done great things at Sissinghurst. The Trust restored the fragile brickwork of the Tower so subtly that within a day of the scaffolding coming down, you would not have known anything or anyone had been there. The clock, too, has just been restored; every wall, every path, has been mended many times; a lot of grass and concrete paths have been replaced by much nicer York stone; every plant has been cared for or, when it has had its day, replaced; and every piece of furniture restored in a sensitive, curatorial way in a style fitting with Sissinghurst's apparent 'shabbiness', and then carefully maintained. Even now, as I write in 2013, every book in the library – a valuable twentieth-century collection – is being worked on to make sure they're here for at least another hundred years.

Harold's remarkable structure is almost totally intact and the horticultural excellence is still very apparent. Undoubtedly, Vita's essence is still there, but the spirit of the garden has changed.

Much is not changed at all: the White Garden, the Purple Border and the Cottage Garden are as good, if not better, now than they were in Vita's day. The people who have gardened here since Vita have taken her idea and strengthened, extended and improved it in all of those three garden rooms. There is still the Ming vase in the centre of the White Garden, placed there by Vita and Harold in 1937. There's still the weeping willow-leaved pear enveloping the statue of the Virgin by Toma Rosandić, put there in the winter of 1949/50 and still surrounded by many of Vita's favourite white and silver plants – *Stachys lanata, Romneya coulteri,* white violas, bearded iris and

The Irish yews in the early 1960s, relaxed and shaggy, not meticulously shaped and pruned, with rosemary 'Sissinghurst' creeping out over the path.

poppies – just as she described it in her *Observer* column of 22 January 1950.

She planted almonds running down the middle of the White Garden to create an architectural backbone, and planted the climbing *Rosa mulliganii* to swathe them in a fragrant curtain for a few weeks of summer; but the curtain got the better of the nut trees and they collapsed under the weight of the rose. In 1970 they were replaced by a metal rose arbour – designed by Nigel, inspired by the paperclips on his desk – and even though this particular rose has a very short season, it's movingly beautiful there at the heart of the garden and especially at its height of floweriness around 1 July. I'm sure Vita would love it, growing on its intricate but sturdy metal frame.

There is still Vita's favourite *Rosa moyesii* in the Purple Border, with the statuesque and towering cardoons rocketing up to ten or twelve feet, and favoured plants such as Chinese bell-flower (*Platycodon grandiflorum*) – '[a]n effective splash of truly imperial purple' – as well as *Iris chrysographes* and *Iris sibirica* which Vita loved in all its colour forms. Pam and Sybille added their wide range of clematis and magnificent new plants such as *Lupinus* 'Blue Jacket' and *Delphinium* 'Black Knight', and lots of mildew-resistant asters which have come to characterise this border, helping to start its purple and blue show earlier and carrying on its colour later in the year.

The Cottage Garden too is still brimming with sunset colours. There are Vita-style crinolines of shrub roses, and orange-flowered potentillas pierced by firework kniphofias, which Harold hated but Vita loved, as well as red and yellow rock roses framing the edge of the path. Even more wallflowers (*Erysimum* 'Blood Red' and 'Fireking') have been added since

The Cottage Garden in 1962, just after Vita's death, photographed by Edwin
Smith. You almost have to tiptoe to make your way through, with plants
colonising the garden from every direction, displaying Vita's 'cram, cram' style.

Vita's day, to fill the enclosed garden with perfume, and there are still pots of 'Lady Tulip' and Vita and Harold's favourite *Tulipa* 'Couleur Cardinal', arranged in a clutch around Harold's chair by the front door.

There are strands of continuity and things that Vita would instantly recognise if she returned to walk through her garden, but I wonder if there should be more. For example, only a third of the plants in the garden now are ones there in Vita's day. You can read about this in the Sissinghurst plant catalogue compiled by the National Trust in 1984 and annotated later by Pam and Sibylle, showing that some of the shrubs and wall plants are the ones Vita planted, or replacements, but almost all the rest have changed since 1959. As Pam said when interviewed by Tony Lord, 'Had Lady Nicolson been alive, she would always have been adding plants. We were so thankful that somewhere along the line somebody decided that Sissinghurst was going to be a place where we would go on adding rather than someone absolutely stopping the clock.'

That has to be right – it would be dull if the Sissinghurst garden was made into a mausoleum, slavishly recreating year on year the same plant combinations, good or bad, that were there in Vita's day. And there are some things Vita definitely got wrong – ideas that were almost impossible to achieve. Her love of decorating a struggling tree, for instance, often turned out to be a bad idea: adding the climber, unless it was quite a contained grower, often killed the tree even more quickly. Pam and Sybille reduced this practice gradually through the 1960s and 70s, and it has almost totally ceased. There is the rose 'Flora' in a prunus by the door to Priest's House, not planted by Vita but inspired by her, and the odd rose in the orchard, but now these are mainly trained over wooden frames.

Of course, the people who take care of the garden should, and do, make their own choices of what to add and, to an extent, what to take away. But I sometimes long to see more of her favourites. So many of the plants that Vita loved and wrote about are as good today as they were when she grew them and there should be a return to more.

Hoherias are lovely and there is still one in the garden now, but what about more crab apples, robinias, tamarisks, kolkwitzias, indigoferas and so many more of her beloved flowering shrubs? Vita's overall philosophy of 'Cram, cram, cram, every chink and cranny' has all but disappeared. Inevitably with so many people, so many pairs of feet in a public, no longer private, garden, plants can't creep out over the paths without being trampled; and there are bound to be complaints about tresses of roses that swathe the paths catching visitors' hair – or worse, an eye – but the flower beds and walls can be filled to overbrimming

It's a difficult balance to strike in twenty-first-century Britain, but I think there's room for greater softness and abundance without a threat to either plants or people.

No reader of this book will be in any doubt about how much Vita loved her borders to be packed. She hated the sight of too much mulch, criticising Edwardian rose gardens with their 'savagely pruned roses of uniform height, with bare ground in between, liberally disfigured by mulches of unsightly and unsavoury manure'.

There's no doubt that many people expect a tidier world now

than in the 1930s, 40s and 50s. You can see that from our coun-
tryside, which many of us expect to be maintained almost to the
level of a golf green – lane edges mown, hedges clipped, bram-
bles cut from our footpaths – but it's even truer of our gardens
opened to the public.

So there's pressure for things to be just-so and, interestingly,
Nigel liked it kept very tidy too. He encouraged changes to the
outside of the garden – removing the piggery and garage to the
west of the Priest's House – to make the place feel more 'presentable' as you arrived. In the garden, he loved the roses
dead-headed almost every day, the paths swept and the yews all
precisely clipped and tidy. The gardeners – all three genera-
tions of them since Vita's day – are in agreement with him
about this, but maybe it's now time for this to change a little –
to soften and relax.

In his book Tony Lord says, 'to most garden visitors in the
late fifties, Sissinghurst seemed more free and more romantic
than ever. But professional horticulturalists who remember it
from this time recall that the garden seemed to have reached
the point at which excessive freedom and informality were
about to give way to chaotic ugliness and, before long, obliv-
ion.' The whole point of the Sissinghurst garden is that it
should and could meld a love and understanding of plants
with a profoundly romantic sense of beauty. The two things
are – and need to be – the same. An enchanting garden like
Sissinghurst is, I would say, at its most beautiful at precisely the
point where its informality is about to tip over into chaos. I am
with Vita and her desire for *sprezzatura* – a studied noncha-
lance, a balance of formality of structure with informality of
planting.

The aim of this book has been to paint that picture – of the garden as it was at its most perfect moment. 'We have done our best,' Vita wrote to Harold nine months before she died, 'and made a garden where none was.'

Vita and Rollo, her Alsatian, in 1956. Her writing room on the first floor of the Tower is behind her.

SOURCES

Vita's gardening boots on a chair in the Brew House, 1962.

VITA SACKVILLE-WEST:

In Your Garden (Michael Joseph), 1951
In Your Garden Again (Michael Joseph), 1953
More for Your Garden (Michael Joseph), 1955
Even More for Your Garden (Michael Joseph), 1958
Some Flowers (Cobden-Sanderson), 1937
Country Notes (Michael Joseph), 1939
Royal Horticultural Journal, 1953
Country Life, 28 August, 4 and 11 Sept 1942
Graham Stewart Thomas, *The Old Shrub Roses*, 1955. Foreword by
    Vita

HAROLD NICOLSON:

Diary 27 September 1933
Letter to Vita, August 1940

OTHER SOURCES:

Jane Brown, *Vita's Other World: A Gardening Biography of Vita
    Sackville-West* (Penguin), 1987
Edward Bunyard, *Old Garden Roses* (Graham Thomas)
Peter Coates, *Great Gardens of the World* (Weidenfeld & Nicolson),
    1963. Introduction by Harold Nicolson
Tony Lord, *Gardening at Sissinghurst* (Frances Lincoln), 1995

William Robinson, *The English Flower Garden* (Bloomsbury Gardening Classics), 1998

William Robinson, *The Wild Garden* (Timber Press), 2010

Anne Scott-James, Sissinghurst: *The Making of a Garden* (Michael Joseph), 1975

Colour Picture Captions

PLATE SECTION 1

Page 1: Lady With a Red Hat by William Strang, 1918. (© William Strang (1859–1921). / Art Gallery and Museum, Kelvingrove, Glasgow, Scotland / © Culture and Sport Glasgow (Museums) / The Bridgeman Art Library)

Pages 2/3: A view from the top of the Tower in June, looking over the Purple Border and out to the farm beyond. (Jonathan Buckley)

Pages 4/5: The yew Rondel and Rose Garden, just coming into flower, seen from the attic room in the south wing. (Stephen Orr)

Pages 6/7: The Spring Garden in April, still planted much as Harold designed it in the 1930s. (Jonathan Buckley)

Page 8: The Sissinghurst Castle Rose – 'Rose des Maures'. (Jonathan Buckley)

PLATE SECTION 2

Page 1: Harold's Yew walk – the backbone of the garden at Sissinghurst, planted soon after they arrived. (Stephen Orr)

Pages 2/3: Looking through the Rose Garden towards the Yew Walk and the Tower at dawn. (Stephen Orr)

Pages 4/5: The Bacchante statue at the top of the Lime Walk, in late May, with the pleached limes in full leaf. (Stephen Orr)

Pages 6/7: The Nuttery, planted around 1900, long before Vita and Harold arrived. Much later, Graham Stewart Thomas worked with head gardeners Pam and Sybille to design the tapestry of spring flowers that carpets the Nuttery floor. (Jonathan Buckley)

Page 8: A view from the Tower over the White Garden, in mid-June, with *Rosa mulliganii* in full flower. (Jonathan Buckley)

PLATE SECTION 3

Page 1: The Rose Garden coming into full flower in early June. (Jonathan Buckley)

Pages 2/3: The Irish sentinel yews, in the Cottage Garden at dawn, in late May. (Stephen Orr)

Page 4: The Purple Border in June with many of Vita's favourites – *Rosa moyesii, Geranium psilostemon* and *Clematis durandii* – in flower. (Jonathan Buckley)

Page 5: The White Garden with *Rosa* 'Iceberg' billowing out of the formal box parterre. (Jonathan Buckley)

Pages 6/7: The moat wall with corydalis and perennial wallflower, *Erysimum* 'Bowles Mauve', frothing from below to meet the white wisteria Vita planted above it. (Jonathan Buckley)

Page 8: A cobalt blue vase filled with spring blossom and euphorbias on the lapis lazuli table in the Big Room. Arrangement by Sarah Raven. Photograph by Pia Tryde. (Courtesy of Frances Lincoln publishers)

Index of Plants, Shrubs and Trees

LOBELIA SIPHILITICA 'ALBA'
LEONOTIS ...CASE'
LAVANDULA × CHRISTIANA
LAVANDULA STOECHAS
TRITELEIA LAXA
TULIPA 'HINA PINK'
TULIPA 'PRINSES IRENE'
Lathyrus nervosus
...hartwegii ...lancaneve
LYTHRUM SALICARIA FIRECANDLE
LEONOT... LEONURI
Leonotis 'Staircase'
TULIP... 'MAYTIM...
...ATHYRUS ...UNDIFOLIUS
LAVANDUL... DENTATA
...LUPINUS ...RIUS
...TULIPA ...STOCRA...
TULIPA SYLVEST...
...JOAN...
Ligularia veitchiana
SPE... MAGNIFIC...
LILIUM ...ECIOS ...RUBRU ...UCHIDA
LILIUM SPECIOSUM 'UCHIDA'
LOBELIA 'JACK McMASTER'
LUNARIA ANNUA var. ALBIFLORA
TULIPA 'MAUREEN'
TULIP... 'DAIRYM...
TULIPA 'CLARA BUT...
MAGNOLIA ...ENUDATA
MIMULUS AURANTIACUS PUNICEUS
MAURANDY... ...LOPHOSPERM...
Maurandya barclayana alba
MAURANDYA BARCLAYANA
...US DOMEST ...ORCESTER PEARMAIN
ULMUS X ELEGANTISSIMA 'JACQUELINE HILLIER'
UNCINIA UNCINIATA
VERBA... CRET...
VERBASCUM CRETICA
...MYRTUS ...COMM...
MALUS DOME 'BROAD-EY... PIPPIN'
MONARDA FISTULOSA
MICHAUXIA CAMPANULOIDES
MALVA SYLVESTRIS MAURITANICA
VERBASCUM PHOENICEUM
VIOLA SEPTENTRIONAL...
VERBENA SISSINGHU...
VERBASCU... CHAIXII
NICOTIANA GLAUCA
NEPETA × FAASSENII
...RCISSUS ...Y MOON'
...ERINE ...OWDENII ...RAECOX'
WALLFLOWER 'PURPLE QUEEN'
WALLFLOWER GIANT PINK'
...PA
NICOTIANA ALATA 'LIME GRE...
NICOTIANA ...I ATA
...EPETA ...CA
ORNITHOGALUM NUTANS
OMPHALODES LINIFOLIA
...NTHORHIZA ...MPLICISSIMA
YUCCA FILAMENTOSA VARIEGATA
YU... RECU...
...OTHERA ...ECIOSA
...OSPERMUM ...NNINGTON JOHN'
OMPHALODES CAPPADOCICA
OXALIS OBTUS...
OSTEOSPERMUM 'WHIRLIGIG'
...ERMUM ...IRLS...
...OT... ONITHOGALUM REVERCHONII
...TEMON ...GRAPES'
PERSICARIA AFFINIS 'SUPERBUM'
PHUOPSIS STYLOSA
PAPAVER COMMUTATUM 'LADYBIRD'
PAPAVER SOMNIFERUM WHITE FORM
AINSE HYSSOP AGASTACHE ANETHIODORA
Adonis aestiva...
BASIL 'DARK OPAL'
...SSIFLORA ...AERULEA
PACHYSANDRA TERMINALIS
PERSICARIA BISTORTA 'SUPERBUM'
PAPAVER SULTANA
CANCERBU...
PINK CLARY SALVIA VIRIDI...
CRIMSON CLOVER TRIFOLIUM INCARNATUM
CU...
PHLOX ...NIFERA ...RIDGE'
...ATA
...ERSICARIA ...LLETII
PHLOX STOLONIF... 'VIOLET V...
PHEGOPTER... CONNECTILIS
POLYSTICHUM SETIFERUM 'DIVISILOBUM GROUP
SUTHERLAN... FRUTESCE...
VARIEGATED MINT MENTHA SUAVEOLENS 'VARIEGATA'
ANISE HYSSOP AGASTACHE FOENICULUM
PHYGELIUS AEQUALIS YELLOW TRUMPET
CHAMOMILE CHAMAEMELUM NOBILE
CATMINT Nepeta multibracteata hybrid
...ALLIS ...ATA
...USHIMA
PLATYCO... GRANDIFLO... DOUBLE W...
Hyssopus officinalis t. albus
...OO FLY PLANT NICARDRA ...YSALOIDES
...NAT... ...ANTH... ...REC...
TOBACCO NICOTIANA TABA...
NASTUR... ...OBACCO
...ONATUM ...RIDUM ...OW'
POLYGONU... SCOPARII
POLYPODIUM CAMBRICUM
...LYPODIUM ...ULGARE
POLYSTICH... SETIFER... DIVISILOBUM G...
COMFREY Symphytum peregrinum
...HUS ...RUTICOSA ...SUNSET'
PRIMULA 'CAPTAIN B...
PERSICARIA
PRIMU... ...OWICH...
PRUNUS SARGENTII
CHERVIL ANTHRISCUS CEREFOLIUM
...ONETTE
...EL FL...
...CULATA ...GELLA ...TIVA
IRIS DOUGLASIANA
C... ...IVUM
GIA... SCH...